PHYSICAL EDUCATION
FOR CCEA GCSE LEVEL

3rd EDITION

COLOURPOINT EDUCATIONAL

Derek Prentice

© 2019 Derek Prentice and Colourpoint Creative Ltd

ISBN: 978-1-78073-187-2

Third Edition
First Impression 2019

Layout and design: April Sky Design
Printed by: W&G Baird Limited, Antrim

All rights reserved. No part of this publication may be reproduced, stored in a retrieval system or transmitted in any form or by any means, electronic, mechanical, photocopying, scanning, recording or otherwise, without the prior written permission of the copyright owners and publisher of this book.

Copyright

Page 191 constitutes an extension of this copyright page.

Colourpoint Educational

An imprint of Colourpoint Creative Ltd
Colourpoint House
Jubilee Business Park
Jubilee Road
Newtownards
County Down
Northern Ireland
BT23 4YH

Tel: 028 9182 6339
Fax: 028 9182 1900
E-mail: sales@colourpoint.co.uk
Web site: www.colourpoint.co.uk

The Author

DEREK PRENTICE, along with a small group of other PE teachers, introduced CSE examination Physical Education into Northern Ireland in the mid-1970s and since then has continued to be involved in its development. He was involved in writing the first specification for GCSE PE and all subsequent specifications. He was a Chief Examiner for an awarding body for GCSE Physical Education from its introduction in 1986 until his retirement from this post in 2017. He continues to be part of a Senior Moderating Team that visits schools for an awarding body.

This is the third edition of the textbook. This edition, along with the two previous editions, has been written to help all students studying GCSE Physical Education. Derek has been greatly encouraged by all those students and teachers who, over the years, have expressed to him how they have appreciated and valued the previous editions. He hopes that this third edition will also be helpful for all students preparing for the CCEA GCSE PE examinations.

Dedication

This book, as were the other editions, is dedicated to my daughter Zahra and, this time, also to her husband Johnny. Thank you both for helping me with some of the photographs. I must also dedicate it to my wife, Ann, who hopes this will be my last edition.

Publisher's Note: This book has been through a rigorous quality assurance process by an independent person experienced in the CCEA specification prior to publication. It has been written to help students preparing for the GCSE Physical Education specification from CCEA. While Colourpoint Educational, the author and the quality assurance person have taken every care in its production, we are not able to guarantee that the book is completely error-free. Additionally, while the book has been written to address the CCEA specification, it is the responsibility of each candidate to satisfy themselves that they have fully met the requirements of the CCEA specification prior to sitting an exam set by that body. For this reason, and because specifications and CCEA advice change with time, we strongly advise every candidate to avail of a qualified teacher and to check the contents of the most recent specification for themselves prior to the exam. Colourpoint Creative Ltd cannot be held responsible for any errors or omissions in this book or any consequences thereof.

CONTENTS

INTRODUCTION 5

TOOLS AND TEMPLATES 6

COMPONENT 1:
Factors Underpinning Health and Performance 12

1.1 The Body at Work 13
The skeletal system 13
The muscular system 17
The cardiovascular system 23
The respiratory system 28
The digestive system 31
The nervous system 33

1.2 Health and Lifestyle Decisions 37
Mental and social health 37
Physical health: exercise 46
Principles of training 54
Fitness testing 60
Risk assessment 63
Physical health: nutrition 66
Physical health: sleep 76
Physical health: tobacco and illegal drugs 80
Planning for physical health: Factors that can affect lifestyle decisions . . 94

1.3 The Active Leisure Industry..........102

    The concept of leisure 102

    Structure of the active leisure industry (in Northern Ireland)..........105

    Event management..........114

    Knockout, league and ladder competitions 123

    Evaluating the success of active leisure events 137

COMPONENT 2:
Developing Performance 141

2.1 Developing Physical Fitness for Performance 142

    Physical fitness 142

    Principles of training 147

    Methods of training 150

    Assessment of physical fitness..........156

    Planning and evaluating training programmes 159

    Planning and evaluating training sessions..........162

2.2 Developing Skilled Performance..........171

    Skilled performance 171

    Factors underpinning the learning of skills..........175

SAMPLE AUDITS..........185

INTRODUCTION

Components 1 and 2

The course for GCSE Physical Education has been divided into three components. This book looks at Components 1 and 2 – 'Factors Underpinning Health and Performance' and 'Developing Performance' – which will be assessed in external, written examination papers.

Assessment Objectives (AO)

There are three assessment objectives for Components 1 and 2:

> **AO1:**
> Recall knowledge and demonstrate understanding of the concepts, facts, terminology, principles and methods relating to the subject content.
>
> **AO2:**
> Apply effectively the concepts, facts, terminology, principles and methods relating to the subject content.
>
> **AO3:**
> Analyse, interpret and evaluate information and data relating to the subject content.

AO1

For AO1, in the two written examination papers, you will be asked to recall and explain your knowledge and understanding of the relevant concepts, facts, terminology, principles and methods for the following areas:

Paper 1
- 3.1.1 The body at work
- 3.1.2 Health and lifestyle decisions
- 3.1.3 The active leisure industry

Paper 2
- 3.2.1 Developing physical fitness for performance
- 3.2.2 Developing skilled performance

It is important that you gain an in-depth knowledge and understanding of the content in each of the sections of the specification, because that will provide a strong foundation from which you will to be able to answer questions associated with AO2 and AO3.

AO2

For AO2, you will be asked to demonstrate that you can apply or use the concepts, facts, terminology, principles and methods safely, appropriately and effectively. This could be generally or for specific situations.

AO3

For AO3, you will be given information and/or data and asked to analyse, interpret and evaluate it with regard to safety, appropriateness and effectiveness. Again, this could be generally or for specific situations.

ASSESSMENT FOR LEARNING

In each section, you will have opportunities to test your knowledge and understanding of the content (AO1). These questions/tasks will be highlighted in green.

You will also have opportunities to apply the concepts, facts, terminology, principles or methods (AO2). These questions/tasks will be highlighted in yellow.

There will also be opportunities to present, analyse, interpret and evaluate information and/or data produced by you, your classmates or your teacher (AO3). These questions/tasks will be highlighted in blue.

Tasks that require you to work as part of a team will be highlighted in pink.

TOOLS AND TEMPLATES

This section contains some tools and templates that can help as you:
- Analyse, interpret and evaluate information or data on a given topic; set SMART objectives and targets to bring about improvements; devise action plans to achieve the SMART objectives and targets; and be able to monitor and adjust the action plans. (**The five steps: external written examination papers.**)
- Analyse, interpret and evaluate performances in your chosen physical activities or sports; set SMART objectives and targets to bring about improvements; devise action plans to achieve the SMART objectives and targets; and be able to implement, monitor and adjust the action plans. (**The five steps: practical activities.**)
- Understand a Physical Activity Readiness Questionnaire (**PAR-Q**).
- Understand the **SMART** principle.

The five steps: external written examination papers

As you work through the book you will see references to the 'five steps' – the process to follow when trying to bring about improvements, e.g. in the person's health or fitness. When you encounter these references in questions, refer back to this page for guidance on how to carry out the activity.

- **Step 1 – know and understand:**
  - the relevant concepts, facts, terminology, principles and methods associated with the topic;
  - what you or others should be aiming to achieve (the 'ideal' model or targets). This will be the accepted recommendations, advice or standards for the relevant topic;
  - what information you need from an audit or assessment to allow an effective analysis and evaluation of the present situation;
  - how to analyse, interpret and evaluate the information and/or data from an audit or assessment and then, based on your findings, set SMART objectives and targets (see page 11) to bring about improvements;
  - how to apply the relevant concepts, facts, terminology, principles and methods to devise a safe, appropriate and effective action plan to achieve SMART objectives and targets;
  - how to monitor the effectiveness of the implementation of the action plan and of the actions themselves.
- **Step 2 – assess** the comprehensiveness and quality of the information and/or data presented from an audit or assessment. Do you have the information and/or data you need to evaluate the issue/situation effectively? Is anything missing, or incorrect? If anything is missing, explain what further information/data you would need. If anything is wrong, explain how this information or data could affect the quality of your analysis, interpretation and evaluation.
- **Step 3 – analyse, interpret and evaluate** the information/data from the audit or assessment by breaking it down into appropriate parts. See how each part matches up to the facts, accepted advice, recommendations and expected standards (e.g. the 'ideal' model and targets agreed from step 1). Identify the person's strengths and weaknesses (note the positive aspects and explain the benefits, and note the negative aspects – what is wrong, missing or below expected standards – and explain the consequences). Be able to make sound recommendations and provide SMART objectives and targets (see page 11) to bring about improvements over a specified period of time.
- **Step 4 – plan a safe, appropriate and effective action plan** that will suit the person and be appropriate for the situation. Apply the relevant concepts, facts, terminology, principles and

TOOLS AND TEMPLATES

methods to achieve the SMART objectives and targets within the specified time frame.

- **Step 5 – implement, monitor and evaluate the action plan** to ensure that it stays safe, appropriate and effective. If at times parts of the action plan are not happening, or the actions implemented are ineffective, explain what changes or adjustments you would make to get back on track. Overall, you want to explain how effectively you implemented the action plan and how effective the actions were in achieving the SMART objectives and targets.

The diagram below represents the five-step process to bring about improvements.

Once the SMART objectives and targets from an action plan have been fully or partially completed within the time frame, the process of the five steps can be repeated to bring about further improvements.

Terms

In the exam, and in this book, you will encounter the following terms:

- *Monitor*: to regularly check how everything is going when implementing the action plan and record what actions were, or were not, implemented. This record can then be analysed and evaluated.
- *Analyse*: to look at each of the various parts that make up the audits, action plans or assessments.

The five steps: external written examination papers

1 – Know and understand
For example:
- Can you recall and explain the concepts, facts, terminology, principles and methods used in each section?
- Can you demonstrate that you can apply them safely, appropriately, efficiently and effectively, either generally or for specific situations?
- Can you analyse, interpret and evaluate information and/or data based on the application of the concepts, facts, terminology, principles and methods used in the sections/chapters?

2 Assess
For example:
- Do you know what information and/or data you need to find out, collate and present for an effective audit? – e.g. details on what the person's/organisation's situation is presently; results from appropriate assessments that were carried out; information on persona circumstances and preferences.
- Can you carry out an effective audit using appropriate methods and assessments?
- Can you judge the comprehensiveness and quality of the information and/or data that was collected and presented?

3 Analyse, interpret and evaluate
For example:
- Do you know and understand the accepted advice and recommendations for an ideal model?
- Can you compare the information and/or data from the audit with the advice and recommendations for an ideal model?
- Can you identify what practices from the audit match the accepted advice and recommendations for an ideal model and the benefits of these practices?
- Can you identify negative practices from the audit and the possible consequences of these practices?
- Can you identify any advice and recommendations for an ideal model that are not being implemented and the possible consequences of this?
- Can you draw conclusions, give meaningful feedback and make sound recommendations in the form of setting SMART objectives and targets for improvement?

4 Action plan
For example:
- Can you devise safe, appropriate and effective action plans to achieve SMART objectives and targets within a set time frame?
- Can you apply the principles for bringing about improvements safely, efficiently and effectively over a particular time frame?
- Can you use safe and appropriate methods and apply them effectively over a time frame?

5 Implement, monitor and evaluate
For example:
- Can you select efficient methods for monitoring both the effectiveness of the application of action plans, and the effectiveness of the actions implemented?
- Can you make safe, appropriate and effective adjustments to the action plan based on this monitoring?

- *Interpret*: to seek to explain the findings.
- *Evaluate*: to give a judgement on the findings.

Analysis, interpretation and evaluation

Throughout the book are sections that only call for 'Analysis, interpretation and evaluation' of data and/or information on a given situation. When you come across these sections in the book, you will notice that you, your classmates and your teacher are asked to produce statements, diagrams, scenarios, information and/or data to allow you and your classmates to practise these skills. This is teamwork, and engaging in this whole process will help you become competent in Assessment Objectives 1 and 3 for the written examination papers (Steps 1, 2 and 3 of the five-step process).

Foundation

Each time you are asked to analyse, interpret and evaluate statements, scenarios, information or data, it is your knowledge and understanding (Step 1) that is the foundation that will allow you to successfully complete Steps 2 and 3.

Use the following process to form your solid foundation.

- Use the relevant parts of the textbook and other means to find what concepts, facts, terminology, principles and methods you need to know, and/or what the 'ideal' model should be for this particular situation. Write down the relevant facts, accepted advice and recommendations, and/or what the 'ideal' model should be. This will be your foundation.
- Self-check your facts and assess your 'ideal' model – check for accuracy, quality and comprehensiveness. Can you find anything that is wrong, unclear or missing? If necessary, make changes or add to your model.
- Analyse and evaluate your chosen 'ideal' model – do you cover all components; is your advice and are your recommendations sound and from acceptable sources? If necessary, make changes or add to your model.
- Finally, get others to check your facts, assess, analyse and evaluate your 'ideal' model. Take advice from your teacher and classmates. If necessary, make changes or add to your model. You should also be willing to do this for your classmates.

By completing this process, you should know and understand the facts and what is considered to be the 'ideal' model, or as close as you can get to one. This foundation will help you successfully assess, analyse, interpret and evaluate any information or data presented in audits, or assessments, produced by your teacher, your classmates or from the written examination papers.

Analysis, interpretation, evaluation and action planning

There are opportunities where an audit has been provided (see Sample Audits at the rear of this book) to allow you to undertake all of the five-step process to bring about improvements.

Teamwork

You, your classmates and your teacher should also produce sample audits to provide further practice in completing the five-step process to bring about improvements.

Help

In applying the five steps, if you find your own knowledge and understanding is lacking in any way, take note where, then look up (or discuss with your teacher) what information you need to carry on with that particular step.

FURTHER THINKING

This textbook can help prepare you for the written examination papers in GCSE Physical Education, but there are other means available to help you. Explore these to broaden and deepen your knowledge and understanding of the subject content. Opportunities for further exploration or thinking will be highlighted in grey.

The five steps: practical activities

Although not covered by this book, the process of the five steps can also be used to improve the efficiency and effectiveness of your performances in your chosen physical activities or sports.

TOOLS AND TEMPLATES

AO4(i)

Perform safely, efficiently, effectively and consistently the skills, strategies, tactical or compositional principles used in physical activities and sports to consistently maintain appropriate fitness levels, desirable attitudes and behaviours and comply with the rules and health and safety requirements of your chosen physical activities and sports.

Steps 1, 2 and 3 can also help you to analyse and evaluate the quality of your performances and the performances of others in your chosen physical activities or sports.

AO4(ii)

Analyse and evaluate the quality of performances of the skills, strategies, tactical or compositional principles used in physical activities and sports, along with fitness levels, desirable attitudes and behaviours and compliance with the rules and health and safety requirements of their physical activities and sports.

The diagram below represents the five-step process as applied to practical activities.

The five steps: practical activities

1 – Knowl and understand

For example:
- Do you know and understand the strategies, skills, fitness requirements, attitudes, behaviours and rules of your physical activities or sports?
- Can you demonstrate how you apply them safely, appropriately, efficiently and effectively in practice and competitive situations?
- Can you analyse, interpret and evaluate the quality of performances based on the application of the strategies, skills, fitness requirements, attitudes, behaviours and rules of your physical activities or sports?

2 Assess

For example:
- Can you set up practice and competitive situations where you use the strategies, skills, fitness requirements, attitudes, behaviours and rules of your physical activities or sports?
- Can you carry out appropriate assessments and use the results to demonstrate present levels of performance?
- Can you judge the suitability and quality of methods used to audit performances in your physical activities or sports?

3 Analyse, interpret and evaluate

For example:
- Do you know and understand what rates as outstanding in the application of the strategies, skills, fitness requirements, attitudes, behaviours and rules of your physical activities or sports?
- Can you compare, identify and explain, using evidence, how the quality of your performances and the performances of others match the 'outstanding' model for your physical activities or sports?
- Can you draw conclusions, give meaningful feedback and communicate these effectively?

4 Action plan

For example:
- Can you devise safe, appropriate and effective action plans to achieve, within a set time frame, SMART objectives and targets to improve one or more of the strategies, skills, fitness requirements, attitudes, behaviours and rules of your physical activities or sports?
- Can you apply the principles for improving performances safely, efficiently and effectively over a time frame?
- Can you use safe and appropriate methods and apply them effectively over a time frame?

5 Implement, monitor and evaluate

For example:
- Can you implement your action plans?
- Can you monitor the effectiveness of the implementation of the action plans?
- Can you monitor the effectiveness of the actions implemented?
- Can you make safe, appropriate and effective adjustments to the action plans based on this monitoring?

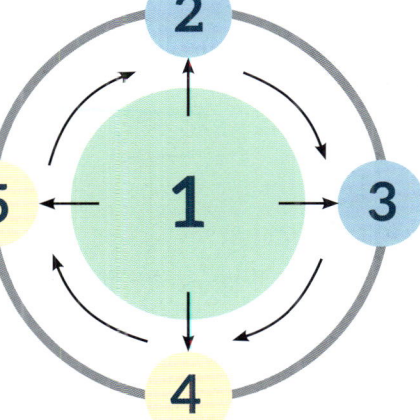

Sample Physical Activity Readiness Questionnaire (PAR-Q)

When analysing a person's physical activity/exercise, it can be useful to conduct a Physical Activity Readiness Questionnaire (PAR-Q) in which you ask a range of 'yes or no' questions.

If a person answers yes to one or more of the questions and they have been inactive for a long time or are concerned about their health, they should consult their doctor before starting an exercise programme.

If a person answers no to all the PAR-Q questions, they can be reasonably assured they can exercise safely.

Sample questions are:

1. Has your doctor ever said that you have a heart condition and that you should only do physical activity recommended by a doctor? ☐ Yes ☐ No

2. Do you feel pain in your chest when you do physical activity? ☐ Yes ☐ No

3. In the past month, have you had chest pain when you were not doing physical activity? ☐ Yes ☐ No

4. Do you lose your balance because of dizziness or do you ever lose consciousness? ☐ Yes ☐ No

5. Do you have a bone or joint problem that could be made worse by a change in your physical activity? ☐ Yes ☐ No

6. Is your doctor currently prescribing drugs for your blood pressure or heart condition? ☐ Yes ☐ No

7. Do you know of any other reason why you should not do physical activity? ☐ Yes ☐ No

The SMART principle

When setting objectives and planning actions for yourself or others, it can be useful to adhere to the SMART principle. It provides a way to organise your objectives and track your progress:

S **Specific:** Try to be clear on what your intended objective actually is. For instance, instead of saying, "I want to do more aerobic training", you must specify the type of exercise and method of training (e.g. I will complete a 30-minute run every Monday, Wednesday and Saturday). It may help to ask yourself the following questions: What exactly do I want to achieve? Where will I do this? How? What is my time frame? What are my limitations? Why do I want to reach this objective?

M **Measurable:** Try to break your objective down into elements that can be measured: this will be an effective way to track your progress, and make your objective clearer and easier to reach. For instance, your objective is to run the marathon in less than three hours.

A **Attainable/Agreed:** It can be very discouraging to fail to meet a desired objective, so think carefully about whether the objective really is achievable. Weigh the time and effort it will take against your other obligations and priorities. If you don't have the time, money or talent to reach a certain objective you'll be more likely to fail. If the objective is for another person, it should be agreed with them.

R **Relevant:** The actions must be relevant to the specific objectives. For example, if your objective is to run a 10 km road race, then swimming is not going to be a relevant activity.

T **Time-bound:** Set deadlines and go after them! Every objective needs a target date, so that you have something to focus on and work toward, but make sure the timeline is realistic and flexible in order to stay motivated.

Although not on the specification, to take this theory a little further, you could follow the SMART**ER** principle by adding:

E **Exciting:** Set objectives that inspire and excite you. After all, a person is more likely to carry out the training if it is interesting for them, especially when faced with setbacks, failures, pain, tedium, or the desire to do other more interesting things.

R **Recorded/Reviewed:** You are more likely to stay committed when you make a record of your intended goals, and the milestones you reach along the way. This allows you to check on progress being made and review the effectiveness of the training programme as it is followed.

COMPONENT 1
Factors Underpinning Health and Performance

1.1 THE BODY AT WORK

Learning outcomes

In this section, you will learn about the:

- skeletal system
- muscular system
- cardiovascular system
- respiratory system
- digestive system and
- nervous system

The skeletal system

Functions during performances in physical activities and sports

Shape/support

The adult skeleton is made up of 206 bones. **Ligaments** hold bones in place at joints. **Tendons** attach muscles to bones across joints – this set-up provides stability at the joints, allows movement and gives the human body its upright shape. The framework of the skeleton also supports internal organs (for example, the lungs and the brain).

People of all shapes and sizes participate in physical activities and sports; however, size and shape can have a significant influence on your potential to be an elite performer. For example, Olympic gymnasts are usually small with a light frame while most elite high jumpers are tall with a light frame.

Movement

Being able to move efficiently and effectively is a key factor for successful performance in sport. The 'freely moveable' or **synovial** joints of the body enable a wide range of movements (see page 14 for information on how synovial joints work and the movements they allow).

Protection

Many physical activities and sports involve physical contact. The skeleton provides protection for our vital organs when we make contact with the ground, equipment or other players. The skull protects the brain; the rib cage, sternum and spinal column protect the heart, lungs and major blood vessels; and the vertebrae protect the spinal cord.

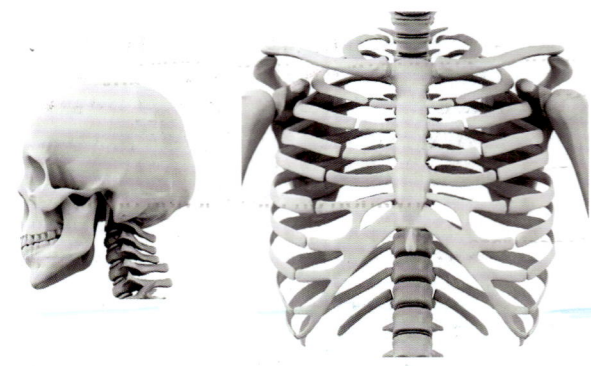

the body from infectious diseases and foreign invaders. Platelets help to form clots and stop bleeding.

Mineral storage

Bone acts as a storage area for excess calcium, phosphorus and iron. To function effectively, the body needs to maintain a balanced level of these minerals in the blood.

For some physical activities and sports additional protection is needed. In sports like hurling, cycling and skiing, performers wear hard helmets. In taekwondo, fencing and cricket, body protection is used to limit serious injury; and in hockey and rugby, performers wear gum shields to limit oral injuries.

> **ASSESSMENT FOR LEARNING**
>
> 1. Physical activities and sports can be physically demanding. Explain how the skeletal system helps allow safe and effective participation.
>
> 2. You, your class and your teacher should produce a spider diagram with statements on the functions of the skeleton. Some statements should be true and some false.
>
> 3. Analyse each of the statements produced for the task above. Identify which statements are true and which are false. If a statement is false, correct what is inaccurate.

Blood cell production

The body makes about two million **red blood cells** per second in the red marrow of the bones (see diagram below). The red blood cells carry oxygen to the muscles and remove carbon dioxide from the muscles.

Synovial joints

Synovial joints, shown below, are 'freely moveable' joints that allow extensive movement.

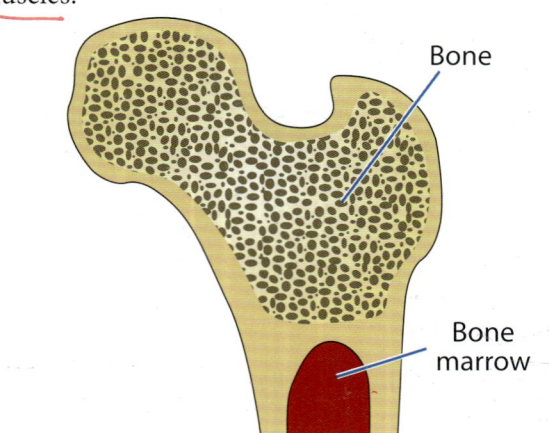

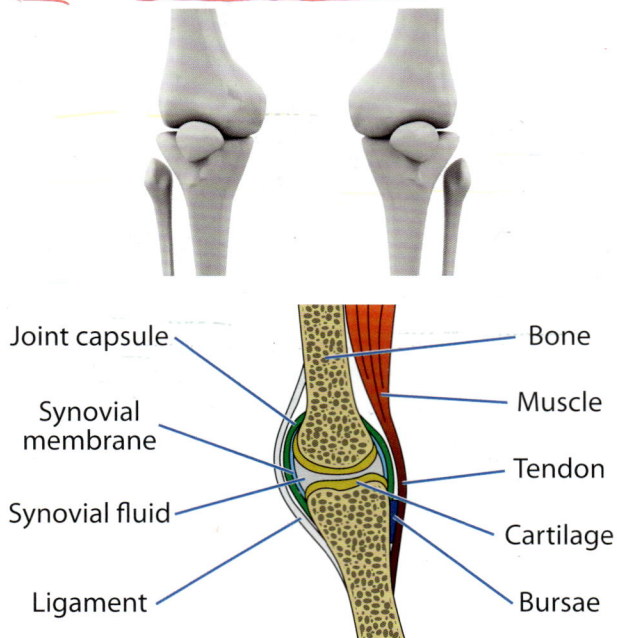

White blood cells and **platelets** are also produced in the red bone marrow. White blood cells protect

How the structure of a synovial joint provides stability and allows movement

A synovial joint consists of the following parts:

Synovial capsule: Encloses the joint and is lined with the synovial membrane. The capsule keeps the synovial fluid around the joint.

Synovial membrane: Lines the entire synovial capsule. Its function is to produce the thick, slippery substance known as synovial fluid.

Synovial fluid: Lubricates the joint, nourishes the cartilage and acts as a shock absorber between the bones.

Bursae: Small sac-like structures filled with fluid, which are situated in joints acting as cushions to alleviate friction between bones, tendons and muscles.

Cartilage: Smooth cartilage covers the end of each bone surface at a joint. The smoothness of the cartilage, combined with lubrication from the synovial fluid, provides a slippery surface that allows almost friction-free movement at the joint. The cartilage is elastic and acts as a cushion or shock absorber between bones.

Ligaments: White, fibrous elastic tissue holds bones in place; provides stability at the joint; prevents over-movement and limits dislocation.

Tendons: Tough bands of connective tissue that attach skeletal muscles to bones. Tendons are put under extreme stress when muscles pull on them.

ASSESSMENT FOR LEARNING

1. Draw a synovial joint and label the various parts.

2. Explain how the structure of the synovial joint allows a person to move safely and freely during performances in physical activities and sports.

3. You, your class and your teacher should produce a pool of diagrams for a typical synovial joint. The diagrams may have any combination of the following: parts not shown; parts not named or incorrectly named; information on the function of the parts not given or the information is inaccurate.

4. Look at each of the diagrams produced for the task above. Identify and correct any parts that are missing, not named or incorrectly named.

5. Identify and correct any information on the function of the parts that is inaccurate.

Movements possible at synovial joints

There are six types of synovial joint. The range of movement possible at each type varies. The following terms describe the main movements.

Abduction: Movement away from the mid-line of the body.

Adduction: Movement toward the mid-line of the body.

Flexion: Bending the limbs at a joint.

Extension: Straightening limbs at a joint.

Circumduction: A circular movement around a fixed point. Circumduction is a combination of flexion, extension, adduction and abduction. Best seen at ball and socket joints, such as the hip and shoulder, it may also be performed by other parts of the body such as fingers, hands, feet and head.

Rotation: Movement around a single long axis either clockwise or anticlockwise.

When referring to the extension or flexion of the foot at the ankle, the following terms are also used:

Dorsiflexion: Movement where the toes are brought closer to the shin.

Plantar flexion: Movement where the sole of the foot is brought closer to the back of the leg.

Classifications of synovial joints

Type of joint	Examples/Location	Movements
Ball and socket	Shoulder and hip	Abduction; adduction; rotation; circumduction. All movements except sliding or gliding movement.
Condyloid	Wrist	Flexion, extension, abduction and adduction movements (circumduction).
Saddle	Thumb	Flexion, extension, abduction, and adduction movements (circumduction). Allows more movement than condyloid.
Pivot	Neck	Rotation of head from side to side.
Hinge	Elbow, finger, toe, knee* and ankle*	Flexion, extension. *The knee and ankle joints have other limited movements, as well as flexion and extension.
Plane/gliding	Hand and foot	Sliding or gliding movement occurs between the surfaces of two flat bones.

ASSESSMENT FOR LEARNING

1. Draw stick diagrams for three different types of synovial joints. The diagrams should show each type being used in a sporting context. Identify and label each stick diagram with the movement(s) (abduction; rotation; flexion etc.) being applied at the joint in this particular sporting context.

2. You, your class and your teacher should produce a collection of different stick diagrams, each showing a type of joint being used in a sporting context. The joint may be incorrectly named and/or the information on the movement being demonstrated inaccurate.

3. Analyse each of the diagrams produced for the task above. Identify and correct any that have been mislabelled or have information that is inaccurate or missing.

Long-term effects of exercise and optimal training on the skeletal system

As a result of regular and prolonged weight-bearing activity – that is, any activity performed whilst on your feet and/or any strength training exercises – the component parts of the skeletal system will change in the following ways, as shown in the diagram on the next page:

Skeletal tissues (bones)
Bones become stronger and denser as the criss-cross matrix structure within is reinforced by an increase in calcium deposits and collagen fibres.

Cartilage
Cartilage, at the end of the bones in synovial joints, becomes thicker and provide increased protection and cushioning.

Tendons
Tendons become thicker and stronger and can withstand greater forces when muscles pull on them.

1.1 THE BODY AT WORK

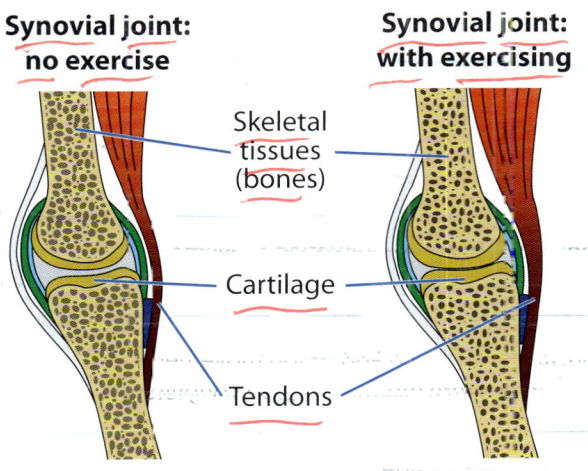

Synovial joint: no exercise

Synovial joint: with exercising

- Skeletal tissues (bones)
- Cartilage
- Tendons

ASSESSMENT FOR LEARNING

1. Explain the changes that take place in the skeletal system as a result of regular, appropriate and effective training.

2. You, your class and your teacher should each produce two statements on the effects of strength training or weight-bearing exercise on the skeletal system – one must be accurate, one inaccurate.

3. As a group, read through each statement produced for the task above and identify and correct any information that is inaccurate.

Keith McClure

The muscular system

Functions during performances in physical activities and sports

Movement

There are three types of muscles in the human body – skeletal, cardiac and smooth – each of which produces either voluntary or involuntary movement:

- **Cardiac muscle** is found in the heart wall and moves blood from the heart around the circulatory system. It is not under your conscious control (autonomic nervous system, see page 34) so movement produced by cardiac muscle is known as *involuntary movement*.
- **Skeletal muscles** are attached to bones and move limbs (for example, the biceps pull the forearm towards the shoulder). They are made of muscle fibres under your conscious control (somatic nervous system, see page 34), so movements produced by skeletal muscles is known as *voluntary movement*.
- **Smooth muscle** is found in internal body systems and it moves various things through the body systems. The walls of the intestines move food through the digestive system; the walls of blood vessels move blood around the circulatory system. It is not under your conscious control (autonomic nervous system), so the movement produced by smooth muscle is known as *involuntary movement*.

Types of muscle

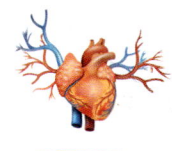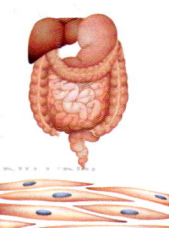

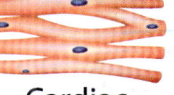
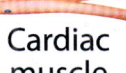

Cardiac muscle | Skeletal muscle | Smooth muscle

17

Support

The skeletal muscles work in pairs across synovial joints and play an important role in supporting and stabilising the joints. Skeletal muscles need to be strong to cope with weight-bearing actions like running, jumping and landing, and flexible enough to allow a full range of movement at each synovial joint.

Muscle tone holds your body in a position, whether it is a position for sleeping, sitting, standing or playing sport. It is good muscle tone that maintains good posture and stability at synovial joints.

Production of heat

When skeletal muscles contract and relax they produce heat. In cold conditions, heat from working muscles can keep the body warm. If it is cold and you are not active you start to shiver. Shivering is the involuntary contraction of muscles to produce heat. When muscles are working hard, performing physical activity, they produce a lot of heat. This heat is dispersed from the muscles through the blood to the skin where the blood is cooled.

ASSESSMENT FOR LEARNING

1. Muscles produce movement. What does each of the three different types of muscle move?

2. Ligaments hold bones in place at synovial joints. Explain how skeletal muscles provide stability at synovial joints.

Skeletal muscle actions and control

The action of prime movers

Skeletal muscles contract and pull on bones. If a muscle pulls a bone in one direction, there has to be another muscle that pulls the bone in the other direction. This means skeletal muscles must work in pairs. Two muscles that work together are known as an **antagonistic pair**. The muscle that is contracting and pulling a bone is known as the **agonist** (or **prime mover**) and the muscle that is relaxing and allowing the movement is known as the **antagonist**.

Concentric and eccentric contractions

A **concentric contraction** occurs when a working muscle gets shorter and fatter (for example, lifting a weight in a biceps curl); and an **eccentric contraction** occurs when a working muscle gets longer and thinner (e.g., lowering the weight in a biceps curl).

Isometric and isotonic contractions

When a muscle is working against resistance and it shortens or lengthens, this is known as an **isotonic contraction** and movement is involved (e.g., during a biceps curl).

When a muscle is working against a resistance and stays the same length, this is known as an **isometric contraction** and no movement is involved (e.g., a gymnast holding a stationary handstand).

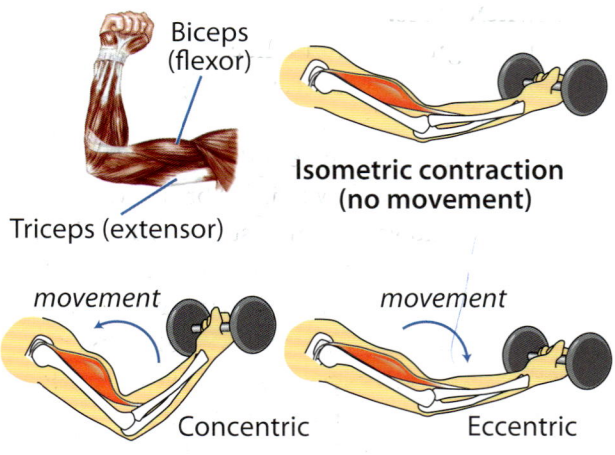

1.1 THE BODY AT WORK

Recruitment of muscle fibres

Some actions in sport require a delicate or soft touch (little force) and others require maximum, or near maximum, force. Skeletal muscles, under the control of the central nervous system (CNS), are able to provide this range of force.

>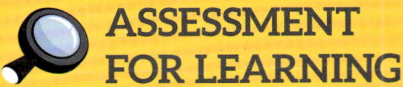
> ## ASSESSMENT FOR LEARNING
>
> 1. Skeletal muscles often work in pairs. Explain this.
> 2. Skeletal muscles contract and relax. Explain the difference between concentric, eccentric, isotonic and isometric contractions.
> 3. You, your class and your teacher should produce labelled diagrams that inaccurately demonstrate concentric, eccentric, isotonic or isometric contractions.
> 4. Analyse, identify and correct what is inaccurate in each of the diagrams produced for the task above.

Muscle fibre types

Slow twitch (Type I) and **fast twitch** (Type II) are the two distinctive types of skeletal muscle fibres.

Slow twitch fibres:
- are designed for endurance.
- contract slowly and relax slowly.
- produce little force.
- keep going for long periods without tiring. This is because slow twitch fibres have more arteries and veins than fast twitch and three times the amount of myoglobin. It is myoglobin that brings the oxygen carried in the blood into the muscle cells. Slow twitch fibres also have bigger, and twelve times more, mitochondria than fast twitch. The mitochondria in the muscle cells are like factories that burn the fuel with the oxygen in order to create energy.

Fast twitch fibres:
- are designed for very high intensity activity.
- contract quickly and relax quickly – in fact, three times more quickly than slow twitch.
- produce much force – ten times more than slow twitch.
- tire quickly – they have fewer arteries and veins than slow twitch, with less myoglobin.

In summary, slow twitch (Type I) fibres are designed for endurance and can produce a large amount of energy over a long period of time, assuming that oxygen is present. Fast twitch (Type II) fibres are designed for very high-intensity activity and can contract rapidly but tire very quickly.

The ratio of fast twitch to slow twitch muscle fibres is controlled genetically. People with high proportions of fast twitch muscle fibres should do well in activities that don't last very long but demand speed, strength or power (for example, sprinting and shot put). People with high proportions of slow twitch muscle fibres should do well in activities that last for long periods of time but demand relatively less strength or power (for example, running a 5000 m or marathon race).

ASSESSMENT FOR LEARNING

1. List the differences between fast twitch (Type II) muscle fibres and slow twitch (Type I) muscle fibres.

2. Your teacher will provide you with a list of three different physical activities, three different athletics events, and three different positions from three different team sports. Analyse the activities and state the physical demands of each activity by elite performers.

3. Look at your evaluation of each activity listed in the task above. Discuss and estimate what percentage of fast twitch muscle fibres compared to slow twitch muscle fibres would be needed for an elite performer in each activity.

Short-term effects of exercise on the muscular system

When you start to exercise, your skeletal muscles have to work harder and contract more often, which means they require more nutrients and oxygen. The respiratory system responds by getting more oxygen into the blood, and the heart (cardiac muscle) in the circulatory system responds by working harder and increasing the blood flow to the working muscles, providing them with more nutrients and oxygen.

When skeletal muscles contract and relax and produce energy for strenuous exercise they become warm and body temperature rises. The heat from the working muscles is dispersed from the muscles via the blood to the skin where the blood is cooled. This helps to regulate body temperature.

Energy systems used for muscle actions

The muscles are the motors or engines of the body. They use fuels to create energy to produce movement.

Skeletal muscles need **ATP (adenosine triphosphate)** as a fuel to produce energy. The ATP is supplied to the muscle by three systems:

- alactic anaerobic system
- lactic acid anaerobic system
- aerobic energy system

Effects of anaerobic exercise

Alactic system

To produce energy for very high-intensity work, the alactic system first uses the stores of ATP in the muscles. This produces energy for approximately one second. After this, stores of **creatine phosphate (CP)** are broken down to provide ATP. This source of fuel produces approximately another nine seconds of energy. The alactic system produces this energy without needing oxygen.

For a short burst of very high-intensity work (for example, a five-to-ten-second sprint or shot put) the main energy system used will be the alactic energy system.

Lactic acid system

Beyond ten seconds of high-intensity work, it is the lactic acid system that supplies the ATP. **Glycogen** (what our carbohydrate food becomes after digestion) is broken down to form ATP. The stores of glycogen can provide energy for up to forty seconds, without needing oxygen, before the build-up of the waste product of lactic acid stops the muscles from working.

For a long burst of very high-intensity work (for example, a 30-to-50-second sprint) the main energy system used will be the lactic acid energy system.

The alactic and lactic acid systems provide fuel for high-intensity work when the respiratory and circulatory systems are unable to meet the muscles' demands for oxygen. In total this can be up to 50 seconds.

As the fuel sources for anaerobic energy production are used up the muscles become tired, painful and eventually stop working altogether because of the build-up of the waste product, lactic acid.

Keith McClure

After very strenuous exercise it is important to replace the fuel sources and to get rid of waste products such as lactic acid. This requires oxygen in large quantities – hence the need for fast and deep breathing, and for the stroke volume (see page 25) and heart rate to remain high to carry lots of oxygen to the muscles during recovery. This need to replace the fuel sources and to remove lactic acid is known as the **oxygen debt**. During your recovery you are said to be paying back the oxygen debt.

Effects of aerobic exercise

The aerobic energy system is used when exercise is not as intense, and the respiratory and circulatory systems deliver sufficient oxygen to the working muscles. Glycogen and fats are broken down to provide ATP. The waste product (carbon dioxide) created from producing the energy is transported in the blood to the lungs where it is breathed out. You can keep going using the aerobic energy system until you run out of glycogen.

For a long period of moderate-intensity work (for example, jogging or running for 20 minutes) the main energy system used will be the aerobic energy system.

The proportion of energy produced by each of the three systems depends on the intensity and duration of the exercise.

The alactic, lactic acid and aerobic energy systems are usually involved at some stage when providing energy for competitive physical activities and sports. However, the proportion of energy produced by each of the three systems depends on the intensity and duration of the exercise.

For a short, maximum effort, activity like the shot put, discus or high jump, the predominant energy system will be the alactic anaerobic energy system. Also, in a sprint event like the 100 m, the predominant energy system will be the alactic anaerobic energy system.

In athletic track events like the 200 m and 400 m, the predominant energy system will be the lactic acid anaerobic energy system. In the 800 m event, the lactic acid and aerobic energy systems will be equally important. For the 1500 m event, right up to the marathon, the aerobic energy system will become more and more predominant, with the alactic and lactic acid systems being used effectively at the beginning and end of the events.

In many team sports, the aerobic energy system will be predominant because of the duration of the games, however, during that time there will be many times when maximum effort will be required and the alactic and lactic acid energy systems will be used.

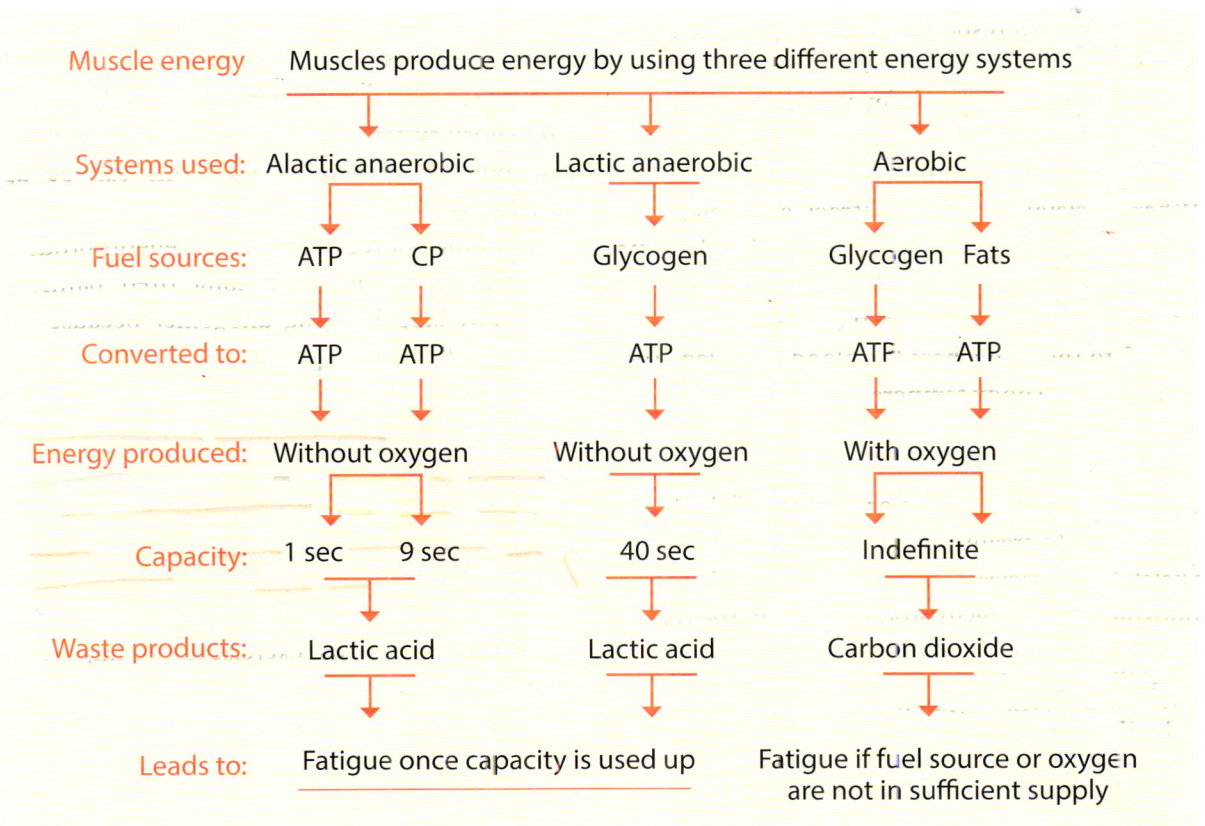

Summary of the energy systems used by working muscles

> ### ASSESSMENT FOR LEARNING
>
> 1. When skeletal muscles start to perform in prolonged vigorous exercise, they need more fuel and oxygen. How do other body systems react to help them get more fuel and oxygen?
> 2. Explain how the anaerobic and aerobic energy production systems work in partnership to fuel from low-intensity exercise up to maximum intensity exercise.
> 3. Analyse and evaluate the use of the energy production systems for the following: 100 m; 800 m; and 5000 m track events. Explain when the different energy production systems are used.

Long-term effects of optimal training on the muscular system

Slow twitch

As a result of regular aerobic endurance training, the slow twitch muscle fibres (Type I) get:

- an increased network of arteries, capillaries and veins. This means more oxygen and nutrients (food) can be delivered to the muscles and more waste products (carbon dioxide and water) can be taken away.
- increased stores of **myoglobin**. This means up to 80% more oxygen can be taken into the muscle.
- an increase in the number and size of **mitochondria**. This means the muscle can produce more energy.

All of these effects mean that you can perform better, aerobically. You can work harder and for longer than before. With high-intensity training the muscles improve their ability to use fats as fuel and become more efficient at using oxygen.

Fast twitch

As a result of regular strength training, the fast twitch muscle fibres (Type II) get:

- an increased cross-sectional area (the diameter increases). This is known as **hypertrophy**. It means the muscle can produce more force.
- increased stores of high-energy phosphagens. This means the muscles can work at a high intensity for longer.

These effects mean you perform better because you can produce more force and can work longer at a very high intensity. With the skeletal muscles being able to produce more force, it means the tendons joining the muscles to the bones become stronger, as do the ligaments surrounding the synovial joints.

> ### ASSESSMENT FOR LEARNING
>
> 1. What changes take place in the slow twitch (Type I) muscle fibres to account for improved aerobic performances, having completed regular, appropriate and effective training?
> 2. What changes take place in the fast twitch (Type II) muscle fibres to account for improved strength, having completed regular, appropriate and effective training?
> 3. You, your class and your teacher should produce a pool of statements on the effects of regular, appropriate and effective training on fast twitch and slow twitch muscle fibres. Some statements and labelling should be accurate and some should be inaccurate.
> 4. Look at each of the statements from the task above. Identify if the statements should refer to slow twitch or fast twitch muscle fibres and whether the statements are accurate or not. Correct the information in the statements that is not accurate.

1.1 THE BODY AT WORK

The cardiovascular system

Functions during performances in physical activities and sports

To perform physical activities and sports, the muscles (the motors or engines of the body) have to work harder and therefore need to be supplied with more nutrients and oxygen. The cardiovascular system does this job in the following ways:

- It transports the nutrients in the blood and the oxygen in the red blood cells in the blood to all the working muscles.
- It transports carbon dioxide – a waste product from muscle metabolism (energy production) – to the lungs where it is breathed out of the body.
- The excess heat produced by the muscles is transported through the blood to the skin where the heat is lost.
- When lactic acid – a waste product – builds up in the skeletal muscles, the respiratory and cardiovascular systems keep delivering more oxygen to the muscles until that lactic acid is broken down and the carbon dioxide is breathed out from the lungs.

The cardiovascular system transports platelets and fibrinogen that aid blood clotting, should you get cut while performing.

> **ASSESSMENT FOR LEARNING**
>
> 1 Explain the cardiovascular system's role in keeping the skeletal muscles working during vigorous aerobic activity.
>
> 2 What other roles does the cardiovascular system have?

How the blood flows around the body during performances in physical activities and sports

Pulmonary and systemic circulation

Blood is pumped from the heart around the body in a double circulatory system. In the **pulmonary circuit**, the blood travels from the right side of the heart to the lungs and back to the left side of the heart. In the **systemic circuit**, the blood travels from the left side of the heart to all parts of the body and back to the right side of the heart, and so it goes on – to the lungs and back, to the body and back – around and around in two 'closed circuits'.

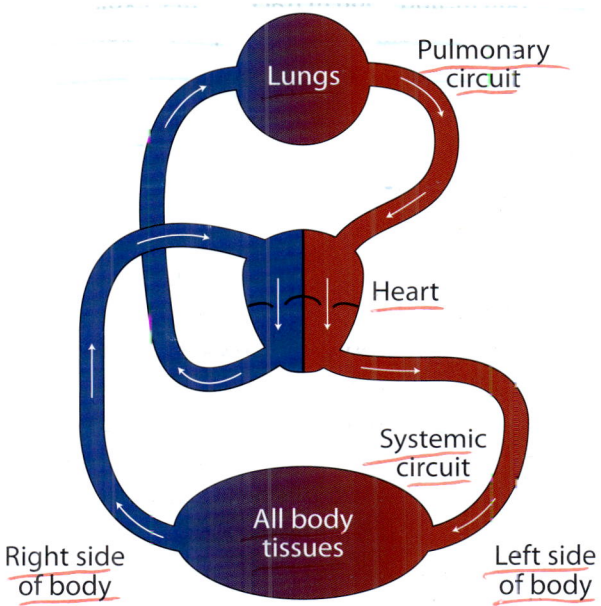

The heart (cardiac muscle) is divided into two separate halves – left and right atriums, and left and right ventricles – by the vertical wall called the **septum**. This is shown in the diagram overleaf.

In the **pulmonary circuit**, deoxygenated blood comes back from the working muscles and enters the heart's **right atrium** via the **superior vena cava**. The right atrium contracts and the blood is pumped into the **right ventricle**. The **tricuspid valve** prevents blood going back into the right atrium. The right ventricle then contracts and pumps the deoxygenated blood into the **pulmonary artery** and the deoxygenated blood goes to the lungs. The **pulmonic valve** prevents blood from going back into the right ventricle. At the alveoli in the lungs, the blood offloads the carbon dioxide (waste product from working muscles) and picks up oxygen. The oxygenated blood then travels back to the heart and enters the **left atrium** of the heart via the **pulmonary vein**.

In the **systemic circuit** the **left atrium** contracts and the blood is pumped into the **left ventricle**. The **mitral valve** prevents blood going back into the left atrium. The **left ventricle** then contracts and pumps the oxygenated blood into the **aorta** and the oxygenated blood goes to the working muscles. The **aortic valve** prevents blood from going back into the left ventricle. The blood offloads the oxygen it is carrying to the muscles and picks up carbon dioxide from the working muscles. The blood then travels back to the heart in veins and enters the right atrium via the superior vena cava. There are valves in the veins to stop the backflow of blood.

The atria (left and right atrium) contract at the same time, and shortly afterwards both ventricles contract simultaneously. The atria and ventricles then relax before the process is repeated. This process is known as the cardiac cycle.

ASSESSMENT FOR LEARNING

1. Explain the main difference between the pulmonary and systemic circuits.
2. Explain how the heart pumps the blood around the pulmonary and systemic circuits.

Blood vessels

Arteries, **capillaries** and **veins** are the main blood-carrying vessels, but all have slightly different roles, as reflected in their structures.

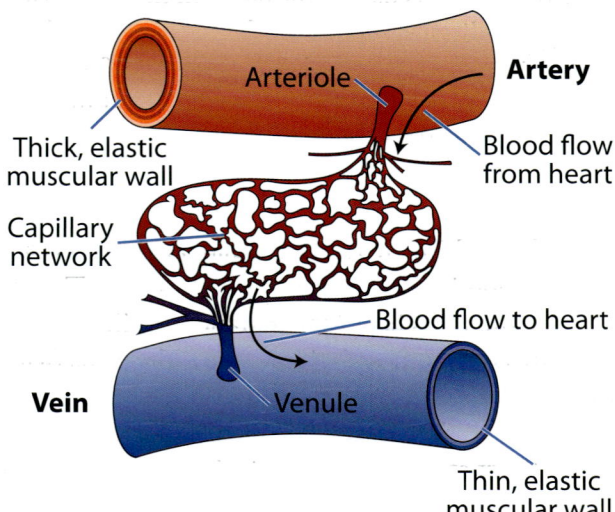

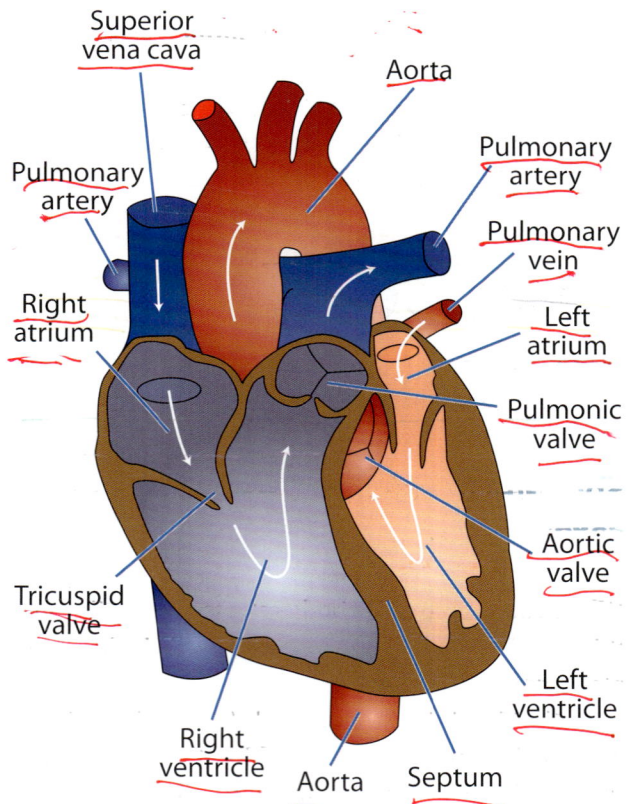

Arteries

Arteries, especially the aorta, have thicker, more muscular and more elastic walls of smooth muscle than other blood vessels because they must cope with blood being pumped at high velocity and under high pressure, away from the heart. Arteries (apart from the pulmonary artery) carry oxygenated blood away from the heart to all areas of the body. An artery's lumen (the space inside it) tends to be smaller than that of a vein.

The arteries branch into smaller arteries, which branch into arterioles, which branch into capillaries. As the blood flows from the arteries to the capillaries the blood pressure decreases and blood velocity slows. The smooth muscles in the arterial walls of the smaller arteries contract (vasoconstriction) or expand (vasodilation) to regulate the flow of blood through their lumen (see page 26).

Precapillary sphincters regulate blood flow into the capillary network. If the muscles are working hard, and are demanding more nutrients and oxygen, the precapillary sphincters can reduce blood flow to areas like the digestive system, allowing more blood with nutrients and oxygen to flow to the working muscles.

Capillaries

Capillaries are very small, narrow and have walls that are just one cell thick. Because of this structure, oxygen and nutrients can pass or **diffuse** through the capillary wall into the muscle cells, and waste products such as carbon dioxide can pass or diffuse from the muscle cells into the blood in the capillaries.

The capillaries merge to form venules, which merge to form veins, which merge to form the superior **vena cava**, which brings the blood into the right atrium of the heart.

Veins

Veins have thinner, less muscular and less elastic walls (smooth muscle) than the arteries. This is because the veins have to withstand very little blood pressure compared with the arteries. The veins (with the exception of the pulmonary vein) transport deoxygenated blood from all areas of the body back to the heart at an increased velocity. The lumen of a vein is larger than that of an artery.

Blood pressure is at its lowest in the veins. It is through the rhythmic movements of smooth muscle and the contractions of the skeletal muscles when they squeeze against the veins, that blood flow increases and the blood is forced back towards the heart. To help in the process and to counteract gravity, many of the veins have non-return valves, which prevent the backflow of blood when the skeletal muscles relax.

> **ASSESSMENT FOR LEARNING**
>
> 1 Explain why arteries, capillaries and veins have their own different and particular physical characteristics.

Heart actions and control
Heart rate

The heart rate (or pulse) is the number of cardiac cycles (beats) per minute. The heart rate rises in direct proportion to the exercise intensity. In other words, the harder you exercise, the faster your heart will beat.

Stroke volume

Stroke volume is the amount of blood pumped from the left ventricle per heartbeat. Stroke volume increases with exercise due to an increased venous return of blood to the heart, and from stronger contractions.

Cardiac output

Cardiac output is the volume of blood pumped out of the left side of the heart in one minute. Cardiac output is determined by the amount of blood pumped from the left ventricle per heartbeat and by the number of heartbeats (cardiac cycles) per minute.

In other words:

Cardiac output = stroke volume × heart rate

Stroke volume increases with exercise and the heart rate increases with exercise. This means cardiac output will increase with exercise.

> **ASSESSMENT FOR LEARNING**
>
> 1 Explain the difference between stroke volume and cardiac output.

Short-term effects of exercise on the cardiovascular system
Cardiac output increases

When you exercise, the body releases adrenaline and this causes the heart rate to rise. This increases blood flow.

With blood being pumped faster, there is an increased venous return of blood, which causes the stroke volume to increase. This increases blood pressure.

This means the cardiac output increases blood pressure and flow. Overall, this means more nutrients and oxygen will be delivered to the working skeletal muscles. This is especially important since working muscles will take 17 ml of oxygen from every 100 ml of blood (expressed as 17 ml/100 ml) compared with 6 ml/100 ml when resting.

exercise, so they will receive a relatively small amount (around 5%) of the blood (vasoconstriction). This is known as the redistribution of blood.

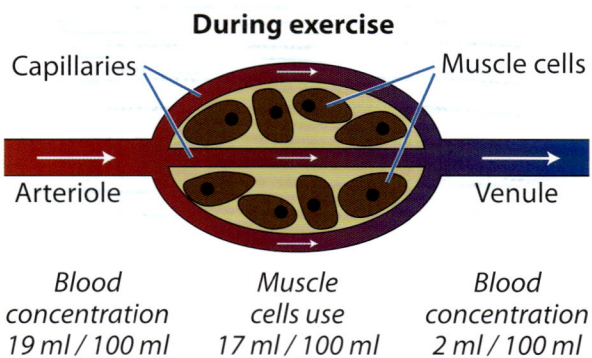

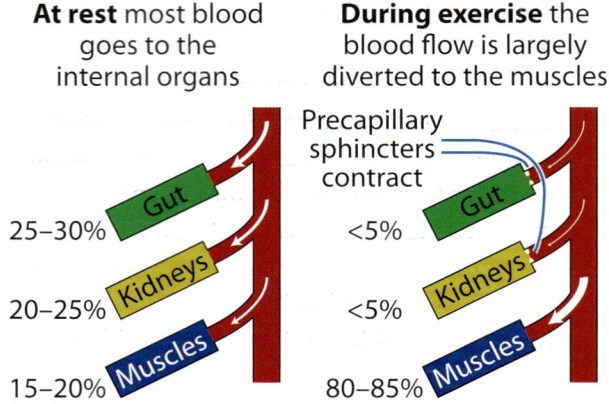

Note: During exercise, coronary blood flow increases by a factor of 5. Blood flow to the brain remains constant, whether at rest or exercising.

With skeletal muscles working harder, levels of carbon dioxide and lactic acid (waste products) increase in the blood. As a result, the cardiac output remains high until those waste products are dispersed from the body. As the skeletal muscles contract and relax to produce energy for high intensity exercise, they become warm and body temperature rises. The heat from the working muscles is dispersed through the blood to the skin where the blood is cooled. This helps regulate body temperature.

Blood plasma volume usually decreases because of increased sweating.

Vasoconstriction and vasodilation

Vasoconstriction restricts the blood flow to an area and **vasodilation** increases blood flow to an area. For instance, the working muscles require 80–85% of the blood during exercise (compared with 15–20% during rest) so, when there is physical exertion, blood flow is largely diverted to these muscles (vasodilation).

At the same time, organs such as the stomach, intestines and kidneys have less urgent needs during

ASSESSMENT FOR LEARNING

1. Cardiac output increases once you start to exercise. What things trigger this?

2. Explain how vasoconstriction and vasodilation help a person when they are doing vigorous aerobic activity.

Long-term effects of optimal training on the cardiovascular system

As illustrated by the diagram opposite, with regular exercise and training:
- the heart becomes larger, with thicker and stronger muscular walls (cardiac hypertrophy). This means more force can be applied on each contraction, and the left ventricle will be emptied more fully on each beat. The heart chambers also become larger, holding more blood before each contraction, meaning the stroke volume of the heart improves. The increased stroke volume means the heart rate when resting will become lower. As stroke volume increases, so will cardiac output since this is determined by the stroke volume multiplied by the number of heartbeats per

1.1 THE BODY AT WORK

minute. The arteries become larger and more elastic, which makes them more efficient in carrying the increased blood supply during exercise.
- more blood capillaries develop in the muscles and, with this increased capillarisation, the muscles get a greater supply of blood (which brings oxygen and nutrients). Also, with more venules, they are able to get rid of more waste products (carbon dioxide, for instance).
- more red blood cells are produced in the large bones of the body, meaning more oxygen can be carried by the blood.
- the body can delay and resist the build up of lactic acid in the cardiovascular system for longer.

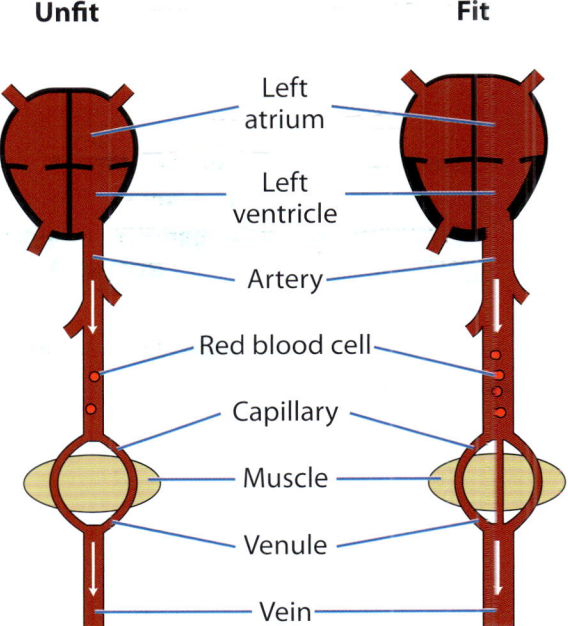

ASSESSMENT FOR LEARNING

1. What physical changes occur to the heart and cardiovascular system as a result of regular, appropriate and effective training? Explain how each of these changes improves aerobic performance.

2. You, your classmates and your teacher should produce some data that would realistically illustrate the differences between resting pulse rates, stroke volumes or cardiac outputs of people when they were unfit compared to when they were physically fit. You should also produce some data that is unrealistic or wrong.

3. Study and interpret the data produced for the task above on resting heart rates, stroke volumes or cardiac outputs. Identify what is realistic and possible and what is unrealistic or inaccurate when you compare the data of the people when they were unfit with the data of when they were physically fit.

All these adaptations mean that, for the same number of heartbeats, you are able to:
- have a higher work rate than before.
- keep going for longer than before.
- recover more quickly than before. The fitter you are, the faster your heart rate will return to normal.

You will not only be physically fitter but you will reduce your risk of suffering from cardiac or cardiovascular diseases.

The respiratory system

Functions during performances in physical activities and sports

The functions of the respiratory system are:
- to breathe air into the lungs.
- to transfer oxygen, through the process of diffusion, from the lungs into the blood.
- to transfer carbon dioxide and other gases from the blood, through the process of diffusion, into the lungs, where the gases are breathed out.

These functions become more pronounced when the body performs in physical activities and sports.

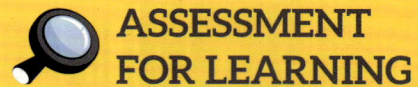

1. What is the role of the respiratory system?

How the respiratory system works

The nose, nasal cavity and mouth warm, filter and moisten the incoming air. This then travels from the throat to the **trachea**, which branches into two **bronchi** for the left and right lungs.

Inside the lungs, the air travels from the bronchi into smaller branches called **bronchioles** – the trachea, bronchi and bronchiole are all lined with a mucous membrane and tiny hairs called **cilia**. The mucous traps dust and dirt and the cilia push this mucous to the back of the throat where it is swallowed or coughed up.

From here, the air travels to the **alveolar sacs**, which contain **alveoli** – individual, hollow cavities – and it is here that the gases are exchanged.

Underneath the lungs sits the **diaphragm** – a broad band of muscle attached to the lower ribs and sternum, which forms the base of the **thoracic cavity**.

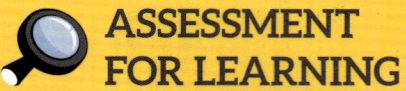

1. What happens to the air on its journey from being breathed in to its arrival in the alveoli of the lungs?

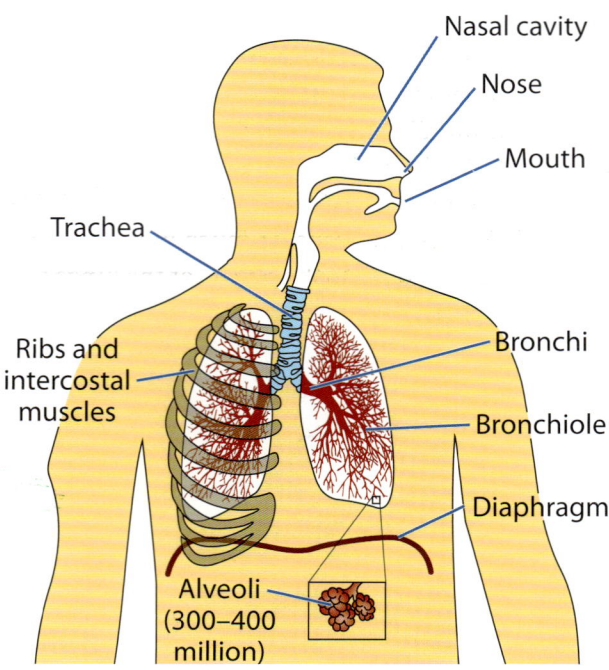

Respiratory processes

Inspiration during rest
- The external intercostal muscles contract gently pulling the ribs up and out.
- The diaphragm contracts, pulling itself down.
- The volume of the chest cavity increases, causing the air pressure to drop so air (with oxygen) is drawn into the alveoli in the lungs to equalize the pressure.

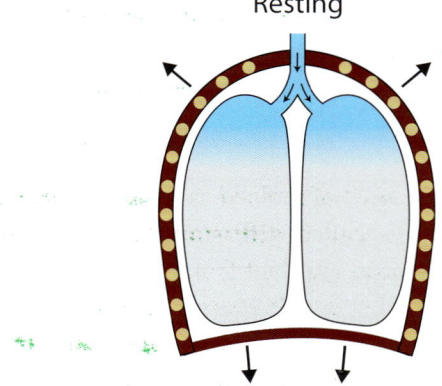

Expiration during rest
- The external intercostal muscles and diaphragm relax, so the ribs go back down and the diaphragm moves up. This pushes the waste product of carbon dioxide out of the lungs into the air.

1.1 THE BODY AT WORK

Inspiration during exercise
- The external intercostal muscles, diaphragm and other muscles not normally used in breathing all contract faster and more forcefully than when at rest.
- The volume of the chest cavity increases visibly and air pressure drops, so much more air (with oxygen) rushes into the alveoli of the lungs to equalize the pressure.

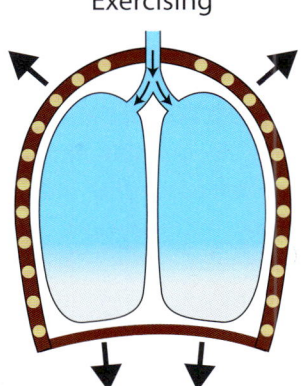

Exercising

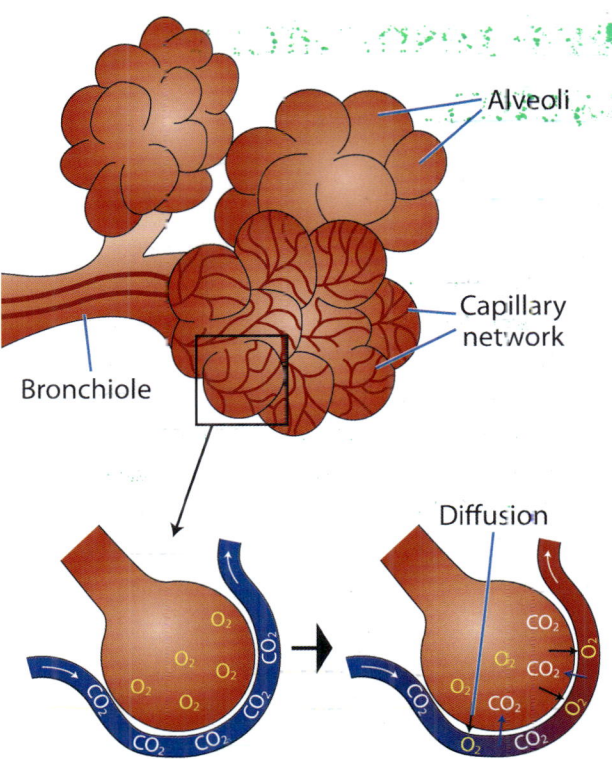

Expiration during exercise
- The external intercostal muscles and diaphragm relax, so the ribs go back down and the diaphragm moves up.
- In addition, the internal intercostal muscles and abdominal muscles contract pulling the rib cage further down, thus forcing more of the waste product of carbon dioxide out of the lungs into the air.
- The process also happens at a faster rate.

Diffusion
The natural movement of molecules to spread evenly through a liquid is called **diffusion**. Gases diffuse down a concentration gradient from an area of high concentration to an area of low concentration.

After breathing in, the alveoli have a high concentration of oxygen, while blood capillaries have a low concentration. Oxygen diffuses from the alveoli into the blood capillaries to even out the concentration, while carbon dioxide diffuses from the capillaries into the alveoli.

Vital capacity and minute ventilation

Vital capacity
Vital capacity is the maximum amount of air you can exhale (totally breathe out) after maximal inspiration (fully breathing in). It is usually 4–5 litres for men and 3–4 litres for women. Endurance athletes can have vital capacities of 6–7 litres. The greater the vital capacity, the greater the amount of air/oxygen that can be breathed in. This means more oxygen is available for performances.

Minute ventilation
Minute ventilation is the amount of air breathed in and out in one minute. Tidal volume is the volume of air breathed in and out for a normal breath. So:

Minute ventilation =
tidal volume × frequency of breaths/minute.

During exercise, minute ventilation increases because we take deeper breaths (greater volume) and we breathe faster (greater frequency of breaths per minute). For example:

29

For the average person at rest:
   Minute ventilation =
   14 breaths/min × 2 litres of air each breath
   Minute ventilation = 28 litres/minute

For the average person when exercising:
   Minute ventilation =
   20 breaths/min × 6 litres of air each breath
   Minute ventilation = 120 litres/minute

With deeper and more frequent breathing, more oxygen is available. It is more efficient, however, to increase our ventilation through deeper breaths than through faster breathing.

ASSESSMENT FOR LEARNING

1. Explain the basic mechanics of inspiration.

2. Explain why and how more air is breathed in when a person is doing vigorous physical activity.

3. Diffusion is an important process for aerobic performances. Explain how it works in the alveoli of the lungs.

Short-term effects of exercise on the respiratory system

The respiratory centre in the brain detects the increased level of carbon dioxide present in the blood during exercise.

In response to these increased levels, the respiratory centre sends nervous impulses (autonomic nervous system) to the intercostal muscles (external and internal) and the diaphragm. They work harder to increase the rate of breathing and to increase the volume of the thoracic (chest) cavity so more oxygen can be taken in with each breath.

In other words, during exercise, you breathe faster and deeper: your minute ventilation increases to meet the demands of the exercise.

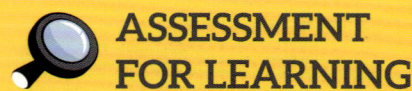

ASSESSMENT FOR LEARNING

1. Explain the importance of a person's vital capacity and minute ventilation for performing in aerobic type activities.

Long-term effects of optimal training on the respiratory system

As a result of regular aerobic endurance training, your respiratory muscles (the intercostal muscles and diaphragm) become stronger. This means your vital capacity and minute ventilation can improve, which in turn means you can get more oxygen in and out of the lungs with each breath and over a period of time, so you can work harder and keep working for longer without tiring.

As a result of regular aerobic endurance training, the surface area for gaseous exchange is increased as the capillaries surrounding the alveoli increase in number and diameter (this means that diffusion capacity increases).

This means you can get more oxygen from the alveoli into the blood and get rid of more carbon dioxide from the blood into the alveoli. It is easier for you to work at a given work rate than before, and you can work longer and harder than before. This principle is illustrated by the following two diagrams.

Unfit

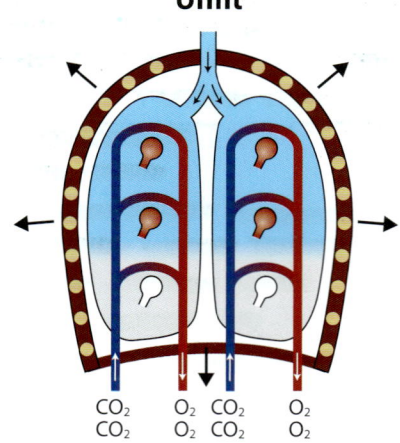

Ventilation = 25 breaths per minute × 4 litres
= 100 litres per minute

1.1 THE BODY AT WORK

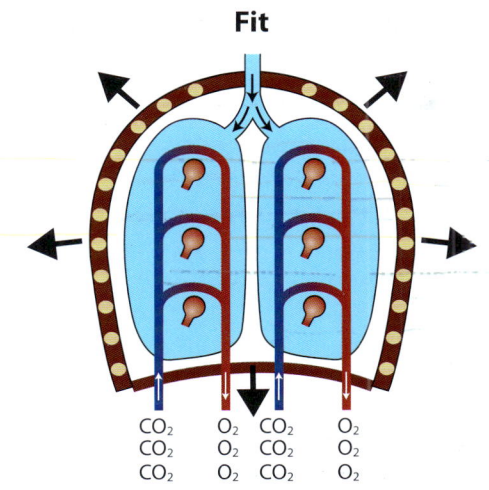

Fit

Ventilation = 18 breaths per minute × 6 litres
= 108 litres per minute

ASSESSMENT FOR LEARNING

1. Explain what physical changes occur as a result of regular, appropriate and effective training to account for the improvements in a person's vital capacity, minute ventilation and capacity for diffusion.

2. You, your classmates and your teacher should produce some data that would realistically illustrate the differences between vital capacities, minute ventilations or diffusion capacities of people when they were unfit compared to when they were physically fit. You should also produce some data that is unrealistic or wrong.

3. Study the data produced for the task above on vital capacities, minute ventilations or diffusion capacities. Identify what is realistic and possible and what is unrealistic or inaccurate when you compare the data of the people when they were unfit with the data of when they were physically fit.

The digestive system
Functions during performances in physical activities and sports

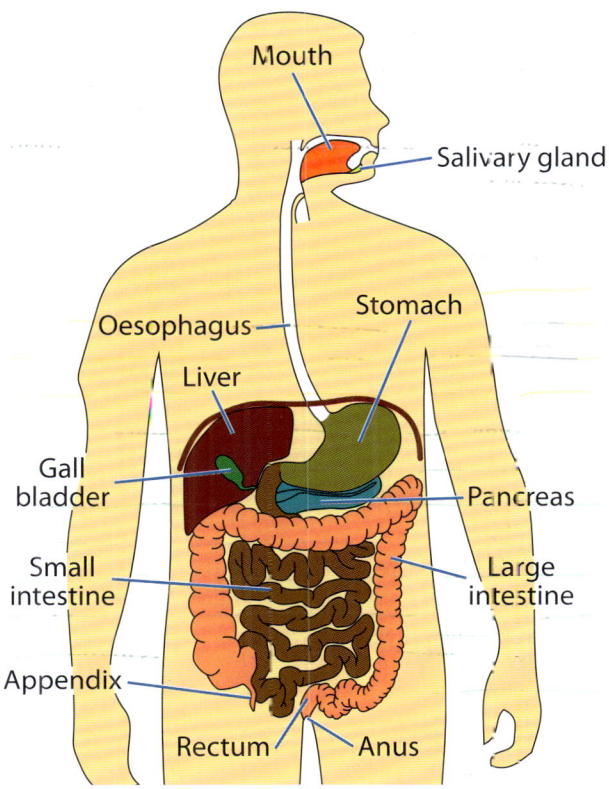

The digestive system performs an important role. However, unlike the other body systems studied, its work slows down during vigorous physical activity.

The food we eat (**ingestion**) is broken down into smaller and smaller pieces (**digestion**). When these pieces are small enough they pass through the intestine wall and dissolve into the blood (**absorption**). The nutrients become the fuel for the muscles to create energy and waste is excreted from the body (**excretion**).

How the digestive system works
Mouth
Food is taken into the body through the mouth (ingestion) and is broken down into smaller pieces by the teeth and tongue (mechanical digestion). Saliva is secreted in the mouth to moisten the food and begin the digestion of carbohydrates (chemical digestion).

Stomach

The stomach is a muscular sac that is able to store food so that the body has time to digest it. In the stomach, the muscular walls mechanically mix and break the food down further. Acid in the stomach kills bacteria present in the food. Digestive enzymes, hormones and hydrochloric acid continue the chemical digestion of the carbohydrates, proteins and fats into smaller molecules to make them easier to absorb.

Small intestine

Mechanical breakdown continues in the small intestine with its muscular walls further mixing and breaking down the food. The small intestine is also concerned with absorption and transfer of molecules to the blood. Bile – produced by the liver and stored in the gall bladder – breaks down fats. The pancreas secretes pancreatic juice into the small intestine. The pancreatic juice contains enzymes to break down carbohydrates, fats and proteins. It also contains insulin, which regulates blood sugar. Most absorption takes place through the walls of the small intestine into the blood.

Large intestine

The large intestine absorbs water and sodium. Small amounts of nutrients are also extracted. The waste (faeces) is then excreted from the body through the anus. The waste is comprised of indigestible material like fibre.

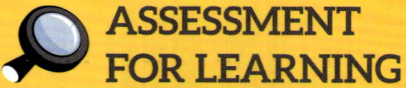

> **ASSESSMENT FOR LEARNING**
>
> 1 The food we eat is broken down and absorbed into the blood in order to fuel the demands of the muscles when performing in physical activities and sports. Explain how this process works.

Short-term effects of exercise on the digestive system

During exercise, digestion effectively stops or slows down as blood flow is largely diverted to the heart, lungs and working muscles (vasoconstriction). At rest, the gut receives 25–30% of the blood flow, but during exercise it gets less than 5% (see page 26).

This helps to explain why you should eat at least two hours in advance of taking part in vigorous exercise and why this pre-exercise meal should consist mainly of carbohydrates. Carbohydrates are digested quicker than fats and protein so you are more likely to have digested your meal and therefore have the energy from it available for your vigorous exercise.

Since the digestive system effectively closes down during vigorous exercise (in order to conserve energy), any food eaten in the period beforehand – particularly food high in fat or protein – is likely to remain in your digestive system for the duration of the exercise. This can be uncomfortable and affect

1.1 THE BODY AT WORK

your performance. In addition, the energy from this undigested food will not be made available to you.

Exercise helps strengthen the muscles involved in digestion, thus making the digestive process more efficient.

Keith McClure

1. Explain why you should eat at least two hours before participating in vigorous physical activity.
2. Explain what type of food you should eat before you participate in vigorous physical activity.

The nervous system

Functions during performances in physical activities and sports

The nervous system is responsible for the control of your body and the communication between your body systems.

Sensory function

During performances in physical activities and sports, your nervous system gathers information from inside and outside your body and sends it to the central nervous system (CNS). This is its **sensory** function.

Interpretive function

The information is processed and interpreted in your brain, and a decision is made on what to do. This is its **interpretive** function.

Motor function

The information on the response is then sent to the muscles in the appropriate parts of the body so they carry out that response. This is its **motor** function.

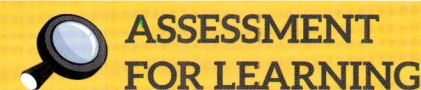

1. Outline the role of the nervous system during performances in sports such as badminton.

How the nervous system works during performances in physical activities and sports

The nervous system consists of two parts:
- **central nervous system (CNS)**
- **peripheral nervous system (PNS)**

The central nervous system

The central nervous system (CNS) consists of the **brain** (cerebrum and cerebellum) and **spinal cord**. The spinal cord carries information from the body to the brain. The brain interprets the information and makes a decision. The information on the response is passed from the brain through the spinal cord to the rest of the body.

33

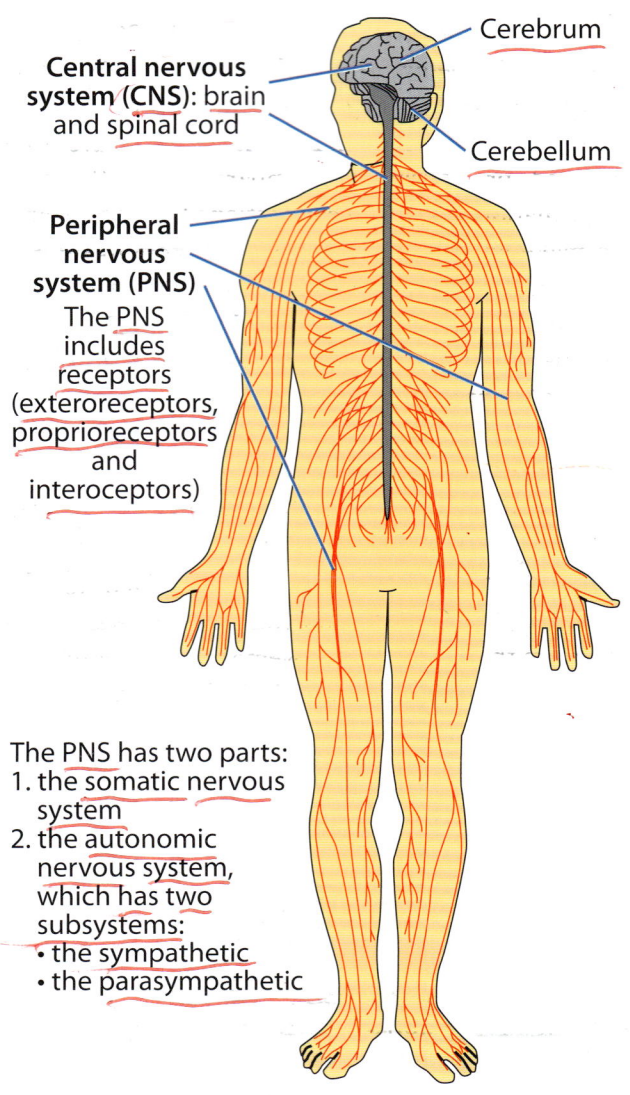

Central nervous system (CNS): brain and spinal cord

Peripheral nervous system (PNS)
The PNS includes receptors (exteroreceptors, proprioceptors and interoceptors)

The PNS has two parts:
1. the somatic nervous system
2. the autonomic nervous system, which has two subsystems:
   • the sympathetic
   • the parasympathetic

The peripheral nervous system

The peripheral nervous system (PNS) consists of the nerves going from the CNS to all parts of the body. There are two types of nerves in the PNS:

- **sensory nerves**: these take information from the **receptors** (**exteroreceptors**, **proprioceptors** and **interoceptors**) to the CNS. The receptors sense changes in the internal or external environments.
- **motor nerves**: these take information from the CNS to the **effectors** (usually the muscles), so it is the muscles that carry out the response of the CNS.

The PNS has two parts:
- the **somatic nervous system** gathers information from the external environment (light, sound, pressure etc.).
- the **autonomic nervous system** gathers information from the internal environment (internal organs like the heart, lungs, stomach, intestines etc.).

It has two subsystems:
- the **sympathetic nervous system**, which prepares the body for 'fight or flight': i.e. it gets the body prepared for action.
- the **parasympathetic nervous system**, which does the opposite of the sympathetic system by calming and relaxing the body.

ASSESSMENT FOR LEARNING

1. The central nervous system (CNS) and the peripheral nervous system (PNS) are the two main parts of the nervous system. Explain the role of the central nervous system (CNS).

2. The peripheral nervous system (PNS) has sensory nerves and motor nerves. Explain the difference between these two types of nerves.

3. The peripheral nervous system (PNS) has two parts: the somatic nervous system and the autonomic nervous system. Explain the difference between these two parts.

4. The autonomic nervous system has two subsystems: the sympathetic nervous system and the parasympathetic nervous system. Explain the difference between these two subsystems.

5. You, your classmates and your teacher should produce a pool of inaccurate statements on: the central nervous system (CNS); the peripheral nervous system (PNS); sensory nerves; motor nerves; the somatic nervous system; the autonomic nervous system; the sympathetic nervous system and the parasympathetic nervous system.

6. Look at each of the statements produced for the task above. Identify and correct the information in the statements that are inaccurate.

The nervous system in action

When learning a skill

Sensory input
When learning a skill, the eyes see the demonstration and the ears hear the instructions. What your eyes observe and what your ears hear is transformed into neural information and transmitted to the brain. This is known as the **input**.

Within a **sensory register** in the brain, **selective perception** takes place. In other words, you select the information that you think is important, while all other information is discarded or forgotten. This happens in milliseconds, and is known as **short-term sensory storage (STSS)**.

Interpretive actions
The selected information is then temporarily stored as working memory or **short-term memory (STM)**. Only a limited amount of information can be held as working memory and only for up to 20 seconds without it being repeated. During this time, **long-term memory (LTM)** is activated to make sense of the information. Experiences that have been learned previously are compared with the new information. The more connections the LTM is able to make with the information, the more likely it is that you know the skill and will be able to perform it efficiently and effectively. The brain's LTM has a limitless capacity and can store all motor skills that can be learnt.

Motor output
A **response generator** handles the way you organise your response to the information. This is known as the **output**. The response is transmitted to the muscles (the **effectors**) and you can then attempt to perform the sequence of movements of the skill.

Feedback on performance helps learning.

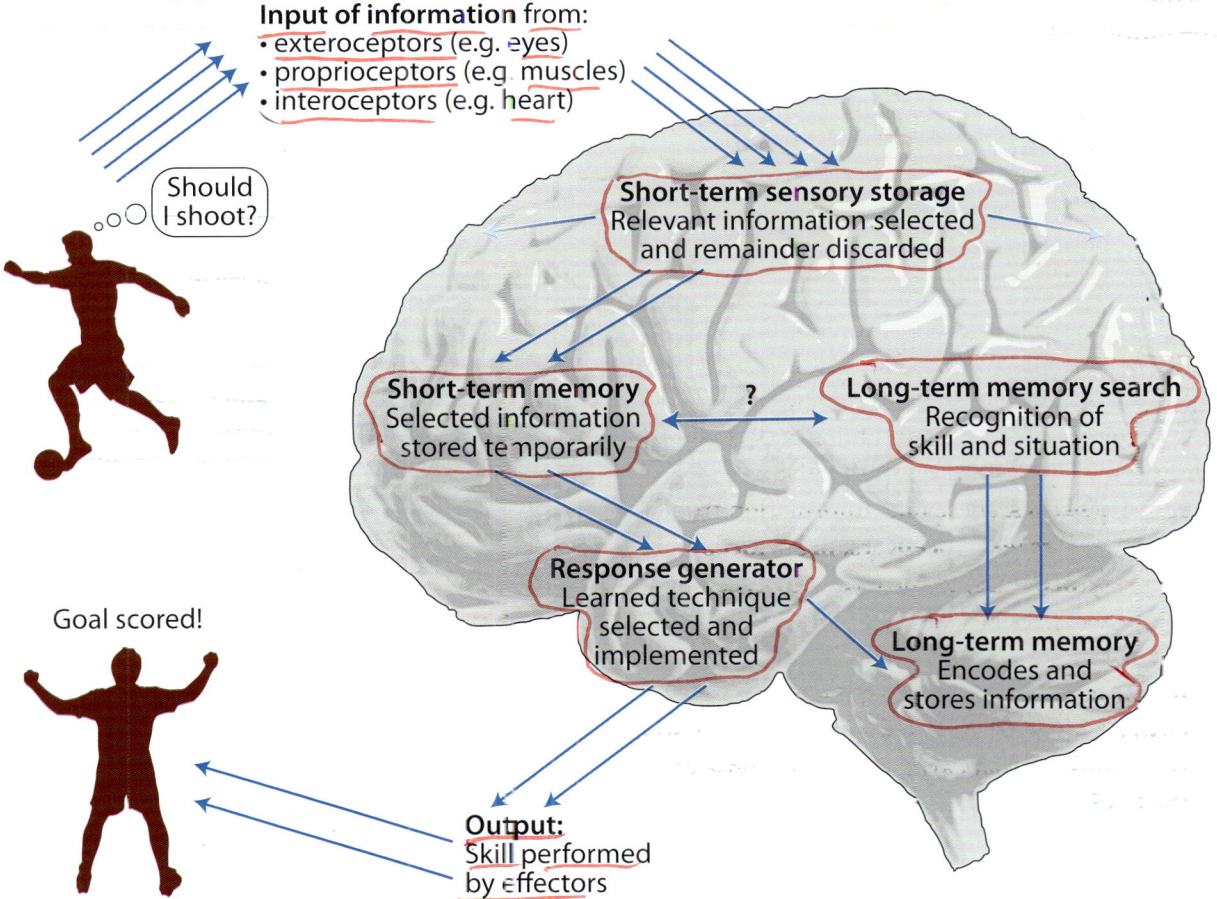

Information processing: should I shoot?

PHYSICAL EDUCATION for CCEA GCSE LEVEL

Brain – cerebrum
- Motor cortex – active when learning new movements or skills
- Premotor area – used when carrying out movements or skills already learnt

Proprioceptors
Inner ear – semi-circular canals and small sacs:
- Provide information on the position of the head (balance)
- Provide information on the direction the head is moving

Brain – cerebellum
- Used as a sorting office: decides what information is relevant
- Smooths and coordinates the actions of the muscles and integrates one movement with the next

Autonomic nervous system
Sympathetic system
Controls internal functions, e.g.:
- Pupils in eyes dilate
- Bronchi in lungs dilate – more oxygen taken in
- Heart rate increases, force of contractions increases
- Liver mobilises glycogen
- Adrenal glands secrete adrenaline
- Blood capillaries dilate – blood flows to muscles more easily
- Digestive system stops working
- Information from interoceptors allows this to happen

Exteroceptors – eyes
- Enable us to assess our surroundings (e.g. locate the ball/hurdle/goal; identify our teammates/opponents, etc.)
- Help us judge distance and speed (having two eyes means we have depth perception)

Exteroceptors – ears
- Enable us to assess our surroundings (e.g. the firing of the starting pistol; the position of our teammate calling for the ball, etc.)

Motor nerve
- Carries impulses (information) from the CNS to the muscles

Motor units
- Brought into play one at a time to increase muscle force
- Small-diameter nerves are recruited first. As the force required increases, larger-diameter nerves are recruited

Sensory nerve
- Carries impulses (information) from the receptors to the CNS

Proprioceptors – muscles, tendons, joints
- Provide information on muscle tension; on how stretched muscles are; and on the angle of the joints

---

ASSESSMENT FOR LEARNING

You have to perform an overhead clear in badminton:

1. Explain how the input of information occurs.
2. Explain how the information is processed in the brain and a decision made on the execution.
3. Explain how the decision on the execution (output) is carried out.
4. If you were able to explain the process for performing the overhead clear in badminton, choose three other skills from three different sports and apply the process to these three skills.

1.2 HEALTH AND LIFESTYLE DECISIONS

Mental and social health

Learning outcomes

> **In this section, you will learn:**
>
> - the concept of health
> - the signs and symptoms that can indicate mental and social health problems
> - the advice and recommendations to apply in order to achieve positive mental and social well-being
> - the benefits of maintaining positive mental and social well-being
> - the consequences of neglecting mental and social well-being
> - the negative coping skills that some may use to deal with mental and social health problems
> - how to analyse, interpret and evaluate information or data on mental and social well-being, and how to apply the advice and recommendations to a range of individuals and their circumstances

The concept of health

In 1946, the World Health Organization (WHO) defined health as "a state of complete physical, social and mental well-being and not merely the absence of disease or infirmity". [WHO, *Constitution of the World Health Organization*, 1946]

However, it can be argued that, rather than dealing in absolutes, well-being should be seen as more of a continuum.

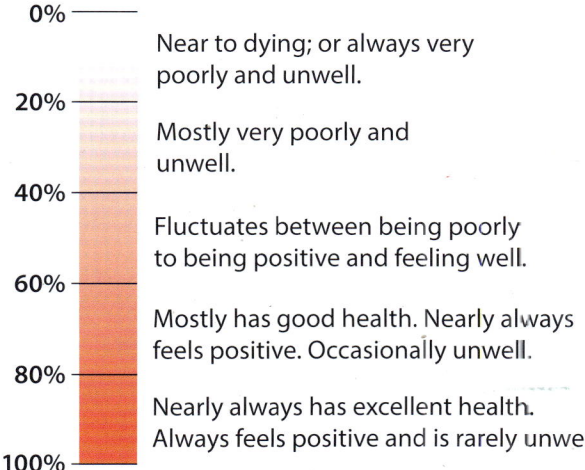

An example of health or well-being as a continuum

One modern medical dictionary seems to have hit upon a compromise, defining health as "an optimal state of physical, social and mental well-being and not merely the absence of disease or infirmity" [Dorland, *Dorland's Illustrated Medical Dictionary*, 2003]. While the UK Department of Health has simply defined health or well-being as "a positive physical, social and mental state" [Department of Health, *Our Health and Wellbeing*, 2010].

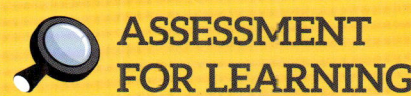

ASSESSMENT FOR LEARNING

1. "A state of complete physical, social and mental well-being and not merely the absence of disease or infirmity" was the World Health Organization's (WHO) original definition for health. Comment on the problems associated with this as the definition.

FURTHER THINKING

Use the Internet to explore the various definitions for health. Discuss the concept of health with your teacher and classmates.

Mental health

WHO defines mental health as "a state of well-being in which the individual realises his or her own abilities, can cope with the normal stresses of life, can work productively and fruitfully, and is able to make a contribution to his or her community". [WHO, *Promoting Mental Health*, 2004]

Mental health includes our emotional, psychological, and social well-being. It affects how we think, feel and act. Mental health problems – for instance, stress, anxiety or depression – are health conditions characterised by alterations in thinking, mood or behaviour.

> **FURTHER THINKING**
>
> Find out what you can about the thoughts, feelings, behaviour and physical symptoms experienced by people suffering from stress, anxiety or depression. Analyse your own lifestyle. Have you ever experienced these symptoms for a sustained period of time or have you noticed them in someone else? What action did you/they take?

Social health

Social health involves your ability to form meaningful, satisfying relationships with others and to interact with them in healthy, positive ways.

Social health or well-being is very much intertwined with mental health or well-being. Poor relationships over a prolonged period, or changes in your relationships, can lead to mental health problems or illnesses.

> **FURTHER THINKING**
>
> Find out what you can about the thoughts, feelings, behaviour and physical symptoms experienced by people with social health problems. Analyse your own lifestyle. Have you ever experienced these symptoms for a sustained period of time or have you noticed them in someone else? What action did you/they take?

Physical health

Physical health involves the well-being of the body. It is the aspect of health that is most visible and of which most people would be aware.

Physical health problems like bruising, a broken bone or torn ligaments can be caused while playing sports. Physical health problems can also be caused by contracting illnesses or diseases, like the flu or malaria. Our focus, however, will be on the problems caused by leading a sedentary lifestyle.

> **FURTHER THINKING**
>
> Find out what you can about the thoughts, feelings and behaviour experienced by people who are leading a sedentary lifestyle. Analyse your own lifestyle. Have you ever experienced these symptoms for a sustained period of time or have you noticed them in someone else? What action did you/they take?

How to improve well-being

The achievement of well-being is a continual process in which a person seeks, and becomes increasingly aware of, things that help them be healthy and well. They make positive choices that will benefit their health and well-being and, in doing this, they feel good, happy, content, valued and loved, and are able to deal with challenges that can arise in any aspect of life.

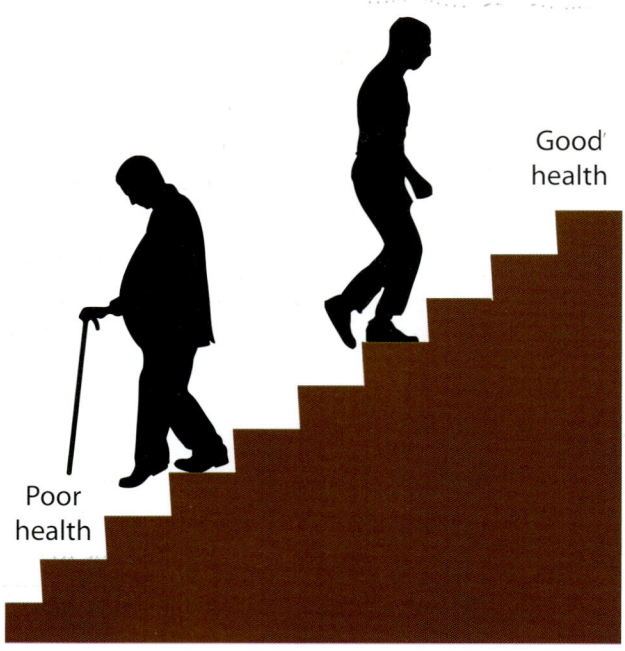

Understanding mental and social health

Advice and recommendations to prevent or deal with mental or social issues

There are several ways through which we can try to prevent or deal with mental and/or social problems. *The advice and recommendations given here are based on those published by the Public Health Agency (PHA).*

1 Know yourself

You should accept who you are – you may not be perfect but understand that you are just as important as anyone else. *Be content* – accept that there are some things that you can change about yourself and there are other things that you cannot; focus on your positive qualities rather than your faults. *Be optimistic* – try to avoid overthinking and comparing yourself with others. *Be kind to yourself rather than being critical* – treat yourself the way you would want friends to treat you. *Know and implement the coping strategies that work for you when you are stressed* – think about and try to do things that make you happy; know what matters to you.

2 Be able to recognise that there is a problem

It is important to recognise the early warning signs, as this can prevent things from getting worse. It will allow you to implement *positive* coping strategies and avoid *negative* coping strategies, such as drinking, smoking or drugs.

If you are worried about your mental health you should talk to your doctor (GP), who will decide what help or treatment is right for you. This could involve making changes to lifestyle; counselling or a talking treatment such as cognitive behavioural therapy (CBT); or the prescription of medication.

It is also good to involve your family, a friend or an adult that you can trust and who will not judge you. Talking with someone or writing about your problem can make you feel supported and less alone. If you are distressed and have no one to talk to, you should contact an online or telephone helpline, or a counselling service: they are usually available 24/7.

3 Work on developing positive, close relationships

Most people want to belong; to be loved, happy and secure; and to have a purpose. People are social by nature and want to be able to share their feelings and know that they will be understood. This happens in good, strong relationships. You should actively nurture/develop good relationships with family, friends, neighbours, school or work colleagues and people in the community. They can help you deal with the stresses of life and offer you other views from your own. They can help you maintain good mental health and be there to support and care for you should you develop mental health problems.

Suggestions for building stronger and closer relationships:

- Eat together as a family. Talk about each other's experiences from the day.
- Be willing to share your dreams and ambitions with your family and friends.
- Be able to share your problems or worries with family and friends
- Be willing to listen to family and friends and give emotional support.
- Do things together as a family: for example, play a game together; go on a family walk or go on a family picnic.

- Arrange to meet with friends to do something: for example, play badminton at the leisure centre or go out for a meal.
- Make the effort to phone friends or colleagues sometimes instead of texting, messaging or emailing them.
- Be willing to visit a friend or family member who needs support or company.
- Be willing to keep in touch with family and friends that live far away – there are a variety of apps available now to enable you to do this.

4 Give to others

Research suggests that acts of giving and kindness are associated with positive mental well-being. Helping others can be rewarding; make you feel needed and valued; and give you a sense of purpose – as can working with others towards a shared goal. What you do for others in a constructive way helps you strengthen relationships and build new ones.

Even simple things – like smiling at, thanking or holding a door open for someone – can make you feel good and connect you to people.

5 Set tasks to achieve things

When you achieve something, you feel good. Successfully completing tasks usually involves having good time-management techniques. Planning what has to be done helps you feel in control and can reduce stress and worry. When you actually complete the tasks, you feel great and encouraged.

6 Have some 'me time'

You should set some time aside for yourself to relax and do something that you enjoy. Having this sort of 'me time' can help you forget your worries for a while, change your mood and help you feel better.

7 Be physically active

Being physically active on a regular basis is not only important for good physical health but is also important for dealing with, or helping you avoid, social and mental health problems.

Regular physical activity can energise you, lift your mood, reduce your stress and anxiety levels and help your worries seem less severe. If you can do physical activity with someone else, this can help even more.

Activities like walking, running, cycling or dancing are great because they can be done alone or with others, at a time that suits you, and they are relatively inexpensive to do. If you work at an appropriate intensity long enough and often enough, it will bring health benefits. It is important to find physical activities that you enjoy and so will continue to do.

Being physically active can also include doing tasks more energetically, for example, when you go up or down stairs, mow the lawn or walk to school/work. In other words, you do the tasks more quickly.

More information on being physically active may be found on pages 46–59.

8 Eat a balanced, healthy diet

If you want to maintain good physical, social and mental health, your nutritional intake needs to be balanced and healthy. This means eating the appropriate amount of food so that you maintain a healthy weight, and eating the right sort and balance of nutrients so that the body functions well. If you eat a poor, unbalanced or unhealthy diet, then your physical, social and mental health can be affected.

More information on nutritional intake may be found on pages 66–75.

9 Get quality sleep

Make sure to create the right environment in your bedroom for quality sleep – ideally the room should be dark, quiet and comfortable. Establish helpful routines for going to bed and for getting to sleep. Aim to go to bed and get up at the same time each day. Ensure you are getting the optimum amount of sleep for someone your age.

More information on sleep may be found on pages 76–79.

10 Control unhealthy ways of coping

Some people turn to unhealthy coping strategies as a means of relief when they are stressed: they may smoke, drink alcohol, take drugs or other illegal substances. In the short-term these may seem to make you forget about your worries, however they all have negative impacts on your mental and physical health. Alcohol, for instance, is a depressant; while drug misuse (whether in illegal drugs, prescribed or over the counter medications) can lead to mental health problems and serious mental illness. If you want to maintain good physical, social and mental health then you should avoid these unhealthy ways of coping.

More information on tobacco, illegal substances and alcohol may be found on pages 80–93.

ASSESSMENT FOR LEARNING

1. Analyse your own lifestyle. How well are you applying each of the ten self-help strategies listed in this section with regard to mental and/or social well-being? For each strategy:
   - list the positive thing that you are already doing and
   - list the things that you are not doing but feel you should be doing.
2. What actions should/will you take to address the list of things that you are not doing?
3. Using the ten self-help strategies, explain what sort of lifestyle you might expect a person suffering from mental health issues to have.

If a mental health issue is suspected

If a mental health issue is suspected, the best thing to do is to see a doctor (GP) as soon as possible. Earlier treatment leads to a quicker and better recovery. The GP can also rule out any other medical cause for symptoms.

Depending on the severity of symptoms, the GP will decide on a suitable treatment. Usual approaches are:
- self-help strategies (see pages 39–41)
- talking therapies (psychotherapies)
- medication

Talking therapies (psychotherapies)

Cognitive behavioural therapy (CBT) has been proven very effective for mental health conditions such as depression and anxiety. It works on the basis that if we change our unhelpful thinking patterns and behaviour it will improve how we feel. Computerised CBT and self-help books are also available.

Other types of therapy are mindfulness and counselling. Mindfulness is a way of paying attention to the present moment using meditation and breathing, and helps a person become more aware of their thoughts and feelings so that, instead of being overwhelmed by them, they are better able to manage them.

Any of these therapies may be used with or without medication.

Medication

Anti-depressants are the most effective and most commonly prescribed treatment for moderate/severe depression and for certain types of anxiety. They work by boosting certain brain chemicals that affect mood.

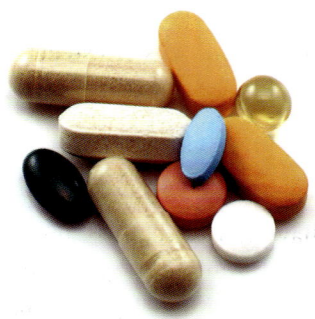

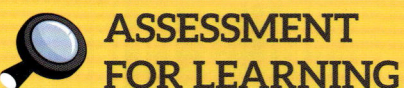

ASSESSMENT FOR LEARNING

1. How would talking therapies (psychotherapies) help a person who is suffering from depression or anxiety?

2. What medication might a doctor prescribe to help a person who is suffering from depression or anxiety? How does medication help?

Positive benefits from maintaining mental and social well-being

If you look after your mental and social well-being, you may experience some of the following benefits:

Having coping skills for life's challenges

If you are motivated to participate and compete in life's challenges, you may develop coping skills to deal with these challenges, or to deal with other matters. You begin to see difficulties as challenges rather than problems, cope well with setbacks and failures, and are willing and able to accept change. People trust you and are willing to work with you.

Resilience

This is the ability to cope with setbacks and not feel down when things go wrong. If you are resilient you can bounce back, no matter how many times things go against you.

It does not mean that you experience less distress, grief, or anxiety than other people. It means that you can handle setbacks in ways that are positive.

The ability to function well with others

If you can work well with others, you get on well with family, colleagues and neighbours. You feel confident and at ease when meeting new people, and have self-belief when working with others.

You understand and respect others, effectively manage your emotions and work well as part of a team. If you use social media sites, you do so positively and respectfully.

You are willing to share give to others and offer help without being asked. This gives you feelings of happiness and self-worth.

Effective management of emotions

If you can enjoy success or cope with failure without allowing your feelings to get out of control, you are able to control your emotions when dealing with challenging situations involving family, friends, colleagues, strangers or people in authority.

An honest self-regard and self-esteem

If you are in a state of positive mental well-being, you feel good and are usually content and at peace with yourself and the world. You have self-belief. You know yourself and are realistic about what you want.

1.2 HEALTH AND LIFESTYLE DECISIONS

The ability to view the world honestly, accurately and realistically

If you are able to discern right from wrong, you may realise that many things and actions are far from perfect, but you do what you can to make your world, and that of others, a better place.

> **ASSESSMENT FOR LEARNING**
>
> 1. What positive benefits are associated with those who maintain their mental and social well-being?
> 2. Analyse your own lifestyle with regard to mental and social well-being. Which, if any, of the positive benefits do you have? As a class, discuss the positive benefits and identify real-life examples.

Consequences of neglecting mental and social well-being

When people cannot cope with the challenges of everyday life, or when they have difficulties with relationships, they can feel unloved, unvalued, rejected, insecure, intimidated and bullied. If these feelings are not dealt with, people can lose their self-belief, self-esteem and confidence.

Stress from continually failing, or from hurtful experiences, can lead to mental health problems, like depression, which can cause sufferers to withdraw even further away from family, friends and from social activities. They may also face more distress, pain, suffering and disturbances in their lives because they have difficulty dealing with trauma and they have now resilience.

Having mental and social health problems can often lead to the following:

Decreased motivation

A decrease in motivation can have a detrimental effect on many aspects of people's lives: for example, a loss of self-belief and self-esteem; a decline in physical health; an effect on nutritional intake; or an impact on social life.

Difficulty dealing with trauma and challenges

People who have not developed appropriate coping skills to deal with the challenges of everyday life or difficulties within relationships may lack confidence when embracing challenges and have limited ability to deal with trauma.

Poor physical health

The causes of poor physical health in people with mental and social health problems – and therefore the symptoms of that poor health – will vary. For example, medications can impact physical health, in some cases causing rapid weight gain which can then lead to health complications. And sometimes high amounts of stress can lead to cardiac problems.

In some cases, physical issues are overlooked and viewed by doctors as just an extension of the mental health issue. Or perhaps the type of mental and social health problem can make it more difficult to eat well or exercise, especially if the person experiences social isolation, low motivation or a lack of routine.

Sleep, too, is a factor: because of poor mood; lack of motivation or personal responsibility; stress or fatigue, some may want to sleep or remain in bed longer than normal. Others may find it difficult to get to sleep, or they have their sleep continually disrupted (for example, due to anxiety). Poor sleeping patterns make everything worse – physically, socially and mentally.

High amounts of stress
High amounts of stress over a prolonged period can lead to headaches; sleeping problems; lack of energy; dizziness; chest or back pains; rapid or shallow breathing; and rapid heartbeat. People experiencing high stress levels can also suffer from unexplained illnesses.

A sedentary lifestyle
By not being physically active, people can lose physical capacity, affecting their ability to work and effectively complete everyday tasks. This then leads to a sedentary lifestyle, which increases the risk of coronary heart disease, diabetes, bowel cancer, osteoporosis or loss of lean muscle tissue (atrophy).

Poor nutritional intake
In some cases, individuals who suffer from mental and/or social health problems may make unhealthy nutritional decisions. This can lead to eating disorders such as bulimia nervosa, anorexia nervosa or obesity. Without a balanced, healthy nutritional plan, physical health is likely to suffer.

> **ASSESSMENT FOR LEARNING**
>
> 1. What are the consequences associated with those who neglect their mental and social well-being?

Negative coping skills used in dealing with mental and social problems

Work
Some people cope with mental or social health issues by spending more time doing other things; for example, spending more time at **work** to avoid dealing with problems.

Denial
Some people may be aware of early warning signs of mental health problems – including mood swings; altered sleep patterns; changes in appetite; weight loss or gain; increased irritability, sensitivity or aggression; difficulty following a conversation, remembering things or concentrating – but they **ignore them** or **deny** them if others enquire about their health.

Avoiding problems
Sometimes, people **withdraw** and either avoid or delay any attempts to resolve their problems. This often means problems build up, and things get worse rather than better.

Alcohol, tobacco, drugs

Some people turn to alcohol, cigarettes or illegal substances as a means of dealing with social or mental health issues. These temporary and unhelpful coping strategies are to be avoided as they usually make matters worse (see pages 80–93).

*Issues with excessive **alcohol** use:*
- Alcohol disrupts sleep, leaving people tired and irritable.
- Hangovers make concentration harder and even simple tasks more difficult.
- Alcohol can make feelings of anxiety and depression worse.
- Repeated alcohol use is expensive, and can result in stressful financial difficulties.
- Alcohol has a negative impact on your physical health and is addictive.

*Issues with smoking **tobacco**:*
- People think that smoking helps them relax, however it is actually a stimulant that speeds up the heart rate, and so has the opposite effect.

1.2 HEALTH AND LIFESTYLE DECISIONS

- It can also cause stress: for example when a smoker is in a place that prohibits smoking.
- Habitual smoking is expensive, and it can result in stressful financial difficulties.
- Smoking has a negative impact on your lungs and is addictive.

*Issues with taking **drugs** and other illegal substances:*
- The effects can be unpredictable.
- They can react against alcohol and lead to overdose.
- People often rely on stimulants to get a high and then sedatives to come back down, and the mix of the two puts the body under immense pressure. This can affect breathing, lead to coma, cardiac arrest, overdose, and even death.
- Drugs are expensive, and addiction can result in stressful financial difficulties.

Self-harm

Some feel that things are so bad that they cause deliberate injury to themselves (**self-harm**) as a way of coping with or expressing overwhelming emotional distress. A further extension of this is in considering, and sometimes committing, suicide. This is not the answer – suicide is a final solution for a temporary problem.

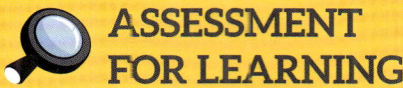

ASSESSMENT FOR LEARNING

1. What negative coping skills are associated with those who neglect their mental and social well-being?

2. Analyse your own lifestyle with regard to mental and social well-being. Which, if any, of the negative coping skills have you experienced? As a class, discuss the dangers of the negative coping skills.

3. You, your classmates and your teacher should produce brief lifestyle scenarios for different people suffering from mental health problems.

4. Analyse each of these lifestyles and recommend what things each person should change in their lifestyle and what things they should introduce into their lifestyle to regain and then maintain their mental health.

FURTHER THINKING

Explore the Public Health Agency (PHA) and other websites to further enhance your understanding of mental and social health. Note, and share, your discoveries.

ANALYSIS, INTERPRETATION, EVALUATION AND PLANNING

ASSESSMENT FOR LEARNING

1. Study the audit on page 187. It provides information on Laura's lifestyle practices with regard to her mental and social health. Analyse, interpret and evaluate the information/data in the audit, make sound recommendations and set SMART objectives and targets to bring about improvements. Back up your findings with references to what is factual, sound or recommended (the 'ideal').

2. Devise a safe, appropriate and effective action plan to achieve the objectives and targets within a set time frame. Explain how you would monitor the implementation of the action plan and the benefits of doing this.

   For guidance on how to do this, use Steps 1–5 on page 6.

3. You, your classmates and your teacher should produce a variety of audits that reflect a range of individuals from those who have mental and social health problems to those who are positively healthy in this area. Use the audits to practise answering questions 1 and 2 above.

Physical health: exercise

Learning outcomes

> **In this section, you will learn:**
>
> - the consequences of a sedentary lifestyle
> - advice and recommendations to apply for exercise and physical activity
> - the benefits of maintaining physical well-being
> - the concept of physical fitness for health and for performance
> - the components of physical fitness
> - the principles of training
> - how to carry out fitness testing
> - the benefits and application of risk assessments
> - how to analyse, interpret and evaluate information or data on exercise and physical activity, and how to plan safe, appropriate and effective health-related exercise programmes

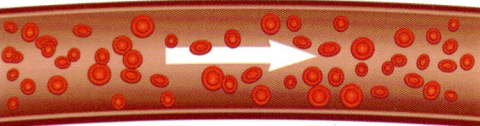

Normal artery

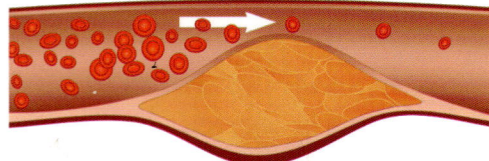

Fatty material building up

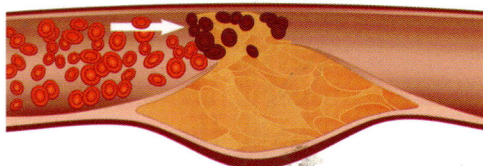

A significantly narrowed artery

You should be aware by now that physical health, social health and mental health are all interlinked, and poor health in one can affect the others.

Consequences of a sedentary lifestyle

Leading a sedentary lifestyle – one in which you are sitting or lying down for long periods – is bad for your health, and has the following consequences:

Chronic disease

A sedentary lifestyle often increases the risk of chronic disease such as:

- **coronary heart disease**: coronary arteries become narrowed by a gradual build up of fatty material within their walls. In time, the fatty material hardens and arteries may become so narrow that they cannot deliver enough oxygen-rich blood to the heart. The pain and discomfort felt as a result of this is called angina. If a piece of fatty material breaks off it may cause a blood clot to form. If it blocks the coronary artery and cuts off the supply of oxygen-rich blood to the heart muscle, the heart may become permanently damaged. This is known as a heart attack.

- **diabetes** (type 2): a long-term metabolic disorder where the body causes blood glucose (sugar) levels to rise higher than normal and does not use insulin properly (insulin resistance). At first, the pancreas makes extra insulin but, over time, it cannot make enough insulin to keep blood glucose at normal levels.

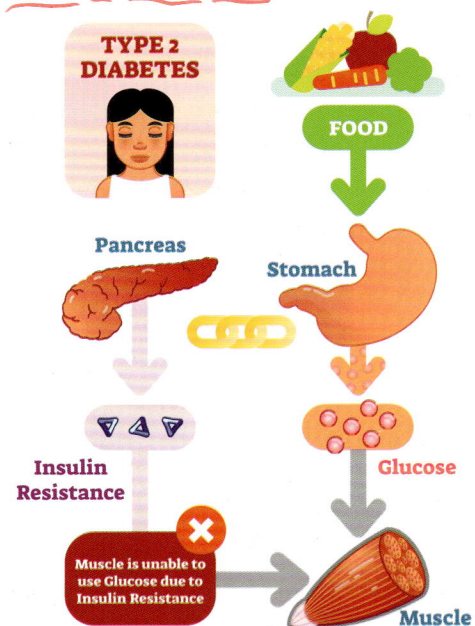

- **bowel cancer**: abnormal cells divide and grow, affecting surrounding tissues or organs.
- **osteoporosis** (porous bones): bones become thin, weak and brittle. In most cases, bones weaken due to low levels of calcium, phosphorus and other minerals.

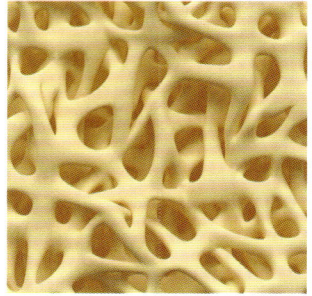 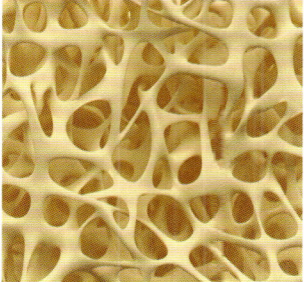

Normal bone   *Bone with osteoporosis*

Cognitive decline

Cognition refers to the ability to think. Mild cognitive impairment is a decline in cognition, including concentration, communication, memory and orientation. One of the most common examples of this is **dementia** where there is a loss of cognitive function due to changes in the brain caused by disease or trauma. The changes may occur gradually or quickly and can affect the ability to dress, bathe or eat.

Atrophy

When muscles are not being used enough, they can waste away – the loss of lean muscle tissue.

Depression

Depression is characterised by low energy and mood, low self-esteem, and loss of interest or pleasure in normally enjoyable activities. Depression can occur when a person is physically inactive: they lose physical capacity, which can affect ability to work and effectively complete everyday tasks.

A less efficient immune system

People who lead a sedentary lifestyle are more likely to catch a cold, flu or other illness, whereas people who exercise develop a more efficient immune system (see page 49).

>  **ASSESSMENT FOR LEARNING**
>
> 1. Explain the effects that a sedentary lifestyle has on the following body systems:
>   - the skeletal system
>   - the muscular system
>   - the circulatory system
>   - the central nervous system
> 2. What diseases and conditions can develop as a result of following a sedentary lifestyle?

Advice and recommendations on exercise and physical activity to develop and maintain physical health and well-being

There are several ways through which we can try to develop and maintain physical health and well-being. *The advice and recommendations given here are based on those published by the Public Health Agency (PHA).*

Even small steps in increasing physical activity can improve health and well-being, and while there are undoubtedly external factors that influence people's involvement – age, gender, affluence and so on (see pages 94–101) – some people may just be reluctant to try. The following excuses are often used:

> "I don't like exercise or sports"… "I am no good at sports or physical activities"…
> "I cannot do this, it is too hard"…
> "It is too much bother"… "I don't have time"…
> "I'm too tired"… "I don't want to do it on my own"… "I don't like the weather."

There are many challenges to overcome in convincing people with sedentary lifestyles to take even small steps towards increasing physical activity.

The first challenge is to find an activity that overcomes most, if not all, of the excuses above; an activity that will be suitable for as many people as possible, but especially for those who are inactive; will be easy to start; and is a good foundation that may lead to participation in other physical activities.

The Public Health Agency (PHA) promotes **walking** as the best activity since it has many benefits, including that it:

- can be done by almost anyone: children, teenagers, adults and older adults.
- can be done alone or with other people or pets.
- does not require specialist equipment, clothing or facilities.
- can be done in any weather.
- can fit into a busy schedule (as a means to get from A to B rather than using a car, taxi or bus).
- is free: there are no fees and no gym membership needed.
- can be done anywhere: in cities, in the mountains, in the countryside, along the coast, or on a treadmill.

- can be done at any time, day or night.
- is part of life, and so should be the foundation, or starting point, in benefiting or improving physical, mental and social health.

Various tips and strategies have been suggested to get people walking and keep them involved – such as choosing interesting places to walk to maintain variety; entering events/charity walks; and joining a walking group – but one of the most popular is the use of a pedometer/step counter. With these, the target is to slowly build up to doing 10000+ steps (approximately four miles/seven kilometres) per day by gradually increasing the daily amount. By monitoring and recording the number of steps walked each week, progress can be charted.

To encourage people to take more steps, the PHA gives the following ten tips:

1. If you're heading somewhere local, walk rather than take the car or the bus.
2. In the supermarket car park, choose a space as far away from the entrance as possible.
3. March up and down while talking on the phone.
4. Ignore lifts and escalators – always take the stairs.
5. Instead of catching up with friends over a coffee, meet them for a walk.
6. Get off the bus or train one stop before your usual one and walk the rest of the way.
7. Instead of emailing or phoning a colleague, walk over to their desk.
8. Help out a friend or neighbour by offering to walk their dog.
9. Find a route near your office or home where you can go for a brisk 15-minute walk at lunchtime.
10. Have a meeting while walking rather than sitting in the office.

Walking, therefore, is a great introductory exercise, and it keeps the respiratory and circulatory systems and the muscles of the legs in working order. However, it does not directly benefit the major muscles and joints of the trunk, upper body and arms, and it does not improve the mobility needed around all major joints. This means that, for all-round physical health, you should do appropriate and sufficient exercise for those areas as well.

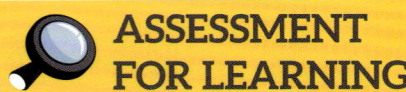

ASSESSMENT FOR LEARNING

1. List the many advantages of walking as a physical activity that can develop and maintain physical health.

FURTHER THINKING

Look online for other physical activities suitable for sedentary people to use to improve their physical health. Compare the advantages of these physical activities with the advantages of walking as the main physical activity. How do they compare? Write down your conclusions.

Benefits of maintaining physical well-being

The human body is built for use. The more it is used the more efficient it becomes. The less it is used the less efficient it becomes and the more likely it is to break down and suffer from diseases associated with a sedentary lifestyle.

With sufficient, appropriate and regular exercise:

- **the respiratory system will work more efficiently**. You will be able to take in more air per breath (and therefore per minute), which means you will be able to work harder and for longer than before.
- **the circulatory system will work more efficiently**. More blood will be delivered to the working muscles with less effort, which means you will be able to work harder and for longer than before.
- **the musculatory system will work more efficiently**. More energy will be produced, allowing you to keep going at physical tasks. Regular exercise tones the muscles so that you can maintain good posture. Lack of exercise

means loss of muscle tone and a decline in posture, so you slouch and cannot stand up straight for any length of time. With regular exercise, your muscles will get bigger (hypertrophy) meaning more strength and power for physical tasks. Your muscles will also become more flexible, which means you are able to bend, twist and turn more easily.

- **you are less likely to suffer from illnesses and diseases associated with sedentary lifestyles.** If you are fit and healthy you are at less risk of suffering from coronary heart diseases – including heart attack, angina or arteriosclerosis (build-up of fatty deposits and loss of elasticity in the artery walls) – stroke, type 2 diabetes and cancer. You are also less likely to become obese or suffer from osteoporosis (brittle bones). Being more physically active helps people to manage stress, back pain, weight and medical conditions.
- **the immune system becomes more efficient.** It is not really known how exercise increases your immunity to certain illnesses. Suggested theories include: exercise flushes bacteria out of the lungs thus reducing your chances of getting an illness; with exercise the white blood cells (fight infection) circulate more quickly and therefore might detect illnesses earlier than before, reducing your chances of getting an illness; exercise raises body temperature and this prevents bacteria from growing, reducing your chances of getting an illness; and exercise slows down the release of stress hormones. Stress hormones are associated with illness.

In addition, when you exercise regularly and appropriately, you are more likely to:

- **respect/look after your body.** Avoid negative habits that are detrimental to your health: for example smoking, drugs, excessive eating and excessive intake of alcohol.
- **control your weight.** Physical activity helps because it increases your metabolic rate and burns up the calories eaten. Even after you stop exercising, your metabolic rate remains high, so keeps burning the calories.
- **sleep well.** Exercise can make you physically tired and therefore help you to get to sleep at

night. Lack of exercise may lead to difficulty in getting to sleep. Physically active people are not only likely to sleep well but look well (shape and posture), feel good, and be more confident.

- **experience good mental well-being, feelings of self-worth and have good social interaction**. Physical activity can help relieve stress. It can take your mind off problems, give you a different perspective, and re-energise you.

People who engage in physical activity have reported greater enjoyment of their work; improved concentration and mental alertness; and improved cooperation and rapport with colleagues. They also have good relationships with family, friends and neighbours.

Active people have fewer sick days than inactive people and, if sick, they recover more quickly. Musculoskeletal disorders (including back pain) and stress are also leading causes of work-related health problems. Increased activity by those who do little physical activity could bring significant benefits not just to their health but also to the economy.

> "When mood state is studied before and after exercise, negative feelings such as depression, tension, confusion and fatigue all drop and there is a spike in vigour or energy. This is a healthy psychological state to be in and exercise does typically produce that in people."
>
> *Dr Clare Stevinson, Senior Lecturer in Behavioural Aspects of Physical Activity and Health, Loughborough University.*

- **extend a healthy active life.** If you are fit and healthy, your body is in good working order and you are able to perform everyday tasks with ease. Keeping active helps you to age well and enjoy life.

The difference between physical fitness for health and for performance

Physical fitness can be defined as the ability to perform physical tasks efficiently and effectively. There are different levels of physical fitness at which people may find themselves, or aspire to achieve, as represented in the diagram below:

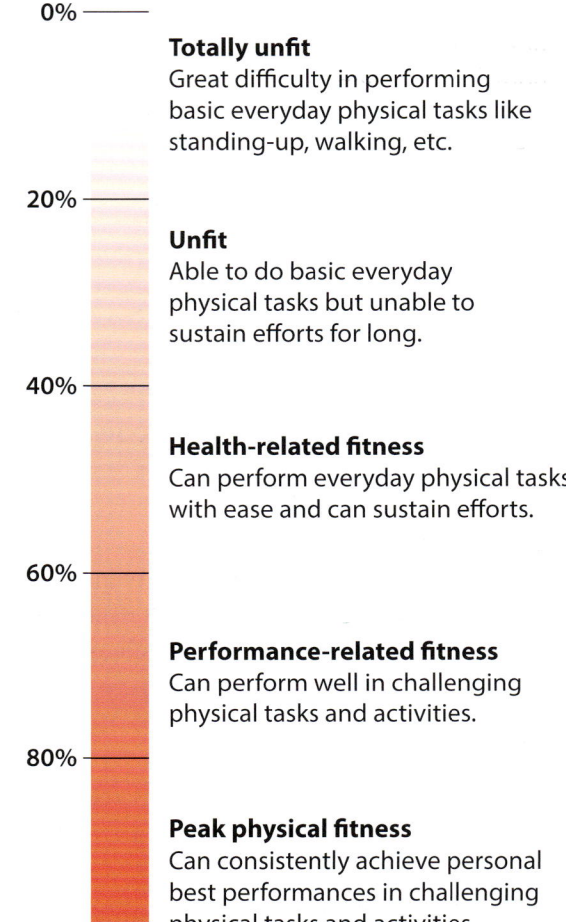

0% — Totally unfit
Great difficulty in performing basic everyday physical tasks like standing-up, walking, etc.

20% — Unfit
Able to do basic everyday physical tasks but unable to sustain efforts for long.

40% — Health-related fitness
Can perform everyday physical tasks with ease and can sustain efforts.

60% — Performance-related fitness
Can perform well in challenging physical tasks and activities.

80% — Peak physical fitness
Can consistently achieve personal best performances in challenging physical tasks and activities.

100%

ASSESSMENT FOR LEARNING

1. The human body is built for use. The more it is used, the more efficient it becomes. Explain how the following body systems become more efficient:
   - The respiratory system
   - The circulatory system
   - The musculatory system

2. Physical activity makes the main body systems work more efficiently. Explain five other benefits associated with being a physically active person.

FURTHER THINKING

Search online for:
- the benefits to be gained from being physically active
- the consequences of leading a sedentary lifestyle

Note your discoveries. Discuss them with others.

The baseline for keeping the body in reasonable working order (**physical fitness for health**) is at 40–60% of potential. For physical activities and sports where people want to be performing as efficiently and effectively as possible (**physical fitness for performance**) the optimum level is in the zone of 80–100% of potential.

1.2 HEALTH AND LIFESTYLE DECISIONS

Components of physical fitness for health

The components of physical fitness are: aerobic energy production; anaerobic energy production; muscular strength; muscular power; muscular speed; muscular endurance; flexibility and body composition. However, the components that relate most to physical health and well-being are:

- aerobic energy production
- muscular strength/endurance
- flexibility
- body composition

See page 54 for recommendations on how much physical activity is needed (frequency, intensity and time) to maintain physical well-being in each of these components.

Aerobic energy production

Aerobic energy is energy produced **with the use of oxygen.**

When you consider the type of energy production needed for everyday life then aerobic energy production would rate as being very important. For example, the physical work or tasks done in most jobs (walking, climbing the stairs and so on) and during leisure time (gardening, decorating and so on) are nearly all aerobic-based. There are not many everyday activities that demand maximum or high-intensity efforts (anaerobic energy production). It is only occasionally that you may need to sprint for a bus or to get out of the rain.

This means an exercise programme to develop or to maintain physical health/well-being should consist mostly of aerobic-based physical activity/exercise.

Types of exercise

You can choose one, or any combination of, aerobic activities, and by doing what is recommended (see page 54), you will be able to keep the body in reasonable working order (achieve the baseline for physical well-being). Aerobic activities include walking, dancing, running, cycling, swimming or rowing – activities in which major muscles of the body are worked and in which the respiratory and circulatory systems meet the energy demands of the activities.

Training methods

The three main methods of training through which a person can develop aerobic fitness for physical well-being are (in order of popular use): **continuous steady-pace (CSP)** training (see page 150); **fartlek** training (see page 151); and, providing the person has no medical conditions, **interval training** (see page 151). Overall, it is probably best to use a combination of these training methods.

Muscular strength/endurance

Most of the time, everyday things that need to be lifted, pushed, pulled or moved are only moderately heavy – shopping bags, saucepans, vacuum cleaners, chairs and lawn mowers, for instance – but these may have to be carried or used for a time and so require muscular endurance.

There are also occasions when heavy things need to be lifted, pushed, pulled or moved – moving furniture, pushing a car or lifting a heavy bag of shopping, for instance. It is heavy work and so these actions require muscular strength.

This means that an exercise programme to develop or to maintain physical health/well-being should contain exercises that develop muscular endurance through to basic muscular strength.

Types of exercise

Exercises that work the major muscles of the body include, for example, bench presses (for the pectoral muscles, triceps and front deltoids), crunches (for the abdominal muscles) and squats (for the quadriceps, glutes, hamstrings and calves). You should be able to name, illustrate and describe how to perform suitable resistance exercises for all the major muscles of the body.

You should also remember that:

Muscular endurance = less demanding exercises with many repetitions.

Muscular strength = very demanding exercises with few repetitions.

Training methods

There are two popular methods of training through which a person can develop muscular endurance/strength for physical health and well-being: the most common is **circuit training** (see page 152); but many use **resistance training** with weights or resistance machines (see page 153).

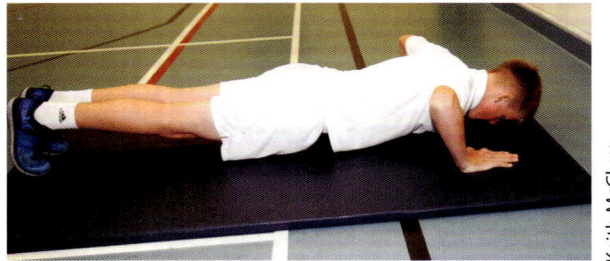

Circuit training

Resistance training

Flexibility

Many everyday tasks require you to bend, stretch, turn or twist, so flexibility is very important. You need to be able to bend to tie your shoe laces or to easily pick something up from the floor; you need to be able to stretch to reach things from a high shelf; and you need to be able to twist your body and turn your head to see what is behind you.

Types of exercise

Exercises that stretch the muscles include, for example, a hamstring stretch, a quadriceps stretch or a gluteals stretch. You should be able to name, illustrate and describe how to perform flexibility exercises for the muscles surrounding the major joints of the body.

Training methods

There are two popular methods of training through which a person can develop flexibility for physical health and well-being: the most common is through **static flexibility** exercises (see page 155); but many achieve this through **dynamic flexibility exercises** (see page 155).

Static flexibility

Dynamic flexibility

1.2 HEALTH AND LIFESTYLE DECISIONS

Body composition
Body composition is how much fat mass you have in comparison to lean mass (muscle, for example). This is an important factor for health because as your body's fat-to-lean ratio increases, so do your health risks.

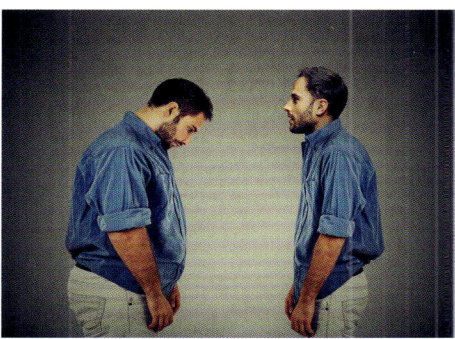

Types of exercise
Exercises that burn fats include skipping, doing burpees or running. You should be able to name, illustrate and describe how to perform aerobic exercise and anaerobic exercise to burn fats, as well as name, illustrate and describe how to perform resistance exercises for the major muscles of the body.

Training methods
It has been found that, to get physically fit for life and to lose excess fat, it can be faster and easier to use **interval training** where you work hard, but for short periods of time (see page 151). A combination of continuous steady-pace training (CSP) with interval training probably works best. The most common training methods used to build muscles would be resistance training – **circuit training** and **weight training**.

> ## ASSESSMENT FOR LEARNING
>
> 1. How many different types of exercise can you name that would develop aerobic energy production?
>
> 2. As a class, build a portfolio of exercises that could be used to develop muscular strength/endurance in the major muscle areas of the body.
>
> 3. As a class, build a portfolio of exercises that could be used to develop the flexibility of the muscles surrounding the major joints of the body.

> ## FURTHER THINKING
>
> Use the Internet to expand your portfolio of exercises that develop aerobic energy production, muscular strength/endurance and flexibility. Note your discoveries. Discuss them with others.

Principles of training

How much exercise/physical activity is recommended?

Walking is an ideal introductory physical activity to get people exercising, but how much walking do they need to do and what other physical activity is needed in order to achieve and maintain all-round physical well-being? *The advice and recommendations given here are based on those published by the Public Health Agency (PHA): you should use this as the model for planning and evaluating health-related exercise/physical activity programmes for physical well-being.*

Rate of Perceived Exertion (RPE): scale 10–1*

10	Maximum intensity	• Working flat-out (anaerobic) • Can maintain intensity only for a very short time (e.g. sprints for 10–30 seconds) • Completely out of breath • Unable to talk
		Resistance exercises: 1RM–4RM† intensity to develop strength
9	Very hard intensity	• Working very hard (anaerobic) • Very difficult to maintain the intensity (e.g. fast run for 30–60 seconds) • Can barely breathe • Can speak only a few words
		Resistance exercises: 5RM–9RM intensity to develop strength
7–8	Vigorous to hard intensity	• Working hard (aerobic/anaerobic) • Uncomfortable at 8 (e.g. race pace maintained) • Fairly uncomfortable at 7 • Breathing heavily • Can speak a sentence
		Resistance exercises: 10RM–15RM intensity to develop strength/endurance; 16RM–22RM intensity to develop endurance/strength
5–6	Moderate to vigorous intensity	• Working (aerobic) • Discomfort at 6 (e.g. good pace maintained) • Some discomfort at 5 • Breathing hard but can hold a short conversation
		Resistance exercises: 23RM–30RM intensity to develop endurance; 31RM–40RM intensity to develop endurance
3–4	Light to moderate intensity	• Some exertion • A little discomfort at 4 (e.g. comfortable pace maintained) • Comfortable at 3 • Can carry on a conversation
		Resistance exercises: 40RMRM intensity to develop endurance
2	Light intensity	• Little exertion • Comfortable • Pace feels easy to maintain • Easy breathing • Can easily carry on a conversation
		Exercises: low resistance, basic movements of limbs
1	Very light intensity	• Hardly any exertion, but more than sleeping, sitting, etc.
		Exercises: limited movement of limbs

* Adapted from the scale introduced by sport psychologist Gunnar Borg in the 1960s: the Borg 'Rate of Perceived Exertion'
† RM refers to repetition maximum – this is the most weight you can lift for a defined number of exercise movements. For example, 1RM is the maximum amount of weight that a person can lift for one repetition; 10RM would be the maximum a person could lift for 10 repetitions, and so on.

1.2 HEALTH AND LIFESTYLE DECISIONS

Key recommendations:

Aerobic
- *A minimum of 3 hours of vigorous physical activity per week*: An hour of vigorous or hard-intensity physical activity (aerobic to anaerobic) – done all at once, or in bursts of at least 10 minutes – should be done on at least 3 days per week.
- *A further 4 hours of moderate physical activity per week*: An hour or more (up to 3 hours) of moderate-intensity physical activity – done all at once, or in bursts of at least 10 minutes – should be done on at least 4 days per week, ideally on days that vigorous or hard intensity physical activity (aerobic) is not being done.

Muscular endurance/strength
A range of muscular strength/endurance exercises, covering the major areas of the body, should be performed three days per week.

Flexibility
Flexibility exercises may be performed after bouts of physical activity, but at least three times per week.

Recommendations on maintaining physical well-being for teenagers and adults

Component	Type of exercise (sample)	**T** Frequency	**F** Intensity	**I** Time	**T** Example
Aerobic	Running	3 days minimum per week	Vigorous to hard (i.e. 7/10 RPE)	Minimum of 10 minutes at any one time. 60 minutes minimum for a day. Total of 3 hours per week.	Running at, for example, a pace of 5 minutes 30 seconds (5:30) per kilometre for 11 km.
Aerobic	Walking	4 days maximum per week* * For those incapable of doing 3 days of vigorous or hard-intensity physical activity, this should be 7 days of moderate-intensity physical activity.	Moderate (i.e. 5/10 RPE)	Minimum of 10 minutes at any one time. 60 minutes or more per day. Minimum total of 4 hours per week.	Walking briskly, for 10000 steps per day.
Muscular endurance/ strength	Press-ups and sit-ups	3 days	Vigorous or hard (i.e. 7/10 RPE)	Adequate time to work legs, hips, back, abdomen, chest, shoulders and arms.	Resistance training; for example, using weights or circuits.
Flexibility	Static and dynamic flexibility exercises	3 days minimum: preferably after any aerobic or muscular strength workouts.	Moderate (i.e. 5/10 RPE)	Adequate time to stretch the muscles surrounding all the major joints.	Sit on floor, legs front and reach towards feet to stretch hamstring muscles: hold for 30 seconds.

Applying the FITT principle

What is the FITT principle?
It is used to plan an effective programme of physical activity in order to develop and maintain physical well-being:

- **Frequency**: How often the person should take part in the various types of physical activity over a week. This is measured by the number of workouts done per week for each of the health-related components.
- **Intensity:** How hard the person should work when participating in the various workouts and types of physical activity. This is usually identified using the rate of perceived exertion (RPE, see table on page 54).
- **Time:** How long the person should spend doing the various types of physical activity in a workout.
- **Type:** The types of physical activity the person should be doing.

Workload
The scale from the rate of perceived exertion (RPE) can be multiplied by the time spent on the workout to give an overall workload (WL). For example, a very hard workout, at 9 on the RPE scale, for 30 minutes would give an overall workload of $9 \times 30 = 270$. A moderate intensity workout, 5 on the RPE scale, for 60 minutes would give an overall workload of $5 \times 60 = 300$. By doing this you can get data that lets you compare and evaluate the workload between workouts; the workloads over weeks; average workloads for weeks, etc.

Measuring intensity
Intensity may also be measured by using:
- distances and times (e.g. 10 km run in 50 minutes).
- pace and distances (e.g. 5 km/hour pace for 10 km).
- the weights lifted for exercises with the number of repetitions and sets (e.g. 20 kg × 10 reps × 3 sets).
- the exercises done in a circuit with the work times, or the number of repetitions and sets, with recovery times between reps and sets (e.g. press-ups × 20 reps × 3 sets; no recovery between reps and 2 minutes recovery between sets).

This information provides the reality of what was actually done rather than just the concept. This information on intensity is very specific to a person as you do not know how hard or easy the task will be for different individuals. For example, running the distance of 10 km in 50 minutes could be easy for some, but impossible for others. Likewise, using 100 kg for 10 repetitions of a leg press may be easy for some and impossible for others. This is why it is important to describe in some way how much effort or exertion was required to complete the specific task or workout (the RPE). With that information, you will know the intensity or how much effort was required to run the 10 km in 50 minutes, or to leg press the 100 kg for 10 repetitions.

1.2 HEALTH AND LIFESTYLE DECISIONS

ASSESSMENT FOR LEARNING

1. Draw a table like the one below for the seven days of the week. Using the FITT principle, plan a feasible physical activity programme that meets all the physical activity recommendations for maintaining physical well-being.

Sun	
Mon	
Tue	
Wed	
Thu	
Fri	
Sat	

2. You, your classmates and your teacher should produce a series of physical activity programmes, with some that do, and some that do not, meet the recommendations for maintaining physical well-being.

3. Assess, analyse, interpret and evaluate the physical activity programmes against the accepted advice and recommendations for maintaining physical well-being.

Planning safe, appropriate and effective weekly health-related exercise programmes: SPORRT

To move up the 'levels of physical fitness' continuum (see page 50), you need to plan an appropriate and effective health-related weekly exercise programme. To do this, you should apply the following key principles of training (the acronym **SPORRT** can help you remember these):

- **S** **S**pecificity
- **PO** **P**rogressive **O**verload
- **R** **R**est/recovery
- **R** the avoidance of **R**eversibility (i.e. maintenance)
- **T** the avoidance of **T**edium (i.e. the need for variety)

Specificity

The effects of exercising/training are very specific. In this case, the principle of specificity requires you to focus on the components of physical fitness that are most important for physical health and well-being (i.e. aerobic energy production, muscular strength/endurance; and flexibility). You must, therefore, do physical activity or exercises that develop and maintain aerobic fitness – for example, participating in activities like running, dancing or swimming (or even all three). You must also do physical activity or exercises to develop and maintain muscular strength/endurance – for example, participating in circuit training or weight training – and you must do stretching exercises to develop and maintain your flexibility. This is applying the principle of specificity.

Aerobic fitness

Muscular fitness

Flexibility

Progressive overload

If you want to develop physical fitness in any of the components, then you must work the body systems harder than usual. In other words you must **overload**. For example, if you were doing continuous steady-pace running for two nights per week at a vigorous or hard intensity (RPE 7/10), for 20 minutes each run, then you would have achieved a certain level of aerobic fitness. If you want to improve on this level then you would apply the principle of overload. You could do this by running an extra night per week; running at an intensity of RPE 8/10 instead of RPE 7/10 on one of the runs; or running for 25 minutes instead of 20 minutes on one of the runs. By doing any one of these, or any combination, you would be applying the principle of overload.

The overload puts added stress on the body, and the body gradually adapts to cope with it as the body systems change and become more efficient. Because of this increased efficiency (improved physical fitness) what was originally a stress on the body becomes normal. If you want to become even fitter, you overload again, and as before your body systems adapt to cope. This process of overloading and adapting, then overloading again is known as the principle of **progressive overload**.

It is important that overload increases gradually and sensibly over the duration of the exercise or training programme, and that it is at an appropriate level for the individual and their circumstances. To ensure this, you should apply the **FITT principle**, using one or any combination of these to increase the overload:

- **F**   Increase the **frequency** of the training (e.g. training more days in the week).
- **I**   Increase the **intensity** of the training (e.g. working harder during a training workout at, say, RPE 7/10 rather than 5/10).
- **T**   Increase the length of **time** you train for in a workout (e.g. 40 minutes instead of 30 minutes) …
- **T**   … in your chosen **type of exercise**.

Rest/Recovery

Recovery is an important part of getting fitter. You will benefit from a hard workout only if you allow your muscles time to recover and your body time to replace the fuel used.

A recovery period or a rest day does not necessarily mean that you do nothing: you may still train but at a low intensity (e.g. RPE 4/10 instead of RPE 7/10). Training at a relaxed and easier pace may even help recovery. Alternatively, you could work on a different component of physical fitness or work a different part of your body: for example, having done a hard run one day, you could work on developing muscular strength in the trunk and upper body the following day.

A good guideline in achieving the balance between training effort/intensity and rest/recovery is: *the harder the training effort/intensity then the more time you should allow for rest and recovery.*

Reversibility (avoiding through maintenance)

If you want to maintain your level of physical fitness then you need to continue to train.

In Section 1.1, you learned about the physical changes that take place in the body systems as a result of effective exercise or training programmes, and how these changes improve performances. If you stop training then the biological adaptations produced by the body will be reversed and you will lose your level of physical fitness.

> **"IF YOU DO NOT USE IT, YOU LOSE IT."**

Tedium (avoiding through variety)

You are less likely to become psychologically and physically bored, and less likely to plateau physically, if you use a variety of types of exercise, training methods and venues.

> **"VARIETY IS THE SPICE OF LIFE."**

If you are exercising to maintain aerobic fitness for physical health/well-being then it does not really matter if you get the variety by going swimming one day, going cycling another day and going running another day. However, if you are training for a particular event or sport (for example a 10 km road run), then cycling and swimming may not be particularly helpful. In this case you can use a variety of training methods and venues.

ANALYSIS, INTERPRETATION, EVALUATION AND PLANNING

ASSESSMENT FOR LEARNING

1. Study the audit on page 188. It provides information on John's lifestyle practices with regard to exercise. Analyse, interpret and evaluate the information/data in the audit, make sound recommendations and set SMART objectives and targets to bring about improvements. Back up your findings with references to what is factual, sound or recommended (the 'ideal').

2. Devise a safe, appropriate and effective action plan to achieve the objectives and targets within a set time frame of 9 weeks. Explain how you would monitor the implementation of the action plan and the benefits of doing this. **Note:** John cannot swim but likes walking and running.

   For guidance on how to do this, use Steps 1–5 on page 6.

3. You, your classmates and your teacher should produce a variety of audits that reflect a range of individuals from those who lead sedentary lifestyles to those who are reasonably active. Use the audits to practise answering questions 1 and 2 above.

Fitness testing
Measuring improvements in physical well-being

Many people like to know that they are making progress when they embark on a plan to improve their physical health. At the foundation level, it is sufficient to know that you feel healthier and can do more than before. The following tests are basic, but allow progress to be measured.

Listening to your body – general feeling
You can 'listen' to your body to judge whether your physical activity/exercise is effective. You know your exercise/physical activity is working if:
- you feel that you are no longer out of breath when you would have been before.
- you have more energy than you would have had before.
- you are able to lift, push or pull things much more easily than before.
- you are able to bend, twist, turn or stretch much more easily than before.

Resting pulse rate – aerobic
Your pulse rate is the number of times that your heart beats in one minute. You can use your resting pulse rate to judge whether your aerobic exercise/training is effective.

To do this, take your resting pulse rate before you start your exercise/training programme; ideally first thing in the morning when you wake up. Once you are several weeks into your programme, take your resting pulse rate as before and, if it is lower, then you know that the programme is effective.

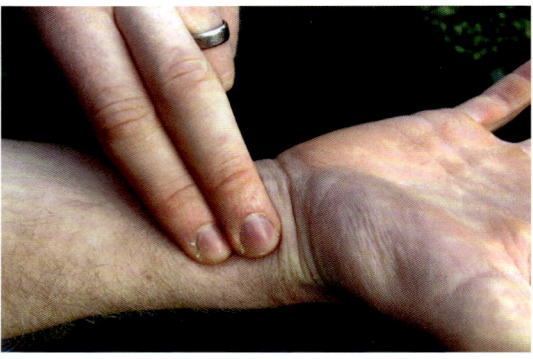

Recovery rate – aerobic
Your recovery rate is how quickly your heart rate can return to its resting pulse rate – e.g. 70 beats per minute (BPM) – after having completed a set piece of work. You can use your recovery rate to judge whether your aerobic exercise/training is effective. The graph below shows a person's heart rate recovery before an exercise programme, and again several weeks into the programme.

Distance and time – aerobic
You can use distance and time to judge whether your aerobic exercise/training is effective. You can either set the distance and measure the time it takes to complete that distance, or you can set the time and measure the distance completed in that time.

As with the other assessments, you must do the test before you start the programme and then use the same test again several weeks in. So, for example, if your initial test was to set the distance and measure the time, then the programme can be regarded as effective if you can now run the distance in a faster

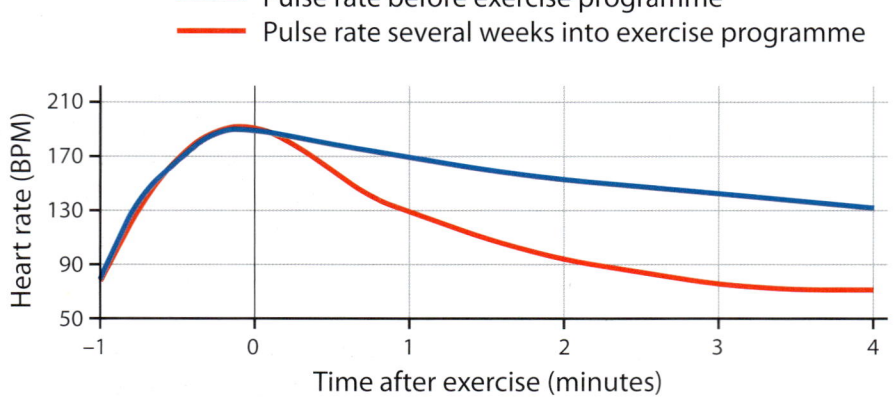

time. Or if your initial test was to set the time and measure the distance, then the programme can be regarded as effective if you are now able to run farther in the set time.

Running a 10 km course	
Month	Time
Jan	60 min
Feb	58 min
Mar	56 min
Apr	55 min

Measuring the time

30 minutes out	
Month	Distance
Jan	3.0 km
Feb	3.3 km
Mar	3.6 km
Apr	4.0 km

Measuring the distance

Repetitions completed – muscular endurance

To assess your level of endurance of local muscles (e.g. the stomach or arm muscles) it is possible to measure the total number of repetitions of an exercise that can be done before fatigue sets in; or you can measure the number of repetitions that can be done in a fixed time.

To do this, count the number of repetitions you can complete for a given exercise in a fixed time: do this before you start your exercise/training programme and then again once you are into the programme. If the programme is effective you would expect to now be able to do more repetitions in the fixed time.

Press-ups done in 60 seconds	
Month	Press-ups
Jan	20
Feb	30
Mar	40
Apr	50

Weight lifted – muscular strength

To assess your level of strength of local muscles (e.g. the arm or leg muscles) it is possible to measure the maximum weight that you can lift or press for a number of repetitions – the number of repetitions is usually low (e.g. five or six).

To do this, you record the weight you can lift or press before you start your exercise/training programme, and then again several weeks into the programme. If the programme is effective you would expect to be able to lift or press heavier weights.

Weight lifted for 6 repetitions – bench press	
Month	Weight
Jan	30 kg
Feb	35 kg
Mar	40 kg
Apr	45 kg

Measuring range of movement – flexibility

To assess your level of flexibility at joints you can measure your range of movement. For example, the sit and reach test could be used (refer to CCEA battery of fitness tests for protocol). Measure your range of movement before you start your exercise/training programme and again once you are several weeks into your programme: if the programme is effective, you would expect to have a greater range of movement.

Sit and reach test	
Month	Distance
Jan	15 cm
Feb	20 cm
Mar	25 cm
Apr	30 cm

Body composition

With regard to overall health, weight is not as important as the composition of that weight. Body composition tests can be used to identify health risks, or to evaluate how well a current exercise and nutrition plan is working. They reveal the relative proportions of fat and lean mass in the body:

- **Lean mass** refers to bones, tissues, organs and muscle.
- **Fat mass** consists of two types of fat: essential fat (males 3%, females 12%); and non-essential fat (the ranges acceptable for good health are 10–22% for males, 20–32% for females). Being within the acceptable range means you have less risk of developing obesity-related diseases.

If you find that you are within a healthy range, you can continue your exercise and nutritional plan. If you find that your body composition should be improved, take a closer look at what you can do to make positive changes to your current level of physical activity and nutritional intake.

You should be aware of the following tests for measuring body composition:

- **Bioelectrical impedance analysis test (BIM):** A device measures the resistance of body tissues to the flow of a small electrical signal – since fat contains little water, the current cannot flow as easily through it. By measuring how easily currents move through the body, percentage body fat can be estimated.

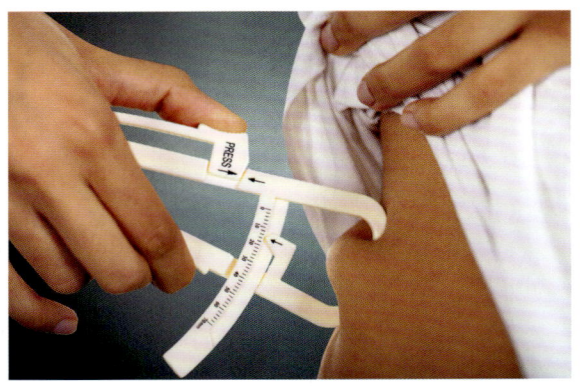

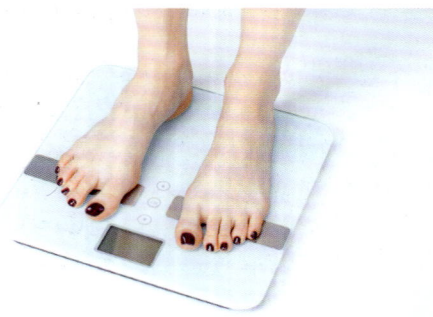

- **Skinfold test:** Calipers are used to measure skinfold thickness at a number of sites on the body. The sum of the skinfolds taken can then be converted to calculate the percentage of body fat. This method is comparatively less accurate than the BIM test, but it is also less expensive.

ASSESSMENT FOR LEARNING

1. Many people walk or jog to keep themselves fit and healthy. Explain three different tests that would allow them to judge if their aerobic fitness was improving.

2. Describe in detail how sit-ups should be used as a reliable test to judge if a person's abdominal muscle endurance was improving.

3. Explain why body composition is better than body weight as an indicator of physical health.

Risk assessment
Carrying out a risk assessment

A **hazard** is something that can cause illness, injury or even death. No matter what your age, there are potential hazards associated with participation in any physical activity or sport. Risk assessments are done to keep people safe.

In carrying out a risk assessment you should:
- **identify** potential risks or hazards regarding:
  1. the well-being of the people taking part.
  2. the nature of the physical activity or sport to be undertaken.
  3. the venue, environment and the equipment to be used.
- **evaluate** the effectiveness of any existing controls and actions that are in place to minimise the risks or hazards identified.
- **recommend** new or additional controls and actions that would be more effective in minimising the risks and hazards identified.

1 The well-being of the people taking part

If a person has not been active for some time, the Physical Activity Readiness Questionnaire (PAR-Q) (see page 10) is a good starting point to see if and when they would be ready to exercise safely.

2 The nature of the physical activity or sport to be undertaken

Many physical activities and sports have regulations, rules and etiquette that help keep people safe. These should be understood and implemented by all.

For all physical activities and sports, you should understand their nature and demands; recognise the possible hazards and the possible consequences; and know the actions that are taken to minimise the risks. For example, association football players should wear shin guards; cricketers when batting should wear batting pads and batting gloves; and when sailing, people should wear lifejackets or buoyancy aids.

Certain types of footwear can be inappropriate for an activity. If walking in the mountains with normal shoes, there is a potential risk of getting injured from slipping on rocks, twisting your ankle or getting bruises, so you should wear appropriate mountaineering boots that provide support, protection, grip and shock absorption.

You should know how to carry out risk assessments for physical activities and sports that may be done in Key Stage 3, Key Stage 4 or for GCSE PE.

3 The venue, environment and equipment to be used

Venues need to be inspected to see if they are suitable for the physical activity or sport to be performed. For example: Is the venue big enough? Is it suitable for both players and spectators? Is there a suitable distance between the courtside and end lines and the walls? Could the lighting be inadequate or, due to the design, could it get damaged or broken when the venue is used?

Outdoor areas also need to be inspected to see if they are suitable for the physical activity or sport to be performed. For example: Are there proper landing areas for pole vault and high jump? Is there a proper caged area for the discus and hammer events?

This type of risk assessment is most likely to be done by someone in event management (see pages 114–122) but the environment needs to be continually inspected by all involved. To give a few examples, there would be a potential hazard if, during a volleyball match, the floor surface of a venue became slippery through sweat or water spills: the risk would be minimised by having it cleaned immediately. Similarly, in a swimming pool, the wet surface at the sides of the pool present a potential hazard: the risk of injury is minimised by preventing people from running when out of the pool. Or a sharp object would present a hazard if left in a long-jump pit, so to minimise the risk of injury, the sand pit should be checked each time before use.

ASSESSMENT FOR LEARNING

1. You have just become the organiser for a charity cycle event that will use public roads. List all the things you will do to carry out an effective risk assessment for this event.

When equipment is necessary for exercising, the providers have a responsibility for its provision, but users should also ensure that it is safe and in good working condition. The equipment should also be used properly. For example, if you go to a gym, weights should be properly secured on barbells, weight-lifting and aerobic machines should be working properly and used as directed.

ANALYSIS, INTERPRETATION, EVALUATION AND PLANNING

ASSESSMENT FOR LEARNING

1. Study the audit on page 188. It provides information on Maria's lifestyle practices with regard to exercise and physical activity. Analyse, interpret and evaluate the information/data in the audit, make sound recommendations and set SMART objectives and targets to bring about improvements. Back up your findings with references to what is factual, sound or recommended (the 'ideal').

2. Devise a safe, appropriate and effective action plan to achieve the objectives and targets within a set time frame. Explain how you would monitor the implementation of the action plan and the benefits of doing this.

3. After the completion of the action plan, if you wanted to help Maria progress further, what steps would you take? **Note:** Maria has chosen walking, running and circuit training as her means to achieve her objectives and targets, and has chosen to do flexibility exercises after completing a running or circuit workout.

   For guidance on how to do this, use Steps 1–5 on page 6.

4. You, your classmates and your teacher should produce a variety of audits that reflect a range of individuals, from those who lead a sedentary lifestyle to those who follow an activity programme for physical well-being. Use the audits to practise answering questions 1, 2 and 3 above.

5. Divide into pairs and conduct an audit on each other's pattern and level of physical activity over a typical week. Analyse, interpret and evaluate the information/data in the audit, make sound recommendations and set SMART objectives and targets to bring about improvements.

6. Devise a safe, appropriate and effective action plan to achieve the objectives and targets within a set time frame. Explain how you would monitor the implementation of the action plan and the benefits of doing this.

Physical health: nutrition

Learning outcomes

In this section, you will learn:

- the concept of a balanced, healthy nutritional eating plan (diet)
- advice and recommendations to apply for nutritional intake – the Eatwell Guide
- the benefits of having a balanced, healthy nutritional plan
- the consequences of unbalanced nutritional plans or erratic eating patterns
- the components of food
- the factors that affect energy needs
- to understand food labelling
- how to analyse, interpret and evaluate information or data on nutrition and how to devise balanced, healthy eating plans

Nutrition

What do we mean by nutritional intake?

Nutritional intake (often referred to as your diet) is the amount and mixture of foods containing the essential nutrients that you need in order to:

- maintain life.
- support growth and repair.
- provide substances to regulate the processes of the body.
- carry out all voluntary physical activity.

What is a balanced, healthy nutritional plan?

It is a plan that gets the balance right between energy intake and energy expenditure.

- If your energy intake equals your energy expenditure, then your body weight will stay constant.

Intake: 2500 kcal

Expenditure: 2500 kcal

- If your energy intake is greater than your energy expenditure, then your body weight will increase.

Intake: 2500 kcal
Expenditure: 2000 kcal

- If your energy intake is less than your energy expenditure, then your body weight will decrease.

Intake: 2500 kcal
Expenditure: 3000 kcal

A balanced, healthy nutritional plan also gets the balance right between the five main food groups.

Advice and recommendations on nutrition

The advice and recommendations given here are based on those published by the Public Health Agency (PHA).

The **Eatwell Guide** (www.food.gov.uk/business-guidance/the-eatwell-guide), shown overleaf, advises us to drink 6–8 cups/glasses of fluid each day. It also categorises foods into five main groups:

- Potatoes, bread, rice, pasta and other starchy carbohydrates
- Fruit and vegetables
- Dairy and alternatives
- Beans, pulses, fish, eggs, meat and other proteins
- Oils and spreads

The Eatwell Guide can help us:

- learn and understand how to apply the guidance to individuals and their circumstances (metabolism, age, gender and so on; see page 71). For example, it advises that, from five years of age, children should be eating the same type of food as the rest of the family but in smaller quantities or portions.
- learn and understand the different types of foods and drinks we should consume (and in

1.2 HEALTH AND LIFESTYLE DECISIONS

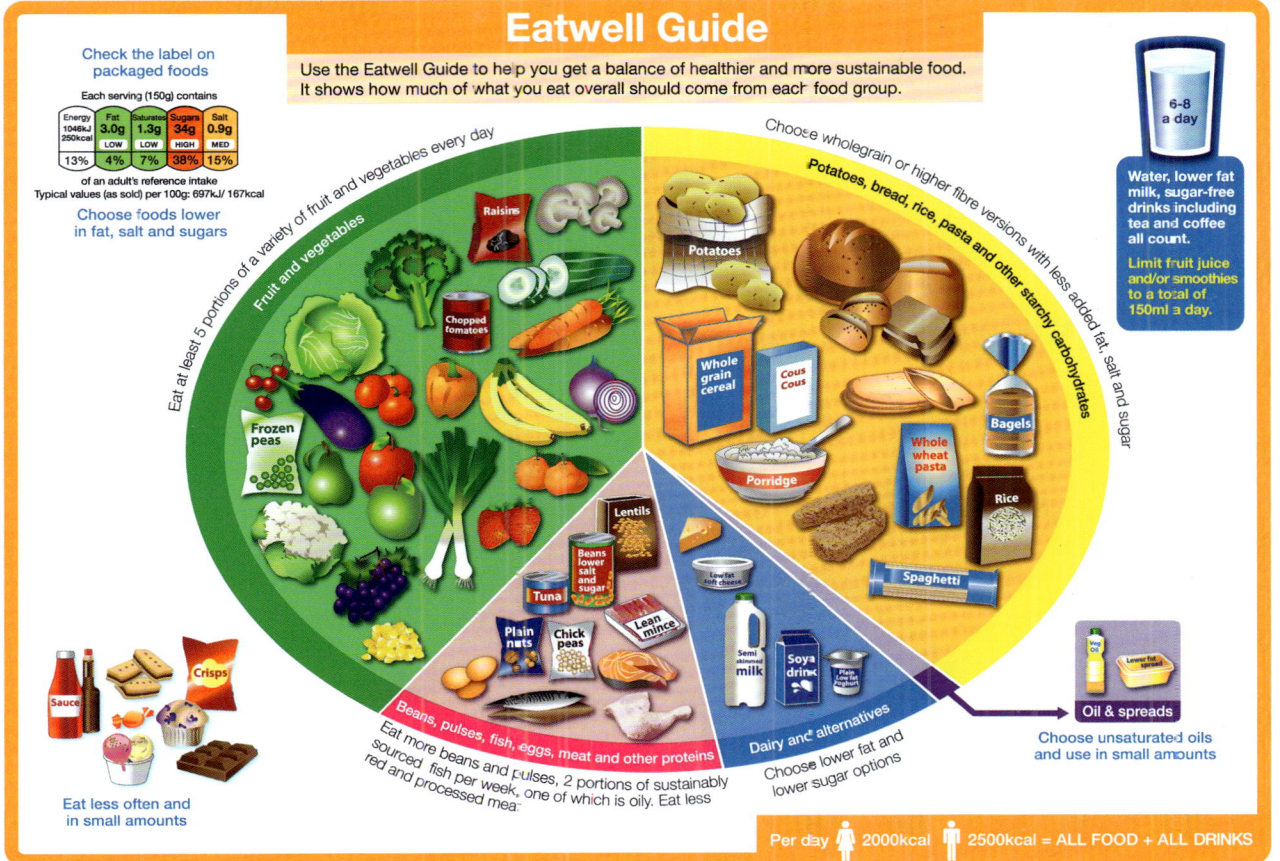

what proportions) to have a healthy, balanced diet. For example, it advises us to consume the following portions of food:
- at least 5 portions of a variety of fruit and vegetables per day.
- 1 portion of starchy food, such as potatoes, pasta, rice, bread or breakfast cereal with every meal (3 portions in total per day).
- 3 portions of lower-fat dairy foods, such as milk, cheese, yogurt, fromage frais or non-dairy alternatives, per day.
- 2 portions of fish per week along with other proteins such as meat, poultry, eggs, beans, pulses or lentils.
- Small amount of oils and spreads.
- Minimal amounts of fatty and sugary foods.

Choosing a wide variety of food from the different food groups is the best way to make sure you are getting all the nutrients you need to stay healthy.

ASSESSMENT FOR LEARNING

1. For yourself, plan in detail the ideal balanced, healthy breakfast, lunch, dinner/tea and snacks (if appropriate) to meet the Eatwell Guide and your energy needs.

2. Be honest, write down in detail what you actually have for breakfast, lunch, dinner/tea and snacks. Analyse and evaluate what you actually eat against your ideal balanced, healthy plan for the day.

The benefits of having a balanced, healthy nutritional plan

If you have a balanced, healthy nutritional plan, you may experience some of the following benefits:
- You can control your weight. You are aware of what you eat and eat only what you need. You eat a balanced, healthy diet and eat at the right times throughout the day.

67

- You have a stronger immune system, which will better protect you from disease and infection. You eat the right nutrients, vitamins and minerals and have the right balance between the nutrients.
- You are less likely to suffer from chronic diseases such as cancer, high blood pressure, diabetes and heart disease. You have very few food or drinks that have high levels of saturated fat; high levels of salt or high levels of sugar.
- You have better cognitive and spatial memory capacity, potentially increasing your ability to process and retain academic information. Your nutritional plan has the right balance of nutrients, vitamins and minerals.
- You enhance your ability to concentrate.
- You have more energy, which will delay the effects of tiredness and fatigue.
- You are more likely to maintain a positive mood.

Breakfast smoothies are one of many ways to enjoy eating more fruit and vegetables

The consequences of poor nutrition and poor eating patterns

Eating disorders are mental disorders defined by abnormal eating habits that negatively affect a person's physical or mental health.

- If you consistently eat too many kilocalories for your energy needs, you will gradually become overweight, then obese. People who are obese have an increased risk of having many serious diseases and health conditions. For example: high blood pressure (Hypertension); Type 2 diabetes; coronary heart disease; stroke; bowel cancer; low quality of life; mental illness such as clinical depression, anxiety, and other mental disorders; body pain and difficulty with physical functioning.
- If you consistently eat too few kilocalories for your energy needs, you will gradually become underweight. Some people suffer from the eating disorder of anorexia nervosa. They try to keep their weight as low as possible by not eating enough food, or exercising too much, or both. People with anorexia nervosa increase their risk of having problems with muscles wasting, osteoporosis and fertility problems. Anorexia can also put a person's life at risk: it is one of the leading causes of deaths related to mental health problems.
- If you consistently have a vitamin A deficiency, you may develop dry eyes and night blindness. With a vitamin C deficiency, you can develop scurvy.
- If you consistently have a mineral deficiency of iron, you may develop anaemia. With a mineral deficiency of calcium, you can develop osteoporosis. With a mineral excess of sodium, you may develop hypertension.
- Drinking less water than what is recommended can provoke dehydration. If you are frequently dehydrated you have more chance of suffering from arthritis and other inflammatory conditions; loss of muscle mass; urinary tract infections and increased risk of kidney stones. The shortage of liquid in brain tissue increases levels of cortisol, elevates stress and can result in depression.

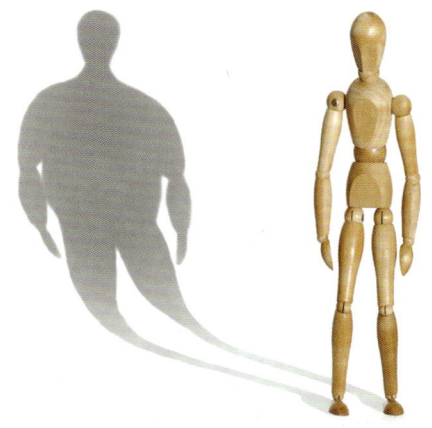

1.2 HEALTH AND LIFESTYLE DECISIONS

ASSESSMENT FOR LEARNING

1. What are the benefits of having a balanced healthy nutritional plan?
2. What can be the consequences if a person becomes obese? How many consequences can you list?
3. What can be the consequences if a person suffers from anorexia nervosa? How many consequences can you list?
4. What can be the consequences if a person has vitamin or mineral deficiencies?
5. What can be the consequences if a person is frequently dehydrated?

The components of food

Foods within the five main food groups – fruit and vegetables; dairy and alternatives; proteins; starchy carbohydrates; and oils and spreads – are composed of combinations of the following:

- **Carbohydrates:** these are the main source for energy production in the body. They can be classified as **complex carbohydrates** – e.g. potatoes and foods that are made from cereals (wholemeal bread, porridge) – or as **simple carbohydrates** – e.g. sugar, honey and jam. It is best to eat complex carbohydrates as these naturally contain more vitamins, minerals and dietary fibre. In the Eatwell Guide, fruits, vegetables, breads, rice, potatoes, pasta and other starchy foods like breakfast cereals, are predominantly carbohydrate foods.

- **Fats:** these are a secondary source for energy production and are vital for normal tissue functioning. Fat is also an insulator and protects vital organs. Fat can be classified as being **saturated fat** – e.g. lard, butter or the fat on meat; **polyunsaturated fat** – e.g. sunflower oil or corn oil; or **monounsaturated fat** – e.g. olive oil. It is better to eat polyunsaturated or monounsaturated fat rather than saturated fat. Cakes, biscuits, chocolate, savoury snacks (e.g. crisps, corn snacks), fizzy drinks, pastries, cream, ice cream, mayonnaise and dressings are high in fat and/or sugar (simple carbohydrates), while oily fish such as sardines, herring, salmon, trout and mackerel are examples of foods that contain good fats.

- **Proteins:** these are needed for growth and repair of the body. They can be classified as **animal protein** – e.g. meat, poultry, fish, milk, cheese and eggs – or **vegetable protein** – e.g. peas, beans and nuts. In the Eatwell Guide, milk and dairy products, meat, fish, eggs, beans and other non-dairy sources are predominantly protein foods.

- **Vitamins:** these are needed for the functioning of muscles and nerves, the growth of body tissue and the release of energy from food. For example, some of the B vitamins are involved in the release of energy from foods; vitamin C releases iron from food; and vitamin D helps with the absorption of calcium from food. All the vitamins the body requires will be contained in a balanced and varied diet.

- **Minerals:** These serve a variety of purposes. Calcium, for instance, gives strength and rigidity to bones. Minerals also assist in many vital body functions. For example: phosphorus assists in the production of ATP (adenosine triphosphate) – the fuel for the release of energy from food. Iron is involved with the use of oxygen and is found in the haemoglobin in the red blood cells. Sodium is found in all body fluids but especially in the blood, and is involved in maintaining the water balance of the body. All minerals will be contained in a balanced and varied diet.

- **Dietary fibre:** this is the part of the food that cannot be digested. It is essential in that it provides bulk to the faeces, which helps prevent constipation and other more serious conditions. Foods high in dietary fibre are usually complex carbohydrate foods.

- **Water:** this is the main medium for transporting **nutrients** (food), removing waste, and regulating body temperature. Water is crucial to life. Without water or fluids, adults will die within a week. The body can lose vast amounts of water through sweating. It is therefore important that you drink plenty of water or other fluids every day and especially when you sweat.

ASSESSMENT FOR LEARNING

1. Copy out the following table. For each of the components, provide example foods; the function of that component; and under which of the five main food groups in the Eatwell Guide you would place it.

2. What advice would you give about each of the components?

Components	Example foods	Function	Food groups	Advice
Carbohydrates				
Fats				
Proteins				
Vitamins				
Minerals				
Dietary fibre				
Water				

1.2 HEALTH AND LIFESTYLE DECISIONS

Factors that determine/affect energy needs

Energy is measured in **joules** (J):

1000 joules = 1 **kilojoule** (kJ)
4.2 kilojoules = 1 **kilocalorie** (kcal)

The number of kilocalories needed is influenced by:

Metabolism

The number of kilocalories you need depends on your **metabolism**. Your metabolism is the rate at which you process or burn up your food. If you have a high metabolic rate, then you process your food quickly and efficiently. If you have a low metabolic rate, then you process your food slowly and less efficiently.

When you exercise, your metabolic rate rises, which means that you burn more kilocalories. When you stop exercising, your metabolic rate continues to remain high for a period of time. This means you continue to burn kilocalories at a faster rate even though you have stopped exercising. This is why exercise, combined with a sensible kilocalorie-controlled diet, is an effective way to lose weight (fat).

Age

You need more kilocalories as a teenager (due to growth spurts) than you will need as an older adult.

Gender

The amount of kilocalories needed per day is **2500 for the average man and 2000 for the average woman**. Though this can rise to 3500 for a man and 3000 for a woman if they are very active.

Body size

The bigger your body is, then the more kilocalories you need to keep it going. Males are genetically bigger than females, so this accounts for the difference in the number of kilocalories needed by each gender.

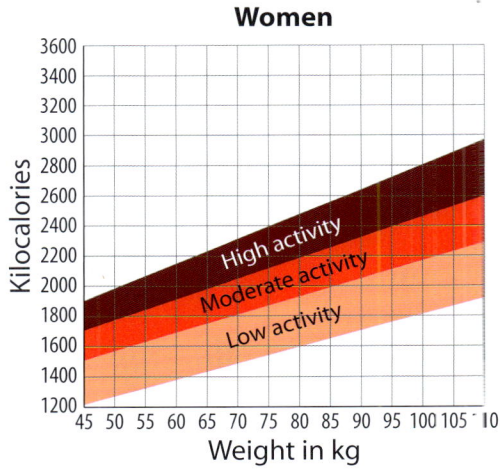

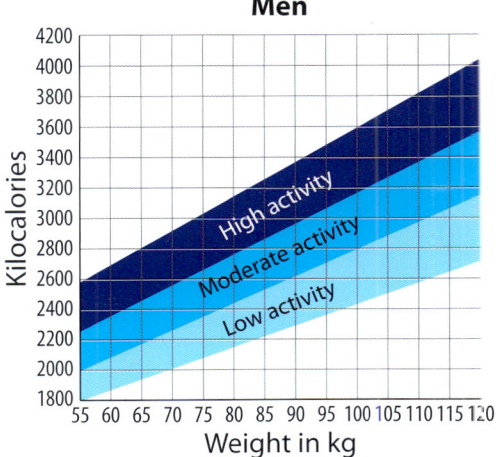

Differences between metabolic rate depending on activity levels

Body composition

Muscles burn kilocalories when they work to move the body. Fat can be used as a fuel source for the muscles, but fat neither does any work, nor burn any kilocalories. Most external fat is dead weight that has to be 'carried' around. This puts extra strain on the muscles to move the body.

Physical activity levels

The more physically active you are, the more kilocalories you need.

Climate

In cold climates, more kilocalories are needed to generate heat to stay warm. In hot climates the body requires fewer kilocalories.

ASSESSMENT FOR LEARNING

1. The kilocalorie (kcal) intake, from all food and drinks, should be around 2500 kcal per day for a male and 2000 kcal per day for a female. What factors would account for males and females needing:
   • more than these amounts?
   • less than these amounts?

2. Using the factors that determine energy needs, analyse your own kilocalorie intake and evaluate to what extent, if any, it needs to change.

Nutritional information provided on foods and drinks

Nutrition labels can help you choose between products and help you keep a check on the amounts of foods you are eating. You should become familiar with the following information that may be provided on food packaging.

General labelling of foods and drink

Most pre-packed food products will be labelled with the manufacturer's name and address, a datemark, instructions for safe storage and the weight of the product.

Other labelling on the pre-packed food products may include:

- **Use by:** you will see 'use by' dates on food that goes off quickly, such as smoked fish, meat products and ready-prepared salads. It is advisable not to consume any food or drink after its 'use by' date because this could put your health at risk.

- **Best before:** these dates appear on a wide range of frozen, dried, tinned and other foods. 'Best before' dates are about quality, not safety. When the date is passed, it doesn't mean that the food will be harmful, but it might begin to lose its flavour and texture.

- **Display until** and **sell by:** retailers often use 'sell by' and 'display until' dates on their shelves, mainly for stock control purposes. These aren't required by law and are instructions for shop staff, not for shoppers. The important dates to look for are the 'use by' and 'best before' dates.

- **Health claims:** food packaging often makes health claims for the food, such as, "helps maintain a healthy heart", or "helps aid digestion".

- **Light** or **lite:** in order to claim that a food is 'light' or 'lite', it must be at least 30% lower in at least one typical value, such as calories or fat, than standard products. The label must explain exactly what has been reduced and by how much; for example, "light: 30% less fat".

- **Low fat:** a claim that a food is low in fat may only be made where the product contains no more than 3 g of fat per 100 g for solids; or 1.5 g of fat per 100 ml for liquids.

- **No added sugar:** this usually means that the food has not had sugar added to it as an ingredient. However, just because a food contains 'no added sugar', this does not necessarily mean it has a low sugar content. The food may contain ingredients that have a naturally high sugar content (such as fruit), or have added milk, which contains lactose – a type of sugar that occurs naturally in milk.

- **Unsweetened:** this usually means that no sugar or sweetener has been added to the food to make it taste sweet. This doesn't necessarily mean that the food does not contain naturally occurring sugars found in fruit or milk.

1.2 HEALTH AND LIFESTYLE DECISIONS

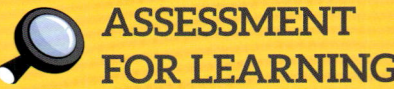
ASSESSMENT FOR LEARNING

1. Collect, or take photographs of, a range of food/drink labels or packaging that illustrate the following:
   - the use of 'use by', 'best before', or 'sell by' dates
   - health claims being made
   - use of 'light' or 'lite'
   - claims of 'low fat'
   - claims of 'no added sugar'
   - the use of 'unsweetened'

2. For the range of food and drink labels you have collected, identify any that have:
   - 'use by', 'best before', or 'sell by' on the labelling/packaging. Why have the manufacturers put these terms on the labelling/packaging?
   - used the term 'light' or 'lite'. What does the labelling/packaging identify as being 'light'? For that element, how well does each product compare with standard products in terms of grams per 100 g, or millilitres per 100 ml?
   - made 'low fat' claims. What does the labelling/packaging for each food identify as the grams per 100 g, or grams per 100 ml? By how much is each within the limit of 3 g per 100 g for foods and 1.5 g per 100 ml for liquids?
   - made 'no added sugar' claims. Do these foods or drinks already have a high percentage of 'Carbohydrates of which sugars' in them?

3. Why would food or drink manufacturers want to put health claims, 'light' or 'lite', 'low fat', 'no added sugar', or 'unsweetened' on their products?

Ingredients

Most pre-packed food products also have a list of ingredients on the packaging and this can help you work out how healthy the product is. Ingredients are listed in order of weight, so the main ingredients always come first. If the first few ingredients are high-fat ingredients, such as cream, butter or oil, then the food in question is a high-fat food.

If flavourings are used, the label must say so.

Food Standards Agency traffic light system

Some front-of-pack nutrition labels use red, amber and green colour coding to tell you at a glance if the food has high, medium or low amounts of fat, saturated fat, sugars and salt.

 **green means low** – the more green on the label, the healthier the choice.

 **amber means medium** (neither high nor low) – so you can eat foods with all or mostly amber on the label most of the time.

 **red means high** – the food is high in fat, saturated fat, salt or sugars, and these are the foods we should cut down on. Try to eat these foods less often and in small amounts.

Each grilled burger (94g) contains

Energy	Fat	Saturates	Sugars	Salt
924kJ 220 kcal	13g	5.9g	0.8g	0.7g
11%	19%	30%	<1%	12%

of an adult's reference intake
Typical values (as sold) per 100g: Energy 966kJ / 230kcal

The guidelines to tell you if a food is high or low in fat, saturated fat, salt or sugar are shown below:

	High	Low
Total fat	more than 17.5 g of fat per 100 g	3 g of fat or less per 100 g
Saturated fat	more than 5 g of saturated fat per 100 g	1.5 g of saturated fat or less per 100 g
Sugars	more than 22.5 g of total sugars per 100 g	5 g of total sugars or less per 100 g
Salt	more than 1.5 g of salt per 100 g (or 0.6 g sodium)	0.3 g of salt or less per 100 g (or 0.1 g sodium)

ASSESSMENT FOR LEARNING

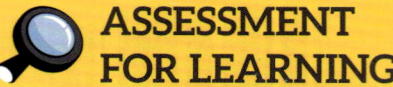

1. Explain why the Food Standards Agency's traffic light system is a helpful tool for choosing healthy food.

2. You, your classmates and your teacher should choose examples of the Food Standards Agency's traffic light system being used on a wide variety of foods and copy them. However, in giving the information for fat, saturates, sugars or salt, change one or more of the original colours designated by the FSA to a different colour.

3. Your challenge is to see if you can identify which colour is wrong for the number of grams that was given for that component.

Nutritional information

Nutrition labels are often displayed as a panel or grid on the back or side of packaging. For example, the image below shows the nutrition label on a loaf of white bread.

Nutrition				
Typical values	100 g contains	Each slice (typically 44 g) contains	% RI*	RI* for an average adult
Energy	985 kJ	435 kJ		8400 kJ
	235 kcal	105 kcal	5%	2000 kcal
Fat	1.5 g	0.7 g	1%	70 g
of which saturates	0.3 g	0.1 g	1%	20 g
Carbohydrates	45.5 g	20.0 g		
of which sugars	3.8 g	1.7 g	2%	90 g
Fibre	2.8 g	1.2 g		
Protein	7.7 g	3.4 g		
Salt	1.0 g	0.4 g	7%	6 g

This pack contains 16 servings
*Reference intake of an average adult (8400 kJ / 2000 kcal)

The label must show the amount of each of the following per 100 g, or 100 ml, of the food:

- **Energy** (in kJ and kcal): This is the amount of energy that the food will give you when you eat it. It is measured in both kilojoules (kJ) and kilocalories (kcal), usually referred to as calories. An average man needs around 10500 kJ (2500 kcal) a day to maintain his weight. For an average woman, the daily figure is around 8,400 kJ (2000 kcal).

- **Fat** (in g): This is the total amount of saturated and unsaturated fat contained in the food. In addition, the nutrition label tells you how much saturated fat is contained in the food under **of which saturates** (in g). As part of a healthy diet, we should try to cut down on food that is high in saturated fat. Reading nutrition labels can help you cut down.

- **Carbohydrate** (in g): This is the total amount of complex and simple carbohydrates contained in the food. In addition, the nutrition label tells you how much simple carbohydrate is contained in the food under **of which sugars**.

- **Protein** (in g): This is the total amount of protein contained in the food.

- **Salt** (in g): On food labels this term includes all the sodium in a food. While most sodium comes from salt (sodium chloride), some can be naturally occurring. It can also come from raising agents and additives.

- **Fibre** (in g): The food label may also provide additional information on certain nutrients, such as fibre.

Allergen information

The **ingredients list must also highlight any allergens** (foods that some people are allergic to) such as eggs, nuts and soya.

ASSESSMENT FOR LEARNING

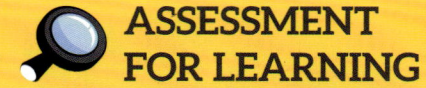

1. List the information provided on the nutrition label on foods and drinks.

2. From the range of food labels/packaging you have collected, find one food that you believe is unhealthy. Use the information on the nutrition label to argue your case.

ANALYSIS, INTERPRETATION, EVALUATION AND PLANNING

ASSESSMENT FOR LEARNING

1. Study the audit on page 189. It provides information on Oliver's lifestyle practices with regard to nutritional intake. Analyse, interpret and evaluate the information/data in the audit, make sound recommendations and set SMART objectives and targets to bring about improvements. Back up your findings with references to what is factual, sound or recommended (the 'ideal').

2. Devise a safe, appropriate and effective action plan to achieve the objectives and targets within a set time frame. Explain how you would monitor the implementation of the action plan and the benefits of doing this. **Note:** Oliver is not known to be allergic to any foods.

   For guidance on how to do this, use Steps 1–5 on page 6.

3. You, your classmates and your teacher should produce a variety of audits that reflect a range of individuals from those who have unhealthy, unbalanced nutritional patterns to those who have healthy, balanced nutritional patterns. Use the audits to practise answering questions 1 and 2 above.

4. Divide into pairs and conduct an audit on each other's nutritional intake over a typical week. Analyse, interpret and evaluate the information/data in the audit, make sound recommendations and set SMART objectives and targets to bring about improvements.

5. Devise a safe, appropriate and effective action plan to achieve the objectives and targets within a set time frame. Explain how you would monitor the implementation of the action plan and the benefits of doing this. Will your partner take up the challenge?

Physical health: sleep

Learning outcomes

In this section, you will learn:

- the advice and recommendations to apply to get quality sleep
- the benefits of getting quality sleep
- the consequences of sleep deprivation
- how to analyse, interpret and evaluate information or data on sleep and how to plan to achieve quality sleep

What do we mean by sleep and rest?

Rest is a period of time when you consciously try and get the mind and/or body to be inactive. **Sleep** is a time of rest during which consciousness of the world is suspended. It is an essential component of health.

Quality sleep promotes and maintains good social, mental and physical health. On the other hand, sleep deprivation can lead to a person developing social, mental or physical health problems. Also, a person who has a social, mental or physical health problem may find it difficult to get quality sleep and this leads to sleep deprivation, which in turn can make the problem worse (see page 78).

How to get quality sleep – recommendations

It is important to get good quality sleep on a regular basis and try to stick to a certain schedule so you feel rested when you wake up.

The advice and recommendations that follow are based on those published by the Public Health Agency (PHA).

To get good, quality sleep you need to:
- get the environment right to encourage quality sleep.
- establish a beneficial night-time routine that encourages sleep.
- sleep the recommended number of hours for your age.
- sleep at the right time.

Getting the environment right

To help you get quality sleep you should:
- make sure the bed is comfortable.
- make sure the bedcovers keep you comfortably warm: not shivering or sweating.
- make sure the bedroom is uncluttered and is a calm place to relax.
- make sure the bedroom is kept at a comfortable, cool temperature.
- make sure the bedroom is dark: by using blackout blinds, curtains or even an eye mask.
- make sure the bedroom is quiet: if necessary, you could wear earplugs to block out 'uncontrolled' noise.
- keep the bedroom free from all distractions such as a television, games console, computer, laptop tablet or smartphone.

Getting the routine right

To help you get quality sleep you should:
- exercise regularly: exercise can relieve the day's stresses and strains.
- maintain a balanced, healthy nutritional plan/diet.
- avoid smoking tobacco and substance misuse.
- avoid taking naps during the day, especially if you have difficulty sleeping at night.
- avoid taking alcohol for at least three hours before bedtime.
- avoid taking caffeine (coffee, tea, energy drinks and some soft drinks) before going to bed. Try a hot, milky or herbal drink instead.
- avoid eating a large meal for at least two hours

1.2 HEALTH AND LIFESTYLE DECISIONS

before bedtime. If you are hungry at night, eat a light, healthy snack.
- make a 'To Do' list for the next day (or write down problems/worries you have to resolve). Do this well before you go to bed, so you will not be thinking of them when in bed.
- set a bedtime alarm to remind you when it is time to get ready for bed.
- relax for at least 30 minutes before bedtime. Do not use your computer, laptop, tablet, smartphone, video games or television. Take a relaxing, hot bath if it helps get you away from the technology.
- put your smartphone on silent for the night and place it away from your bed.
- go to bed early enough for you to get at least eight hours of sleep (or the minimum recommendation for your age)
- if you don't fall asleep after 20 minutes in bed, don't start using your smartphone or the like. Get out of bed and go to a different room for a while and do something that's relaxing and not mentally challenging. Don't lie in or nap the next day to compensate.
- get up at the same time every day, even on weekends or during holidays. Having a regular wake-up time is more important than a regular bedtime. Set an alarm for each morning to avoid any panic of sleeping in.

Getting the number of hours right

The amount of sleep required by people varies according to age and from person to person.

The following recommendations are for healthy individuals:
- **3–5 years**: 10–13 hours/day
- **6–13 years**: 9–11 hours/day
- **14–17 years**: 8–10 hours/day
- **18–64 years**: 7–9 hours/day
- **≥ 65 years**: 7–8 hours/day

Getting the right time of day

Your body sets your 'biological clock' according to the pattern of daylight where you live. This helps you naturally get sleepy at night and stay alert during the day. Problems with sleep can arise if you have to work at night and sleep during the day. This can also be the case when you travel to different time zones.

🔍 ASSESSMENT FOR LEARNING

1. Getting quality sleep depends on a number of factors. Identify the factors and give positive examples of how to apply each factor.

2. Analyse and evaluate your own weekly sleep pattern. For each of the factors, identify the positives and the negatives. What actions will you take to address the negatives?

What are the benefits of getting quality sleep?

- **Sleep helps growth:** Sleep allows growth to occur. Human growth hormone is released under conditions of sleep.
- **Sleep helps repair:** Sleep allows the repairing of muscles, neurons in the nervous system and other tissues, and the replenishing of immune cells, thus **boosting the immune system**. This repairing is maximal during sleep as energy consumption is lowered and is directed towards the healing or recovery process. This lowers your risk of getting sick as often, or of

developing serious health problems, like diabetes and heart disease.

- **Sleep improves concentration, learning and memory:** Sleep enables the brain to encode new information and store it properly. The parts of the brain that control emotions, decision-making and social interactions slow down during sleep, allowing optimal performance when awake. This leads to you thinking more clearly and doing better in school or work.

- **Sleep boosts mental well-being:** Sleep allows the brain to recharge. Sleeping the recommended number of hours per day is associated with improved attention, behaviour, learning, memory, emotional regulation, quality of life and mental and physical health. Quality sleep reduces stress levels and improves your mood, so can help you get along better with people.
- **Sleep improves physical performance:** (see rest and recovery on page 58). Sleep allows the body to recover and to adapt to the stresses of training. This adaptation is what makes you fitter and able to perform better than before. Getting enough sleep can help you make good decisions and perform well in sports. As the American Academy of Sleep Medicine (USA) says, sleep has "no additives, preservatives or chemicals; sleep is an all-natural energy supplement. It's 100% pure. Sleep is legal in every state [USA], with no prescription required. Best of all, it's completely free. Sleep is the original performance enhancer. All others are just cheap imitations." [sleepeducation.org/healthysleep/].

What are the consequences of sleep deprivation?

Sleep deprivation can be caused by, for example, stress; being in pain; suffering from health conditions like heartburn or asthma; as a result of taking certain medicines; as a result of taking caffeine (coffee, tea, energy drinks and some soft drinks); as a result of taking alcohol or other drugs; or as a result of sleep disorders, like apnea or insomnia.

Sleep follows a pattern and has a number of stages. To fully recover and recharge, your brain must experience all these stages. If sleep deprivation or poor-quality sleep prevents this for a time from any of the causes mentioned above, you will end up with severe fatigue, which can lead to:

- decreased attentiveness and concentration.
- decreased short-term memory.
- poor coordination.
- delayed reaction times.
- poor decision-making.
- moodiness, irritability and anxiety.

1.2 HEALTH AND LIFESTYLE DECISIONS

The Royal Society for Public Health (RSPH) reports that poor sleep:

- increases the risk of chronic illnesses including: high blood pressure, diabetes, depression, cancer, heart attack and stroke.
- is related to obesity in both children and adults.
- reduces quality of life and early death.
- in older people, may be related to accelerated cognitive decline.

[RSPH, *Waking up to the Health Benefits of Sleep* (2016)]

Teenagers who get insufficient sleep are associated with an increased risk for self-harm, suicidal thoughts and suicide attempts.

ASSESSMENT FOR LEARNING

1. Explain the benefits associated with getting quality sleep.
2. Explain the consequences associated with sleep deprivation.

ANALYSIS, INTERPRETATION, EVALUATION AND PLANNING

ASSESSMENT FOR LEARNING

1. Study the audit on page 190. It provides information on Ciara's lifestyle practices with regard to her sleep pattern and quality of sleep. Analyse, interpret and evaluate the information/data in the audit, make sound recommendations and set SMART objectives and targets to bring about improvements.

2. Devise a safe, appropriate and effective action plan to achieve the objectives and targets within a set time frame. Explain how you would monitor the implementation of the action plan and the benefits of doing this. **Note:** Ciara is willing to make changes.

   For guidance on how to do this, use Steps 1–5 on page 6.

3. You, your classmates and your teacher should produce a variety of audits that reflect a range of individuals from those who have unhealthy, unbalanced sleeping patterns and poor quality of sleep to those who consistently get quality sleep. Use the audits to practise answering questions 1 and 2 above.

4. Divide into pairs and conduct an audit on each other's sleep patterns over a typical week. Analyse, interpret and evaluate the information/data in the audit, make sound recommendations and set SMART objectives and targets to bring about improvements.

5. Devise a safe, appropriate and effective action plan to achieve the objectives and targets within a set time frame. Explain how you would monitor the implementation of the action plan and the benefits of doing this. Will your partner take up the challenge?

Physical health: tobacco, alcohol and illegal drugs

Learning outcomes

In this section, you will learn:

- the categorisation for drugs
- an outline of the laws on controlled/illegal drugs
- why people smoke tobacco, take illegal substances or drink alcohol
- the effects and negative consequences that smoking tobacco, taking illegal drugs or the excessive consumption of alcohol may have on the body, mind and health
- what help is available to stop
- the benefits of giving up illegal drugs, tobacco and the excessive consumption of alcohol
- how to analyse, interpret and evaluate information or data on taking controlled/illegal substances; smoking tobacco or drinking alcohol

What is a drug?

A drug is any chemical that affects how your body works, or how you behave or feel. Some drugs come from plants and others are made in laboratories. They can broadly be categorised as:

- **stimulants** – for example, caffeine, **nicotine** (tobacco), amphetamines ('speed'), ecstasy, cocaine, mephedrone.
- **depressants** – for example, **alcohol**, tranquillisers, codeine, heroin, cannabis, methadone and solvents.
- **hallucinogens** – for example, cannabis, ketamine, LSD and 'magic mushrooms'.

Commonly used legal drugs

Caffeine (a stimulant) is the most used drug. It is in coffee, tea, many soft drinks and colas, some confectionery, many medicines and available in over-the-counter stimulant preparations such as 'energy drinks'.

The next most commonly used drug is alcohol (a depressant); followed by nicotine (a stimulant) found in cigarettes and other tobacco-based products.

Laws on controlled drugs, tobacco and alcohol: Northern Ireland

Controlled drugs

The Misuse of Drugs Act 1971 covers the majority of laws that the Police Service of Northern Ireland (PSNI) will enforce regarding controlled drugs. Under this act, "passing drugs amongst your friends is supplying, even if no money is exchanged in return. Allowing your house or premises to be used for drug misuse is also illegal."

[psni.police.uk/crime/drugs/controlled-drugs-and-the-law/]

Tobacco

From 1 September 2008, the Children and Young Persons (Sale of Tobacco etc.) Regulations (Northern Ireland) 2008 became effective, raising the minimum purchase, consumption and possession age for tobacco from 16 to 18 years of age. These regulations highlighted "the offence of selling tobacco or cigarette papers to young persons [under the age of 18]" and "provides for the seizure and disposal of tobacco or cigarette papers from young persons" found smoking in any street or public place.

[legislation.gov.uk/nisr/2008/306/made]

Alcohol consumption and age

There are strict laws on alcohol consumption in Northern Ireland. These are contained mainly in the Licensing (NI) Order 1996 and the Registration of Clubs (NI) Order 1996.

Laws relating to those under 14 years of age

Under the Children and Young Persons Act (Northern Ireland) 1968, "anyone under the age of 14 may only consume alcohol in a private house and only for medical purposes."

1.2 HEALTH AND LIFESTYLE DECISIONS

Laws relating to those under 18 years of age

"Anyone under the age of 18 is not allowed in any bar area of licensed premises or registered clubs. However, some licensed premises hold a children's certificate that allows:
- a young person accompanied by an adult to be in the bar area (but not at the bar) in premises up to 9.00 p.m.
- a young person to stay on the premises until 9.30 p.m. to consume a meal purchased before 9.00 p.m."

In addition, "a young person under 18 is allowed to be in:
- an off-licence if accompanied by an adult.
- a refreshment room at a railway station, airport, harbour terminal or bus station.
- a sporting club until 10.00 p.m.
- any part of an indoor arena or outdoor stadium containing a kiosk or other sales point that sells alcoholic drinks as well as food and non-alcoholic drinks."

Laws relating to buying or consuming alcohol

Under the Licensing (NI) Order 1996, "anyone under 18 is not allowed to buy alcohol or consume alcohol in a place other than a private house."

The order also states that "it is an offence for a person to buy alcohol for consumption by a person under 18" or to "send a young person under 18 to get alcohol from licensed premises."

In addition, "It is an offence for a licence holder to:
- sell alcohol to a person under 18 for consumption on or off the premises.
- sell alcohol to any person for consumption by a person under 18 either on or off the premises.
- permit a young person under 18 to consume alcohol in licensed premises."

Towns and cities may also have local bye-laws banning drinking alcohol in public.

[nidirect.gov.uk/articles/alcohol-young-people-under-18-and-law]

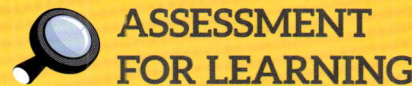

ASSESSMENT FOR LEARNING

1. What is the law regarding the consumption of alcohol for those under 14 years old?
2. What is the law regarding the buying or consumption of alcohol for those under 18 years old?

Why do some people take controlled/illegal drugs, smoke tobacco or drink alcohol?

Curiosity/experimentation

Most young people are naturally curious and often want to try things that they know may be illegal. If they know and mix with young people who smoke tobacco, drink alcohol, or take controlled/illegal drugs, this provides the opportunity for them to do the same. They are likely to be encouraged by the group and, partly from curiosity and partly from wanting to be accepted, they will start smoking tobacco, drinking alcohol or taking illegal drugs or substances.

Natural rebellion

If young people are told that they should not smoke tobacco, drink alcohol or take illegal drugs or substances, this can make some even keener to try them as they do not want to be told by adults what they can or cannot do. They may want to make their own judgements and will try smoking tobacco, drinking alcohol or experimenting with drugs just to be defiant.

Promotion and availability

The advertising of tobacco products was found to encourage young people to start smoking and to reinforce the habit among existing smokers. Advertising tobacco products is now banned, but advertising alcohol products is not. In fact, some people believe that alcopops (alcoholic drinks that do not taste of alcohol and so are more appealing to the young) have been deliberately marketed towards teenagers to entice them to drink.

Despite there being laws about the age at which young people may purchase tobacco or alcohol, it is still possible for them to obtain these products. This is also the case with illegal drugs.

Enjoyment

Many people take drugs, drink alcohol or smoke tobacco for enjoyment: for the 'buzz', the 'thrill' or the 'high' that these products can offer. But while the pleasure experienced mostly comes from the direct effects of the drugs, alcohol or tobacco, it can also be linked to being part of a particular youth subculture.

The defence mechanism

Young people, just like adults, can suffer from stress, depression, anxiety and trauma because of what is happening in their lives, and just like adults some will use tobacco, alcohol or drugs to ease their pain and suffering. This is considered a negative coping strategy that can make things worse rather than better (see page 40).

Cost

Users generally feel that the experience they get from the use of drugs, alcohol or tobacco is worth the money spent on them. Some feel that they get better value for money by taking illegal drugs rather than consuming alcohol or smoking tobacco: that the effects experienced when taking illegal drugs are better than those from alcohol or tobacco.

Environment

Smoking tobacco, consuming alcohol and experimenting with illegal drugs is not limited to just one social group or environment – there are few areas, rich or poor, free from these drugs. However a study carried out by the Advisory Council for the Misuse of Drugs ['Drug Misuse and the Environment' (1998)] indicated that addiction and regular use are more likely to develop among young people from disadvantaged backgrounds. It found that deprivation "is more likely to relate to a lower age of first use, progression to dependence, criminal involvement and … the extremes of problematic use. The chances of overcoming drug problems are less among people who are disadvantaged. They have fewer positive alternatives and less access to meaningful employment, housing etc. … Poor areas with high unemployment levels can provide an environment where drug dealing becomes an established way of earning money, [while] deprived areas often suffer from greater and more visible public nuisance from drug taking and supplying."

ASSESSMENT FOR LEARNING

1. Review the list of factors that can account for people getting involved in taking controlled/illegal drugs, smoking tobacco or drinking alcohol. Explain how each factor may influence young people.

2. How would you rate the significance of each factor as influences in getting vulnerable teenagers involved in:
   - taking controlled/illegal drugs?
   - smoking tobacco?
   - drinking alcohol?

   Use a scale of 1–10, with 10 being 'highly significant' and 1 being of 'no significance.'

   Share your ratings and account for your decisions.

FURTHER THINKING

Are there other factors that may account for people becoming involved in taking controlled/illegal drugs, smoking tobacco or drinking alcohol?

Effects and negative consequences

The effects and consequences of taking controlled/illegal substances, smoking tobacco and drinking alcohol depend on the interaction between:

- **the substance taken** – what is taken; how much is taken; how often it is taken; other ingredients added; the mix of substances taken; and how they are taken (injecting; eating, drinking or snorting).
- **the person** – their mental or psychological state; mood; physical health problems; energy levels; body weight; gender.
- **the setting** – dangerous places (taking any sort of mind-altering substance near, for example, river banks, motorways, or derelict buildings can lead to serious injury, even death); at school or at work (exposure could lead to expulsion or being fired); driving a car, riding a bike or operating machinery (can cause accidents); sexual encounters (lack of inhibitions/precautions could inadvertently lead to pregnancy or HIV or STIs).

Addiction

Taking illegal substances, smoking tobacco or drinking alcohol often leads to addiction and dependency, where the user experiences a strong compulsion to keep taking them. This dependency can be physical and/or psychological:

- **Physical dependency** comes from the repeated use of drugs – including, but not limited to, cigarettes and alcohol. Continual use can change the body chemistry so that if a user does not get a repeat dose they will suffer physical withdrawal symptoms, for example, trembling and anxiety. The person will usually have to keep taking the drug just to stop feeling ill.
- **Psychological dependency** is more common and can happen with any drug. Users turn to drugs as a way to cope with the world – they feel they could not cope without those drugs, even though they may not be physically dependent. You can become psychologically dependent on just about anything – chocolate, gambling, or playing computer games. If any activity becomes more important to you than everything else – school, family or friends – things may need to change.

Addiction to alcohol

People are more likely to become physically dependent or addicted to alcohol if they:

- begin drinking at an early age.
- have a parent or other close relative who has problems with alcohol. This may be influenced by genetic factors.
- have friends who drink regularly.
- drink too much on a regular basis for an extended period, or binge drink on a regular basis.
- have a mental health problem, such as depression or anxiety (the defence mechanism).

People with an alcohol addiction are also more vulnerable to using other addictive substances like drugs or tobacco. It is common for addiction in one area to spread to addictions in other areas as well.

> **ASSESSMENT FOR LEARNING**
>
> 1 Explain the difference between physical dependency and psychological dependency.

Effects of taking stimulants
Stimulants can:
- increase the heart rate and energy levels, making a person feel more alert. However this is soon followed by bouts of exhaustion and even depression. Repeated and regular use can lead to problems of dependence.

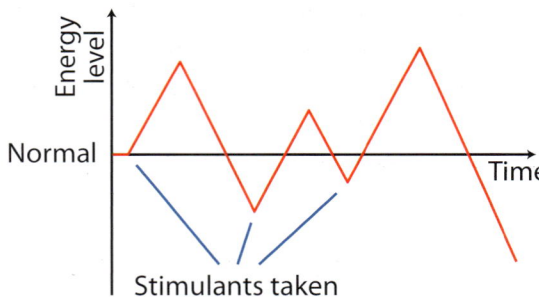

- cause abnormal heart rhythm disorders or even heart attacks. When stimulants such as amphetamines (e.g. speed) are used, the lack of blood to the heart can cause angina (severe chest pain).
- increase the body's movements making injuries more likely, especially during sport. Cocaine at higher doses can act as an anaesthetic so the user does not feel pain and may play on after an injury, causing even more damage.
- make the user irritable and restless – making them less focused.
- keep the user awake, resulting in insufficient rest, which can in turn affect performance.
- decrease appetite, so sufficient calories may not be replaced after exercise.
- produce anxiety or panic attacks particularly if taken in large quantities and can lead to delirium, paranoia and hallucinations.

Other side effects from stimulants include high blood pressure, palpitations, increased body temperature and even death.

Effects of smoking tobacco (stimulant)

Tobacco smoke contains over 4000 chemicals, around 50 of which are known to cause cancer. The main components and most dangerous ones are **nicotine, tar** and **carbon monoxide.**

- **Nicotine** is a powerful, fast-acting drug that is very addictive, and smokers become dependent on it. It can affect the brain within ten seconds of being breathed in. Nicotine:
  - constricts the blood vessels.
  - raises the heart rate.
  - raises blood pressure.
  - speeds up metabolism.
  - affects mood and behaviour.
  - combined with carbon monoxide, leads to clotting of the blood and clogging of the arteries.

- **Tar** is the sticky brown substance that carries many of the harmful materials into the lungs. It also stains smokers' fingers and teeth a yellowy-brown colour. Tar carries:
  - irritants that narrow the bronchioles (small tubes) of the lungs.

1.2 HEALTH AND LIFESTYLE DECISIONS

- irritants that aggravate the delicate mucus membrane lining the air passages, causing them to produce more mucus.
- irritants that damage the cilia (small hairs lining the air passages) that help protect the lungs from dirt and infection.
- the carcinogens that can cause cancer.

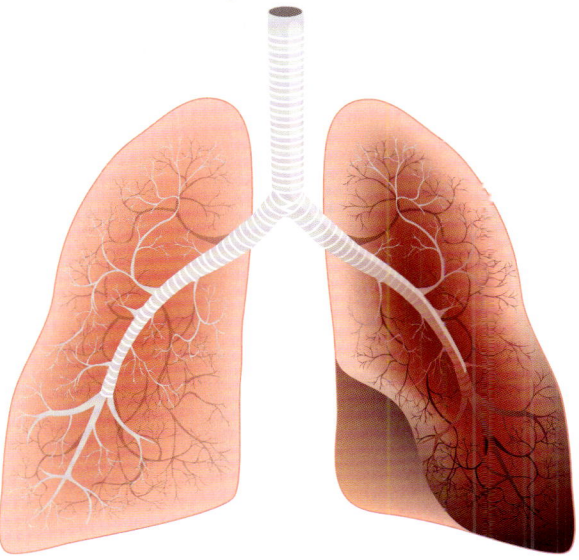

Healthy Lungs   Smoker's Lungs

- **Carbon monoxide** is a poisonous gas. It is taken up by the red blood cells, which should normally be carrying oxygen.

Effects of smoking tobacco on physical performance

- Smoking constricts the lungs' air passages, making it more difficult to breathe air into the lungs.
- The tar from the smoke lies in the alveoli (air sacs) in the lungs. This means there is less surface area than before for the exchange of oxygen and carbon dioxide.
- Due to blood vessels being constricted by the nicotine, the heart has to work harder and blood pressure will be raised.
- With carbon monoxide taking the place of oxygen in the red blood cells, there is less oxygen available than before.
- To be able to work aerobically at a particular work rate, the muscles demand a certain amount of oxygen per minute. If, due to smoking, less oxygen is getting into the lungs and less oxygen is taken into the blood from the lungs, then the respiratory (including the lungs) and the circulatory (including the heart) systems will have to work harder than before to meet the demand of the muscles. As a result, a smoker will be at a disadvantage in aerobic activities.

Long-term effects on health from smoking tobacco

No amount of smoking is free from risk, but the amount of risk depends on how long you have smoked; how many cigarettes you smoke; how deeply you inhale; and on genetic factors. Some of the long-term effects of smoking are listed below.

Effects on respiratory system
Smokers have a much greater risk of getting:
- lung cancer.
- mouth, nose and throat cancer.
- chronic bronchitis and emphysema.
- colds, flu, laryngitis and infections that last much longer.

Effects on heart and circulation
Smokers have a much greater risk of:
- having a heart attack.
- getting leukaemia.
- getting arteriosclerosis (build-up of fatty deposits and loss of elasticity in the artery walls). Arteriosclerosis is the forerunner to a range of diseases, for example strokes, and clotting of the blood in the legs.

Some other effects

- Death. Smokers tend to have a shorter life expectancy: the British Medical Journal has estimated that each cigarette cuts an average of 11 minutes off the life of a male smoker [BMJ Vol.320; No.7226, (2000)]; while NI.direct reports that around 2300 people die from smoking related illnesses in Northern Ireland each year [nidirect.gov.uk/articles/smoking].
- Smoking whilst pregnant can cause a range of problems: babies are more likely to be born prematurely or underweight; develop asthma in childhood; experience ongoing ill health; and/or have a general lack of coordination. Smoking during pregnancy or after birth can also significantly increase the risk of sudden infant death syndrome (SIDS).
- Smoking can have adverse effects on fertility and cause impotence in some men.
- Smoking leads to premature ageing as the chemicals in a cigarette can damage the skin's elasticity, colour and texture.
- Smoking can interfere with the healing of bone and muscle injuries.
- Smoking can lead to loss of appetite (though some see this as beneficial for weight control, and can refuse to quit for fear they will put on weight if they stop).
- Smokers can often have bad breath; their hair and clothes smell; and their teeth and fingers become stained.
- Smokers have a much greater risk of causing fires in their homes.
- Smoking is an expensive habit and can have a significant negative financial effect.

The dangers of second-hand/passive smoke

- Passive smoke affects the health of family, friends and work colleagues and can cause disease, disability, and even death.
- Passive smoking is particularly dangerous for young people. Babies and children raised with people who smoke are more prone to ear infections, colds, bronchitis, and other lung and breathing problems than children from non-smoking families.
- Second-hand smoke can also cause eye irritation, headaches, nausea, and dizziness.

ASSESSMENT FOR LEARNING

1. Identify the effects that can result from taking stimulant drugs.
2. Tobacco is classified as a stimulant. Identify, in detail:
   - the immediate effects that inhaling tobacco smoke can have on people.
   - the long-term effects that inhaling tobacco smoke can have on people.
3. Explain the effects of smoking tobacco on physical performance.

Effects of depressants

The effects of alcohol and other depressants on physical performance

- Depressants slow down the central nervous system, affecting the body's coordination and reaction times: the body's motor ability is reduced, making it harder to coordinate movements and the user becomes less alert; less able to concentrate and slower to react. Due to slow reactions, depressant use is particularly dangerous whilst driving or operating machinery.
- Depressants can also slow down the heart rate, meaning less oxygen-rich blood reaches the muscles, which will affect the user's performance.
- Depressants can slow down breathing and narrow airways, thereby reducing oxygen supply. If exercising, this may affect the user's performance.

1.2 HEALTH AND LIFESTYLE DECISIONS

- Alcohol is a diuretic (meaning that it stimulates the body's elimination of liquid) and it limits sugar glucose – together, this means that muscles have trouble contracting and endurance performances therefore suffer. Alcohol also diminishes the ability of muscles to recover and grow if stressed through exercise.

- Some depressants reduce pain and can cause loss of feeling, so the user may not notice when they are injured: this may lead to delays in getting rapid treatment.
- Other side effects include: nausea and vomiting; loss of sleep; depression; and constipation.
- Alcohol, as a depressant, is high in calories so excessive use may affect the person's weight.

Effects of alcohol (depressant)
Brain and central nervous system
The brain controls all the body's functions. When a person consumes alcohol, that control is impeded. This results in:
- loss of coordination
- loss of balance
- poor information processing
- poor judgement and decision-making
- slowed reflexes/reaction time
- distorted vision
- slurred speech
- memory lapses
- blackouts
- nausea

Excessive drinking can affect the nervous system, causing numbness and pain in the hands and feet, disordered thinking, dementia, and short-term memory loss.

Alcohol also impedes a normal sleep cycle. It impairs a person's ability to hold onto glycogen – the energy source that the body uses during tests of endurance – so endurance performance will suffer.

Hormones
- Underage drinking can cause hormonal imbalances. During the teenage years the brain is undergoing a crucial period of development that will continue until the person is in their late twenties. Alcohol can interfere with this brain development.

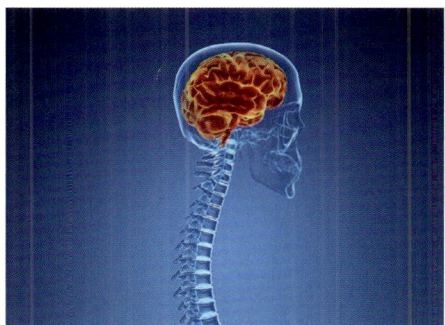

- The sleep interruptions from alcohol consumption increase the levels of cortisol (a stress-related hormone) in the body. Increased cortisol levels correlate with reduced healing (leading to an injury-recovery problem) and reduce the body's production of human growth hormone.
- Alcohol inhibits the production of testosterone.
- Both the human growth hormone and testosterone are crucial to the body's ability to build and repair muscle. Their depletion affects muscle hypertrophy and performance can suffer as a result.

Liver

- Heavy drinking can cause increased fat in the liver (hepatic steatosis), inflammation of the liver (alcoholic hepatitis) and, over time, irreversible destruction and scarring of liver tissue (cirrhosis).
- Alcohol interferes with the release of glucose from your liver and can increase the risk of low blood sugar (hypoglycemia). This is dangerous if you have diabetes and are already taking insulin to lower your blood sugar level.
- Excessive alcohol consumption can lead to permanent liver damage. The liver's main job is to clean the body of toxins, but when it is overwhelmed with alcohol, it can become scarred and unable to perform this vital role.

Heart

Excessive drinking can lead to high blood pressure and increases the risk of an enlarged heart, heart failure or stroke. Even a single binge of alcohol can cause a serious heart arrhythmia called atrial fibrillation.

Digestive system

Heavy drinking can result in inflammation of the stomach lining (gastritis), as well as stomach and oesophageal ulcers. It also can interfere with absorption of B vitamins and other nutrients.

Heavy drinking can damage the pancreas or lead to inflammation of the pancreas (pancreatitis).

Immune system

Excessive alcohol use can make it harder for the body to resist disease and illnesses, especially pneumonia.

Increased risk of cancer

Long-term excessive alcohol use has been linked to a higher risk of many cancers, including mouth, throat, oesophagus, liver, colon and breast cancer. Even moderate drinking can increase the risk of breast cancer.

Judgement

Excessive drinking can reduce your judgement and lower inhibitions, leading to poor choices and dangerous situations or behaviours, including:

- motor vehicle accidents and other types of accidental injury, such as drowning or falling.
- relationship problems with family, friends and work colleagues.
- poor performance at work or school.
- increased risk of suicide.

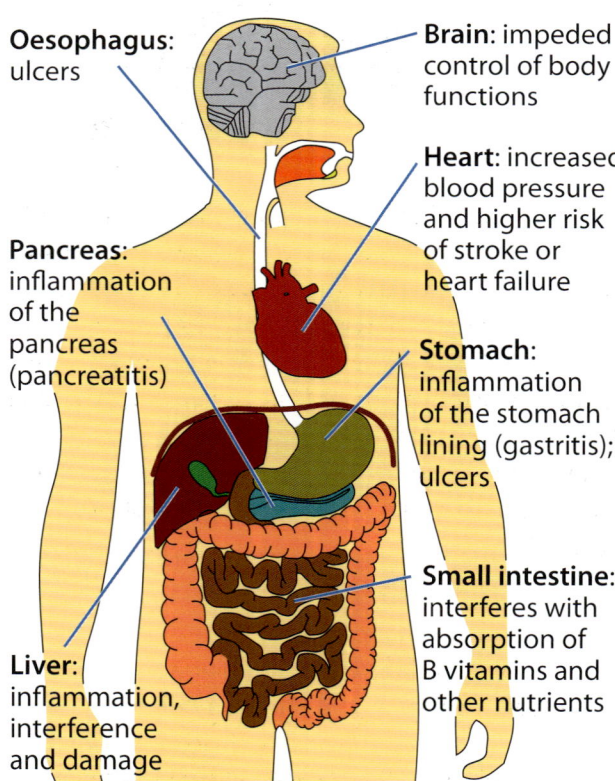

Effects of alcohol on the body

1.2 HEALTH AND LIFESTYLE DECISIONS

ASSESSMENT FOR LEARNING

1. Identify the effects that can result from taking depressant drugs.

2. Alcohol is classified as a depressant. Identify, in detail:
   - the immediate effects excessive alcohol consumption can have on people, including physical performance.
   - the long-term effects that continual alcohol abuse can have on people.

Effects of hallucinogens

Cannabis, ketamine, LSD and 'magic mushrooms' are collectively known as hallucinogens and can change the way people think, feel and perceive their surroundings. They can enhance appreciation of surroundings but can also cause anxiety or paranoia and can contribute to mental health problems.

Hallucinogens distort the user's sense of time and perception and are dangerous if the user is engaged in a 'safety critical' job. Performances in sports can also be impeded as perception and timing are crucial in the effective performance of skills in sports.

Hallucinogens like cannabis and magic mushrooms can play havoc with the senses. They affect the sight and hearing, which would disrupt your ability to perform in sport (and, since cannabis reduces lung capacity, it makes it harder to get oxygen to the working muscles).

Whilst hallucinogens may not cause physical dependence, a user may become psychologically dependent on their effects.

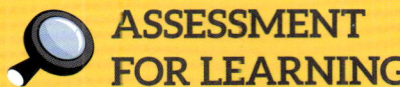

ASSESSMENT FOR LEARNING

1. Identify the effects that can result from taking hallucinogens.

Antisocial aspects of taking illegal drugs and alcohol

Antisocial behaviour is another possible consequence of taking illegal substances or being drunk on alcohol. Substance abusers are more likely to:
- intimidate others.
- demonstrate aggressive behaviour.
- be disruptive at school or work.
- get into debt to pay for their habit.
- get involved in stealing to fund their habit.
- be thoughtless about disposing of needles, litter and about going to the toilet.
- miss days from school or work.
- not work to their potential.
- withdraw from participating in extra-curricular activities.

This type of behaviour causes conflict with family, friends, colleagues and law enforcement authorities. It often leads to the breakdown of family relationships and other personal relationships. Getting expelled from school/college, being dismissed from work, and getting a criminal record are often the outcomes from this antisocial behaviour.

Substance abusers are also more likely to suffer from mental health problems and emotional and social issues. They are more likely to engage in self-harm or to attempt suicide.

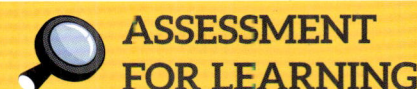

ASSESSMENT FOR LEARNING

1. Explain what type of anti-social behaviour is often associated with people who are addicted to controlled/illegal drugs or alcohol.

FURTHER THINKING

Use the Internet to further your depth of understanding on addiction, including the effects of stimulants (especially smoking tobacco), depressants (especially alcohol) and hallucinogens on the human body and performance.

Quitting and the help available

Alcohol abuse, and the use of controlled/illegal drugs and tobacco, has a negative effect on physical well-being. Quite often, people want to quit, but they need help to stop.

Help to stop taking controlled/illegal drugs

There are different kinds of help available for people who are drug dependent or need advice and information on drugs. They include:

Telephone helplines

There are telephone helplines, available 24 hours a day, where drug dependents can talk or get advice, support and help. Some of these provide help for families of drug users. FRANK, an independent government-funded website (talktofrank.com), offers a live chat facility, email support, an SMS number and a 24-hour telephone helpline.

Drug advice and counselling services

These give information and advice and offer counselling and other forms of support to drug users and/or their partners, family or friends. They usually offer simple advice over the phone as well as seeing people by appointment. The services are nearly always confidential. They are sometimes called Community Drug Teams or Drug Advice Services.

Self-help groups for drug users, parents and families

The local drugs advice service should be able to provide information on what is available in an area. For example, it could be a national organisation like Narcotics Anonymous – this is a network of self-help groups for drug users based on the Alcoholics Anonymous approach.

Family doctor or GP

The family doctor should be able to offer help on drug problems and on other health issues. They can give advice, sometimes prescribe substitute drugs (particularly for heroin users), and should have information on local specialist services.

Hospital-based drug services

These are usually for people who are prolific, long-term drug users: particularly injecting heroin users. Many of these services can prescribe substitute drugs, especially to stabilise or bring people off heroin. These services usually require a letter of referral from a GP, social worker, probation officer or local drug service.

Residential rehabilitation centres

These are for people with longer-term drug problems, usually involving dependency. Users live in them for up to a year in an attempt to kick the habit.

ASSESSMENT FOR LEARNING

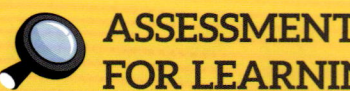

1. List the range of range of services available to help drug users to quit.

2. Explain which of the services may be best-suited to help long-term, totally addicted/dependent drug users to quit.

Help to stop smoking tobacco

The nicotine withdrawal that comes when a person quits smoking can make them feel restless, irritable, frustrated, sleepless, or accident prone, but there are several methods that can offer help during this withdrawal stage:

- **Nicotine replacement therapies (NRT)** are medically-approved ways to take nicotine instead of through tobacco: these include nicotine gum, inhalers, lozenges, mouth spray, nasal spray, patches and tablets, and are widely available.
- **Non-nicotine medications** such as Champix and Zyban are prescription medications that ease the withdrawal symptoms from nicotine and make smoking less pleasurable.
- **Stop smoking services** provide support for people who want to stop smoking and are available mainly through GP practices and pharmacies. There are more than 600 stop smoking services available in Northern Ireland. They help people prepare to quit, work with them to choose a quit date and offer weekly appointments, individual counselling or group sessions.
- **Other methods** that people may choose include self-help books or hypnosis.

As of 2019, the Public Health Agency (PHA) offers a free booklet, 'Want 2 Stop!: Quit plan' (available at want2stop.info), which provides information on the health benefits of stopping smoking. It includes questionnaires that can help smokers gauge their level of addiction, and identify any 'triggers' that have them reaching for a cigarette. It also takes a look at money that can be saved when a person quits smoking.

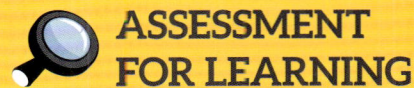

ASSESSMENT FOR LEARNING

1   What services/products are available to help those who wish to quit smoking? How do they work?

Help to stop taking excessive amounts of alcohol

There are different kinds of help available for people who are alcohol dependent. The type of treatment used depends on the individual and the severity of their alcohol dependency.

- **Detoxification:** If a person is physically dependent on alcohol (suffering alcohol withdrawal symptoms when they stop drinking), the first step in treatment is medically-assisted withdrawal (also known as alcohol detoxification). This involves replacing alcohol with other drugs, then reducing the dose over five to seven days in hospital. The aim of detoxification is to reduce the unpleasant withdrawal symptoms. Sedating medications may also be used. The symptoms are generally worse at the beginning of the treatment but improve over time.

- **Abstinence:** Here, treatment is structured and often involves several stages similar to those used in self-help or counselling organisations (such as Alcoholics Anonymous). The main aim is to help the person give up alcohol completely, rather than simply cut down on their drinking. It may include goal setting,

behaviour change techniques, use of self-help manuals, counselling and follow-up care.
- **Rehabilitation:** The process used for this will depend on the person's needs. It can include support through self-help groups or intensive treatment in a rehabilitation facility. Therapy is aimed at helping the person find out why they drink alcohol and to provide alternatives that will eventually lead to a fulfilled life without alcohol. During rehabilitation, the person will face a variety of difficult issues and may experience intense mood swings. Family or group support is important to help them cope with the lifestyle changes and to manage any relapses.

ASSESSMENT FOR LEARNING

1. Detoxification, abstinence and rehabilitation are three methods used to help people who are addicted/dependent on alcohol to break this dependency. Explain how each method works.

FURTHER THINKING

Use the Internet to further explore the methods used to help people to stop:
- taking controlled/illegal drugs
- smoking tobacco and
- drinking excessive amounts of alcohol.

Benefits to be gained by quitting

The health benefits to be gained from quitting drugs, tobacco or alcohol are really about recovering from poor health; or at least decreasing the risks of getting illnesses or diseases associated with these addictive substances. The short-term or immediate negative effects may be reversed reasonably quickly but it takes more time for the body to recover from the long-term effects. Sometimes damage cannot be repaired.

The benefits of quitting stimulants

People who eliminate any kind of stimulant tend to find they are less irritable, agitated, restless, tired, tense, aggressive, confused or delirious. For the most part, their quality of sleep improves, as does their appetite, and they are less likely to suffer from anxiety, panic attacks and paranoia. Their risk of high blood pressure; palpitations and heart rhythm disorders; heart attack or angina are reduced.

Quitting smoking (stimulant)

There are also certain health benefits specific to quitting smoking, and these benefits can be measured almost immediately:

After 20 minutes
Blood pressure and pulse rate return to normal.

After 8 hours
Nicotine and carbon monoxide levels in the blood reduce by more than half, and oxygen levels return to normal.

After 48 hours
Carbon monoxide will be eliminated from the body. Lungs start to clear out mucus and other smoking debris. There is no nicotine in the body. Ability to taste and smell is improved.

After 72 hours
Breathing becomes easier. Bronchial tubes begin to relax and functional abilities are starting to increase

After 2–12 weeks
Circulation improves. Blood circulation in gums and teeth are now similar to that of a non-user. Heart attack risk has started to drop. Lung function is beginning to improve. Quitting smoking can rewire the brain and help break the cycle of addiction. The large number of nicotine receptors in your brain will return to normal levels.

After 3–9 months
Coughing, wheezing and breathing problems improve as lung function increases by up to 10%. Any smoking-related sinus congestion, fatigue or shortness of breath has decreased. Cilia have regrown in the lungs, thereby increasing their ability to handle mucus, keep the lungs clean and reduce infections.

After 1 year
Risk of coronary heart disease, heart attack and stroke is about half that of a person who is still smoking.

After 10 years
Risk of stroke has declined to that of a non-smoker. Risk of lung cancer falls to about half that of a smoker. Risk of cancer of the mouth, throat, oesophagus and pancreas have declined. Risk of developing diabetes is now similar to that of a non-smoker. Risk of smoking-induced tooth loss has declined to that of a non-smoker.

After 15 years
Risk of coronary heart disease and heart attack is now the same as someone who has never smoked.

After 20 years
Risk of death from lung disease and cancer has now reduced to that of a non-smoker. Risk of pancreatic cancer has declined to that of a non-smoker.

The benefits of quitting depressants
People who stop find their motor ability improves – they have better balance and coordination; they are more alert; they are able to concentrate and their reactions improve; their breathing becomes normal again; their heart rate returns to normal; there is no more nausea and vomiting; they get better sleep and there is less risk of depression.

Stopping excessive alcohol consumption (depressant)
People who stop generally find that their coordination, balance and reflexes improve and their reasoning, memory and ability to make sound judgments returns. In teenagers, brain development is no longer compromised.

Normal growth patterns return (notably in the muscles) and sleep improves. The liver recovers, or at least suffers no more damage. There is less risk of getting an enlarged heart; experiencing heart failure or a stroke. There is less risk of getting stomach ulcers; pancreatitis or cancers of the mouth, throat, liver, colon or breast.

The benefits of quitting hallucinogens
People who stop find that their thinking is more realistic; their feelings from their senses (sights and sounds) more genuine; and perception of their surroundings more accurate. They are less likely to suffer from anxiety and paranoia.

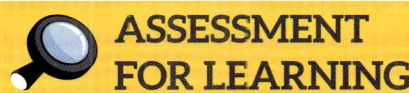

ASSESSMENT FOR LEARNING

1. Tobacco is categorised as a stimulant. Outline why it is worthwhile for a tobacco smoker to stop smoking.

2. Alcohol is categorised as a depressant. Outline why it is worthwhile for an alcoholic to stop drinking.

Planning for physical health: Factors that can affect lifestyle decisions

Personal characteristics and the nature of physical activities

There are a variety of physical activities and sports available for people: there are team sports, individual sports, full contact sports, limited contact sports and non-contact sports. Across the range are opportunities for people to enter competitions or to simply participate without any competitive element.

The personality traits/characteristics that people have can influence the physical activities or sports they are likely to enjoy, participate in and be successful at. These characteristics/traits can be separated into the following five main areas (the acronym **OCEAN** can help you remember these):

- **Openness:** For example, people who are curious, adventurous or open to new experiences may explore a range of outdoor pursuits activities – like mountaineering, rock climbing, canoeing, sailing and snowboarding – whereas others may limit their participation to whatever sport is played locally.
- **Conscientiousness:** For example, people who are organised, efficient, self-disciplined or dependable are more likely to be high-level performers, or good club and team members in either individual or team sports, whereas people who are unorganised, easy-going, careless or even unreliable may only occasionally participate in physical activities or sports and will have limited commitment.
- **Extroversion:** For example, people who are extroverted, enthusiastic, outgoing, optimistic or confident are more likely to be involved in competitive team sports, whereas people who are introverted are more likely to participate in individual physical activities and sports.
- **Agreeableness:** For example, people who are sympathetic, warm or compassionate are more likely to be involved in competitive team sports, whereas people who are outspoken, blunt or antagonistic are more likely to participate in individual physical activities and sports as, in the team situation, they may cause conflict by forcefully expressing their views on coaching, training, tactics, team selection and the like.
- **Neuroticism (or Emotionality):** For example, people who are easily upset, anxious, emotionally unstable or insecure are more likely to participate in non-competitive physical activities and sports, such as recreational walking, as there is limited pressure on them, whereas people who are calm, controlled and confident can cope with the pressures and expectations of competitive individual or team sports.

ASSESSMENT FOR LEARNING

1. Identify and explain the range of different physical activities and sports that are available for people.

2. Identify and explain the five main traits associated with people's personalities.

3. Analyse the nature of the following physical activities or sports then match the likely personal characteristics/traits of people who will sustain participation in them.
   - competitive team sports
   - competitive individual sports
   - non-competitive, recreational physical activities
   - high level, competitive sports
   - no physical activities or sports

Motivation, arousal and success

Motivation is the desire or drive people have to do something. It can be extrinsic or intrinsic.

Extrinsic motivation is when people are motivated by external factors – things *outside* of themselves. This could mean participating in physical activities and sports to achieve things (for example to complete over 20 000 steps per day, or to run a marathon in less than four hours). People who only have extrinsic motivation are often highly aroused and motivated at the beginning, but can become disheartened and, in time, give up.

Intrinsic motivation is when a person's desire comes from *inside* themselves – they participate because they love the physical activity or sport. Like those who are extrinsically motivated, they can have external goals, but if they fail to achieve the goals they do not lose their motivation and stop participating. In fact, people with intrinsic motivation who participate in physical activities and sports are continually aroused and more likely to be healthy and achieve any goals they set.

Most people know there are health benefits associated with participation in physical activity and sport, but this is often not given as the motivation for participation. Most say they participate for enjoyment and for social interaction. It is therefore important to ensure people participate in physical activities or sports that they enjoy and where they have the social interaction that they want. That way they are more likely to become long-term committed participants and gain the health benefits.

Parents, siblings and peers

If your parents or older siblings participate in a physical activity or play a sport, this may influence you. They are likely to encourage you to get involved and to participate. Family is a strong influence during childhood but is significantly less influential during adolescence and adulthood. Teachers and coaches have a significant influence, but usually only during adolescence.

Peer pressure is the influence that people of similar social standing and age can have on each other. Peers are a major influence throughout each stage of your life. People like to be part of a social group and, within a group, there will be those who exert more influence than others.

Disability

The United Nations defines persons with disabilities as "persons who have long-term physical, mental, intellectual or sensory impairments, which, in interaction with various barriers, may hinder their full and effective participation in society on an equal basis with others". [*United Nations Convention on the Rights of Persons with Disabilities* (2016)]

Physical activity and sport can have a positive impact on the lives of people with disabilities but many face challenges or barriers to getting involved, compared with people without a disability.

For example:

- **The attitudes people have towards disability**: Statistics provided by Scope, the UK disability equality charity, reveal that 36% of people in the UK tend to think of disabled people "as not as productive as everyone else"; while 24% of disabled people have experienced attitudes or behaviours where "other people expected less of them because of their disability." [*Current Attitudes Towards Disabled People,* scope.org.uk]

    These kinds of attitudes can have a significant impact on a disabled person's self-confidence and self-image, which may mean they never start, or they withdraw from, participation in physical activities or sports.

- **Lack of understanding and awareness of how to include people with a disability in sport**: People with disabilities often find that, for example, rules, equipment, facilities, skills, and teaching or coaching styles are not adapted or modified for them. This results in negative experiences of physical activities and sports, and people then have low expectations of them.

- **Limited opportunities and programmes for participation, training and competition:** Most schemes and programmes for participation in physical activities and sports have been aimed at the general public or at developing elite sports competitors. The fact that there are relatively few people with disabilities taking part in sport, especially competitive sport, means that opportunities for people with disabilities to get involved and progress within a particular sport are sometimes ignored.
- **Lack of accessible facilities:** Many buildings were designed and built with non-disabled users in mind. Therefore, if people with disabilities have difficulty entering a facility, it may put them off participating there and make them feel unwelcome at the facility.
- **Limited access to transportation:** Many people with disabilities are dependent on a family member or a friend to transport them. This means the car needs to be suitable for the person with the disability and the driver needs to be available at specific times, or participation has to be arranged around those times when the driver is available. This can affect participation. Most public transport systems can now be used by people with disabilities, but the journey can still be challenging.
- **Cost:** It is becoming more and more specialised and expensive to compete in disability sport or adapted physical activity (APA). The cost and availability of prostheses/prosthetics (artificial limbs) or adapted equipment (e.g. wheelchairs) for use by athletes with a disability can have a major impact upon their ability to participate.

Progress is being made on providing access for people with disabilities and the number of international organisations serving athletes with disabilities has increased dramatically. More coaching resources and materials are available that focus on including disabled people. The principles of adapting and modifying activities to include people with a disability are constantly developing as research and programme development continues.

The rise in the success and popularity of the Paralympic Games has provided role models and inspiration for people with disabilities to become involved in sport at all levels. It has also helped to change the perceptions of many amongst the non-disabled population regarding what people with disabilities can achieve.

Mental health

Depression rates are lower among the physically active, so an important strategy to maintain good mental health is to be physically active (see page 49). Regular physical activity energises you, lifts your mood, reduces your stress and anxiety levels, and your worries can seem less severe. If you can do physical activity with someone else, this often helps even more.

Activities like walking, running, cycling or dancing are great activities because they can be done alone or with others, at a time that suits you; and they are relatively inexpensive to do. If you work at an appropriate intensity long enough and often enough, they bring health benefits. What is important is that you find physical activities that you enjoy and will continue to do.

However, if people suffer from mental health issues, their thinking, feelings, behaviour and physical symptoms may mean that they lead a sedentary lifestyle instead (the consequences of this may be found on page 46).

Facilities

Facilities are the buildings or amenities that allow organised sport and physical activities to take place: for example, swimming pools, indoor basketball courts, tennis courts, pitches for team games, and golf courses. Public sector facilities (see pages 105–109) are usually provided and operated by local government and are open to the public, while private sector facilities are operated for their members and are profit-making businesses.

The existence of facilities in an area can affect participation. For example, if an area has a swimming pool, there will probably be a swimming club. The pool will also be used by recreational swimmers and people who take part in other water-based activities. Having easy access to the facility means that anyone with an interest in swimming will use the pool. However, if there is no swimming pool nearby people will be reluctant to travel great distances in order to swim.

In the same way, if a facility or amenity has good access – the means of approaching or entering a place, such as a good road, bus or rail service – it is much easier for people to use it. And, as many people now choose to travel by car, parking spaces at and around the facility or amenity are very important and will affect its use. Access into the facility itself is also important: for people with disabilities, or for those who are old or very young, the facility needs, for example, to have things like special parking areas, ramps, automatic doors, lifts, special toilets and specialist equipment.

Geographical location and the natural features of a place can also influence what sports and physical activities can be done in the area. For example, if you live near the sea or a lake where water sports consistently take place, then there is a good chance that you will get involved. If, however, you live a long way from the sea or lake, then you are less likely to get involved in a water sport and become a committed participant. Likewise, if you live in a high mountainous area that has lots of snow each winter, then there is more chance of you participating in a sport such as skiing than if you live in an area like Northern Ireland.

Experiences

There are 12 years of compulsory education for all children and young people. What they experience of physical activities and sport in those 12 years can influence them for life. If they experience quality physical education and sport during that time and they enjoy participating, then there is a good chance that they will become involved in physical activity and sport inside and outside of school, and that they will continue as committed participants in clubs when they leave school. If their experiences are bad or limited and they do not enjoy participating in school or being coached at a club, then there is less chance of them continuing their participation.

Affluence

Affluence is when there is an abundant supply of money available to spend once all essential outgoings have been paid for. Someone who is affluent is considered rich or wealthy. With more money comes more opportunities to participate in expensive physical activities or sports. For example, you could buy your own yacht for sailing; have your own horse for equestrian events; or have your own car or bike for motor-sport racing.

If you have very little money to spare after paying for all essential outgoings, then you will be limited in what physical activities or sports you will be able to do. For example, you could be limited to walking or running from your home; or swimming or attending the gym at your local leisure centre.

Being affluent or wealthy does mean that you can sample a wider range of activities compared to someone who isn't, but it does not necessarily mean that you will become more of a committed participant in those activities.

Work-leisure balance

Leisure time is free time. It is the time available for you to choose what you want to do, and excludes time at work or school; the time needed for other chores or commitments; and the time needed for essential maintenance like sleeping, washing and eating.

If you work from nine to five and are off at the weekends, then, generally speaking, you would be available for team training and for matches. However, not everyone works these hours. For example, some doctors and nurses work longer hours and weekends, as do some businesspeople. Some people work erratic shifts: for example, they may work from 7 a.m. to 3 p.m. one week; then 3 p.m. to 11 p.m. another week; then 11 p.m. to 7 a.m. the next. People who have long hours or who work shifts can find it difficult to make a commitment to competitive team sports as they are often not available for training or for matches at the weekends.

If you have a lot of leisure time, then you have the freedom to be involved in whatever activities you wish. However, if you don't have much time, or if your leisure time is at unusual times because of shift work, you may be limited in your choice of activity or sport.

Cultural heritage

Cultural heritage is the passing on and reinforcing of shared traditions from one generation to the next. These traditions can be national, local or family-based.

The process can be similar in the local community or at national level. For example, some schools have developed a tradition of playing rugby, others a tradition of playing football, and others a tradition of playing Gaelic games. If you go to a school that has a particular tradition, then there is a good chance that you will become part of that tradition.

Local communities can set up clubs that become successful, and this success attracts young members. If this continues, then the next generation will also be attracted and it soon becomes a community that has a tradition in that particular sport. If lots of local communities have clubs that develop similar traditions in a sport, then the sport can become a *national* tradition.

It is possible for countries to have more than one national sport. For example, rugby and cricket are traditional national sports in Australia; ice hockey and skiing are national sports in Austria; and basketball and baseball are traditional national sports in the USA.

Alternative passive leisure activities

Passive leisure activities are activities where the person participating is totally inactive or where minimal physical activity is involved (for example, watching television; reading; listening to music or playing an instrument; gaming; browsing the Internet or social media). Eating out and going to the cinema are also examples of non-active leisure activities.

There is nothing wrong with participating in any of these passive leisure activities. The problems arise when you participate in them to the exclusion of exercise or physical activity. The more you sit, the more inefficient your body becomes and the more difficult it becomes to carry out physical tasks efficiently and effectively. For example, if you get out of breath easily and feel uncomfortable doing aerobic tasks, you tend to avoid doing these tasks and therefore you become even less fit. Having muscles that are not being used means that you become less strong, less flexible, and you find you can do less and less. There are consequences for leading a sedentary lifestyle (see page 46).

The media (including social media)

The **media** refers to the main means of mass communication that reaches large numbers of people in a short time, such as the Internet, television, radio, newspapers and magazines. The media can influence participation because it decides what sports to cover and to what depth. The media are concerned about viewing figures and ratings, and the number of hits or copies sold, so they will cover what they think people will be most interested in.

Their coverage can reinforce cultural traditions, or alternatively can open up communities to new sports.

Some argue that the coverage of sport inspires people to participate; others argue that the coverage turns people into 'couch spectators' who are more interested in watching sport in the comfort of their homes than actually participating in it.

The media generally gives considerable coverage to sport, so top sportspeople become well known. They can inspire others to participate in their sports and many can be good role models for the young. On the other hand, some sportspeople can be poor role models and discourage people from participating.

Social media refers to technologies that facilitate the creation and sharing of information, ideas, career interests and other forms of expression via virtual communities and networks. It has a big influence. Anyone can post a message or a video using any number of social media platforms, communicating their news and views with their friends and with the world. You no longer need a reporter to write your story or a camera crew to film you.

Social media today is powerful and all-pervading. However, the platforms are just a tool and like any other tool, how you use it depends on you. For example, you could become addicted; end up leading a sedentary lifestyle; suffer from sleep deprivation; experience cyber-bullying; or develop depression. On the other hand, you could have limitless information at your fingertips and a wealth of applications to help you lead a balanced, healthy lifestyle. It is also very easy to keep in contact with your family and friends; to inform and encourage each other and to make arrangements to meet.

Age

All age groups list fun, enjoyment and socialisation as the main reasons for participating in physical activities and sports, but physical appearance also plays a significant role. Older people may find motivation in trying to delay the effects of aging, while many teenagers and young adults are concerned with body image.

However a person's age can also have a negative impact on their desire to participate, and the following reasons are frequently given by those who avoid taking part in physical activity and sport:

Teenagers

- Negative experiences in PE classes: e.g. the competitive nature of the classes, and/or the timetabling of only traditional sports.
- Unflattering PE kits can cause embarrassment and reluctance to participate.
- The dominance of others in PE classes: there is a perception that boys will dominate in coeducation schools, but it is also as likely that the more sporty boys or girls in single-sex schools may make other, less-confident students feel inadequate.
- Peer pressure from other students and from girlfriends/boyfriends who do not like physical activity or sports.
- Identity conflict: girls may be afraid that, becoming active and muscular will make them less conventionally feminine; boys may feel that taking part in certain sports or activities (e.g. dance) may make them less conventionally masculine; while academic students may not wish to be perceived as sporty.
- Teenagers and young adults feel they must aspire to have similar bodies to those portrayed in the media (slim, beautiful women and overly-muscular men). They fail to achieve this, become demoralised and give up on participating in any physical activity or sports.
- Perception that 'adults' do not participate in physical activity and sport.

Adults
- Negative experiences at school.
- Anxiety and lack of confidence about entering unfamiliar settings, such as gyms.
- Not knowing other people.
- Poor body image.
- Unflattering sportswear can cause embarrassment and reluctance to participate.
- Not fitting in with the 'gym' culture or the 'macho' culture in sport.
- High costs and poor access to facilities.
- Lack of free time or childcare, especially for men and women in their twenties and thirties.

Older adults
- Anxious about returning to physical activity or sports.
- Physical activities and sports are geared towards younger people.
- High costs.
- Not having time.

Females
- Traditionally, the masculine nature of the organised sport culture marginalised women. Male sport was predominant on television, and the majority of sports presenters and pundits were male, so females had fewer role models in this area. This has changed dramatically over the last few years, but there is still a lot of ingrained resistance to women's sport.
- There can be a 'macho' culture in school and extracurricular sport. Boys often dominate PE and sport in coeducational schools and, although girls have a willingness to be active, they sometimes report that what is offered in the school curriculum (or for extracurricular activities) does not meet their needs and desires.
- Body image can create a barrier: a conflict occurs with girls wanting to be physically active in order to have the 'perfect' body, yet some do not consider it 'feminine' for them to participate. In the same way, some sports/activities are labelled as 'traditionally male' (e.g. football or rugby) and some still consider it 'unfeminine' to participate in these.
- Unflattering PE kits or sportswear can cause embarrassment and reluctance to participate.
- There is a pressure to conform to social stereotypes due to cultural attitudes; families; or from female and/or male peers.

Gender

There are gender differences in participation and achievement in physical activities and sports, which emerge at a very young age and seem to be a consequence of perceived gender roles. Until recently, participation in sport was perceived as a male-only activity (at the ancient Olympics, women were not allowed to compete or watch) and, although perceived gender roles are changing, they are still rooted in culture and the past.

However, while women tend to encounter significant barriers with regard to participation in physical activities and sports, both sexes can experience issues:

Males

- Boys (and men) can also have body image issues. There are expectations that they should have the perfect 'masculine' muscular body and as they find this difficult or impossible to achieve, they become self-conscious about their body image.
- Some can feel embarrassed because they have no interest in participating in certain 'traditional male' sports (e.g. football or rugby); or that it is not deemed 'masculine' to participate in other activities (e.g. gymnastics or dance).
- Unflattering PE kits or sportswear can cause embarrassment and reluctance to participate.
- The pressure to conform to social stereotypes due to cultural attitudes; families; or from female and/or male peers.

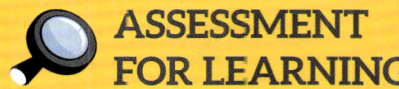

ASSESSMENT FOR LEARNING

1. Choose five factors that can affect participation in physical activities and sports. For each factor, explain how it affects participation.

2. For your chosen five factors, what steps do you believe could be taken to ensure there is equality of opportunity for all?

3. Share your answers for question 2 with your class and allow them to analyse and evaluate them. You should also be willing to analyse and evaluate their answers.

1.3 THE ACTIVE LEISURE INDUSTRY

Learning outcomes

In this section you will learn:

- the concept of leisure
- factors that have contributed to increased leisure time
- classifications within the leisure industry
- factors that determine the successful operation of active leisure facilities
- career opportunities in the active leisure industry
- the principles and actions to ensure an active leisure event is successfully organised
- the skills and qualities of a successful event manager
- how to plan successful tournaments – knockout, league and ladder competitions
- how to analyse, interpret and evaluate information and data related to the active leisure industry

The concept of leisure

Aspects of leisure

Leisure can be defined in terms of time, a state of mind or an activity.

Leisure defined in terms of time

Leisure is time that is free from obligations, work, domestic chores and/or education. It excludes time spent on necessary activities such as eating, sleeping or personal hygiene. It is free time when a person can choose what they want to do.

Leisure defined in terms of a state of mind

Leisure depends on the individual's perception of what they are doing. The person chooses what they want to do and participating in the experience results in personal feelings of satisfaction, enjoyment and gratification.

Leisure defined in terms of an activity

Leisure can be those activities that people participate in during their free time. The problem with this is that it is impossible to draw up a definitive list of leisure activities since participation in a specific activity may bring personal feelings of satisfaction, enjoyment and gratification for some, while participation in the same activity would be of no interest to, and sometimes hated by, others.

Leisure defined

These three definitions could be summed-up as:
Leisure is free time when a person chooses to participate in activities that result in personal feelings of satisfaction, enjoyment and gratification.

Active and passive leisure activities

There are active leisure activities that involve physical effort when you are participating: for example, walking, swimming, dancing and (most) sports. There are also passive leisure activities that involve little or no physical effort: for example, reading, watching television, listening to music or being a spectator at a sporting event.

The challenge for the active leisure industry is to provide opportunities and facilities that will get people to be physically active and thus gain the benefits from this type of lifestyle.

Factors that have contributed to increased leisure time

The concept of leisure originated in the UK in the late eighteenth century as an indirect result of the Industrial Revolution. The following factors help account for modern-day leisure time:

1.3 THE ACTIVE LEISURE INDUSTRY

Shorter working hours
Before the Industrial Revolution, people were expected to work from ten to sixteen hours per day. In 1810, mill-owner Robert Owen cut working hours at his mill to eight per day – his saying was "eight hours labour, eight hours recreation, eight hours rest" – however, it wasn't until Henry Ford adopted the five-day, forty-hour week in 1926, that it began to gain widespread acceptance.

Since the early 1900s, massive advances have been made in labour-saving technology and, at the same time, the labour pool is larger than it ever has been. Yet in the UK and Ireland, the five-day, forty-hour week (nine-to-five) is still the norm, productivity is not great, and unemployment is high.

Some companies in Sweden have been successfully trialling a six-hour working day. It is reported that the workforces are happier, and their productivity often improves.

Job share and part-time work
Many people choose to job share or work part-time hours – perhaps because of family commitments – while others have no choice other than to job share or work part-time if they are unable to get full-time employment.

Unemployment
Many have increased leisure time because they are unable to get employment.

Increased life expectancy
People are generally living longer and therefore have many more years of leisure time after retirement.

Early retirement
Many people choose to take early retirement – perhaps because of the stress of their jobs and/or health problems; or because they wish to do other things while they are still able. Some employers also offer incentives to encourage older employees to retire earlier.

Longer holidays
Many people now get more holidays at Christmas, Easter and during the summer, which means more leisure time.

Development of technology
Technological advances in all areas of life means many people have more leisure time. This ranges from the use of technology in the home (which can provide more leisure time) to the use of technology in the workplace (which can result in unemployment and enforced leisure time).

ASSESSMENT FOR LEARNING

1. Account for most people today having more leisure time than the people who lived at the time of the Industrial Revolution.

2. Leisure can be defined as time, a state of mind, or participation in an activity. For each of these three aspects, compare and contrast what could be considered as being leisure and what could be considered as not being leisure.

FURTHER THINKING

1. Explore the concept of leisure as defined online and in other sources. Compare and contrast your findings with leisure being defined as, "free time when a person chooses to participate in activities that result in personal feelings of satisfaction, enjoyment, and gratification."
2. Explore the pros and cons of a company in the UK or Ireland introducing a six-hour working day.

Classification within the leisure industry

With the Industrial Revolution and the growth of cities, parks were provided for people to use during their leisure time and a walk in the park became a popular leisure activity. As leisure time increased, entrepreneurs began to offer people facilities, opportunities, experiences and activities in which to participate. The range of experiences and activities is continually expanding and changing, but they can mostly be grouped into categories/areas.

'Sports and physical recreation' is only one of five categories, all of which are in competition with each other to attract people to use their leisure time in their category. Within each category are different businesses that are also in competition with each other. For any organisation or business to survive, it needs to attract sufficient people and finance.

The categories are as follows.

Arts and entertainment

This includes everything from a top show in the SSE Arena, to a play in the Lyric theatre, or a visit to Titanic Belfast or to the Ulster Museum. This category usually has purpose-built facilities such as a museum, art gallery, theatre, cinema, nightclub or concert venue.

The experience for the customer can range from being simple fun and enjoyment through to thought-provoking experiences, depending on what is on offer. For most venues, the programme of events will change over the year. Most of these facilities will also offer some form of catering, like a café or a bar.

Catering

This includes everything from mobile fast-food outlets to fine dining in Michelin star restaurants, where the experience for the customer is the enjoyment of eating food prepared by someone else. This experience can be enhanced by the surroundings: a special event may warrant fine food in luxury surroundings; at other times, a high street restaurant or café is just as enjoyable; sometimes a burger from a fast-food outlet is just right. Regardless of the type of venue, catering establishments are all inspected for hygiene control as a way to keep the customers safe and well.

Home-based leisure

This covers all leisure activities done at home and can include anything from reading a book, watching television, gaming, browsing the Internet, to playing board games, baking or exercising. No matter what leisure activity is done, it is done in the privacy of your home. Retail outlets exist to provide for home entertainment: for example, bookshops, electrical shops and online retail or rental outlets for films or games.

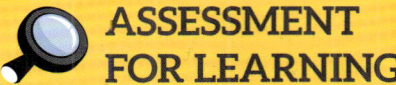

1.3 THE ACTIVE LEISURE INDUSTRY

Sports and physical recreation
This includes everything from walking, dancing and swimming, to playing organised sports such as Gaelic football, basketball or hockey. Some physical activities, like walking, can be done from home with very little gear needed. It is also possible to be equipped to go walking in the countryside, on the beach or in the Mourne mountains.

Physical activities and sports can use amenities such as the mountains, rivers and sea as well as facilities like leisure centres and sports clubs. The experience for the customer can range from walking alone in peace to the thrill and excitement of playing a competitive team sport.

Hospitality
This includes providing overnight accommodation in camp and caravan sites, hostels, bed and breakfast establishments or five-star hotels. The facilities can range from a field with toilet facilities to a luxury suite in a five-star hotel. For some, the customer experience can be the thrill and excitement of travel and staying in accommodation away from home. For others it can be comfort and functionality while on a business trip.

ASSESSMENT FOR LEARNING

1. Name the five different categories into which leisure time activities may be grouped. For each of the five categories, explain what the customers' experiences are likely to be.

2. Find examples of businesses or organisations operating in each of the five categories. Explain how you could incorporate physical activity (sports and physical recreation) into each of the other categories.

3. Analyse and assess the range and quality of opportunities and facilities provided for the community in your local area in each of the five categories (arts and entertainment; catering; home-based leisure; sports and physical recreation; hospitality).

4. Compare and contrast your findings for your local area with your findings for other areas studied, to find:
   - an area that has overall a wider range and quality of opportunities and facilities than your local area.
   - an area that has overall a narrower range and quality of opportunities and facilities than your local area.

Structure of the active leisure industry (in Northern Ireland)

With the growth of leisure time, the active leisure industry has expanded, offering many and varied experiences and activities that involve physical activity. Providers of the opportunities are normally from one of the following three sectors – public, private or voluntary – and the main differences between the three are included in the tables that follow.

Ownership and financial operation

Public sector	• **Owned, funded, controlled and operated by the government** – for example, the amenities and leisure centres operated by district and borough councils (such as Ards and North Down Borough Council) and city councils (such as Belfast City Council). • Set up by government bodies in response to the policies of the ruling government. • Not profit driven – most of the operating finance is funded by government. • Held to account by the media, the public and the government, as they were set up with public money.
Private sector	• **Owned, funded, controlled and operated by private citizens** – for example, DW Fitness First gyms; LA fitness gyms; the David Lloyd fitness and tennis centres; and health and well-being centres in hotels such as the Galgorm Resort and Spa or Culloden Estate and Spa. • Set up by owners, who may be a single person, a private partnership or a board of directors. • Profit driven – most of the operating finance comes from customers. • Held to account by the owners, shareholders or financiers of the organisation, as they were set up with their money.
Voluntary sector	• **Owned, funded, controlled and operated by trustees** – for example, football clubs (Gaelic and Association); hockey clubs; swimming clubs; and golf clubs. • Set up by groups to meet a desire in the community. Trustees on a voluntary basis operate and control the organisation, abiding by government regulations. • They usually focus on a particular activity. • Not profit driven – most of the operating finance comes from membership fees, fundraising and sponsorship. • If self-sufficient, they are held to account by members of the organisation.

Aims/goals

Public sector	• **To serve the public.** • They tend to have very general and vague aims and goals as set by the government: for example, "to improve the health of the nation." • They fulfil these aims and goals in an adequate manner. • They can be slow to react to changes in the marketplace because of the involvement and control of the government.
Private sector	• **To make large profits and outperform competitors in the same field.** • They have clear, well-understood aims and goals. • They are driven to fulfil their aims, goals and specific targets in order to increase both short-term and long-term profits. • They are market-driven and react quickly to changes in the marketplace, technological breakthroughs in the industry, the moves of competitors, and the overall economic climate in the country, as they have to make a profit to survive.
Voluntary sector	• **To promote and offer opportunities for the community to participate in, and be involved in, their particular activity.** • They aim to sustain and grow the organisation. • They aim for their members to achieve success in their particular activity. • They react to falling membership and seek to attract new members: for example, through liaising and working with schools.

1.3 THE ACTIVE LEISURE INDUSTRY

Facilities and provision of services

Public sector	• **Provide amenities and facilities for general public use.** • Amenities (such as parks, playing fields and play areas) and facilities (such as leisure centres) are usually multi-purpose and cover a range of sports and physical activities. The general public, from individuals to clubs, can hire the amenities and facilities. The facilities will be used to run coaching courses, public events and competitions. • The facilities will be well maintained, but unlikely to be changed or refurbished very often as this requires funding from the government (public money).
Private sector	• **Provide selected facilities for the use of their members.** • Facilities are usually specific, upmarket and with the latest technology. They are designed and operated to attract people to become members of the organisation. • They provide the latest equipment and offer the latest trends in the provision of services, which will be changed to match competitors, offer what is 'trending' in the marketplace and what is popular with customers. Personal trainers and coaches will be available for hire. • The facilities and equipment are refurbished on a scheduled timetable in order to maintain high standards and keep customers.
Voluntary sector	• **Provide facilities for members for their activity.** • Facilities will be specific for their activity. They may be hired from the public sector or provided by their organisation. • Facilities can be basic and minimal for some clubs; and for other thriving clubs, facilities can match or better any public sector facility. • Provision of services, such as coaching and competitions, are generally of a good standard. • Refurbishment only happens after massive fundraising or getting a grant from the government.

Management

Public sector	• **Managers work for the government and are paid a set salary.** • Managers often know what needs to be done and desire to do it, but are faced with restrictions, regulations and policies that prevent prompt action being taken. • Managers generally have greater levels of concern and willingness for helping others. • Managers are mainly motivated by serving and forwarding a public cause.
Private sector	• **Managers are employed by the organisation and may get bonus payments according to performance.** • Managers are generally result-orientated, more outgoing and optimistic. Financial rewards play a significant role in motivating. • Managers often focus on creating added value (i.e. a product or service that can be sold competitively to the public). This requires them to have the ability and skill to constantly change, evolve, adapt and improve.
Voluntary sector	• **Managers are often not employed, but work voluntarily for the organisation.** • Managers are nearly always volunteers who serve on committees and act in various roles, such as chairperson, secretary or treasurer. They do this work because of their love for the physical activity or sport.

ASSESSMENT FOR LEARNING

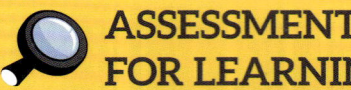

1. Outline the differences between public, private and voluntary sectors in terms of:
   - Ownership and financial operation
   - Aims/goals
   - Facilities and provision of services
   - Management

2. In a class discussion, compare and contrast the ratio of public sector, private sector and voluntary sector providers for your local area with:
   - an area that has overall a wider range and quality of opportunities and facilities than your local area.
   - an area that has overall a narrower range and quality of opportunities and facilities than your local area.

ANALYSIS, INTERPRETATION AND EVALUATION

ASSESSMENT FOR LEARNING

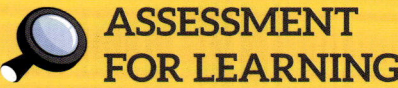

1. You, your classmates and your teacher should research information on organisations operating in the leisure industry. You could provide information on what they do, or how they operate in one or more of the following: ownership and financial operation; aims and goals; facilities and provision of services; or on the management of the organisation.

2. Study the information provided on the organisation. Assess, analyse, interpret and evaluate the information on each organisation and based on your knowledge and understanding, explain your reasons for classifying them by category and by sector. Back up your findings with references to what is factual, sound or recommended (the 'ideal').

   For guidance on how to do this, use Steps 1–3 on page 6.

The active leisure industry in the public sector

The Department of Culture, Arts and Leisure (DCAL) is the central government department in Northern Ireland with responsibility for setting policy for the active leisure industry in the public sector. Three important bodies within the public sector are **Sport NI**, the **NI Councils** and **Disability Sport NI**.

Sport NI

"Sport NI is the leading public body for the development of sport in Northern Ireland. Our **vision** is: *Northern Ireland: renowned as a place where people enjoy, engage and excel in sport*. Our **mission** is: *To lead sports development at all levels producing more participants and more winners*. Our **strategic objectives** are:

  "*Sporting Communities*: To increase and support the number of people adopting and sustaining a sporting lifestyle.

  Sporting Clubs: To enable more people to reach their sporting goals through a structured environment.

  Sporting Winners: To help more Northern Ireland athletes to win at the highest level …

"We have developed a values and principles framework that will guide how we work to achieve our corporate vision, mission and strategic objectives:

- **Leadership:** Being strategic and using our resources and expertise to achieve the maximum impact.
- **Creativity:** Pushing boundaries and being flexible and innovative in our approach.
- **Teamwork:** Ensuring genuine collaboration and partnerships and embracing the contribution of others.
- **Excellence:** Providing an outstanding service for all.
- **Integrity:** Being accountable, transparent, honest and fair."

[*information taken from* sportni.net/about-us/]

1.3 THE ACTIVE LEISURE INDUSTRY

City and borough councils

Northern Ireland councils are part of the public sector and have a responsibility for provision in the active leisure industry. One example of this is **Belfast City Council**, which in 2005, released its *Physical Activity and Sports Development Strategy*.

"The strategy has five key goals to improve sports development in the city:

- partnership – encouraging effective coordination and communication between the strategy's partners.
- capacity – developing community, volunteer and club involvement in sport.
- facilities – making sure Belfast has the 'right' facilities in the 'right' places.
- participation – boosting participation in sports.
- performance – looking at ways in which performance can be developed.

"It also identifies seven main ways to help it achieve these goals. These are:

- supporting schools and third-level institutions.
- building sustainable club and community development.
- raising the profile of sport and physical activity in Belfast.
- promoting health and physical activity.
- developing coaches and volunteers.
- supporting leisure centres to become development and community-focused.
- developing 'pathways to performance.'"

[*information taken from* belfastcity.gov.uk]

Disability Sport NI

Sport and physical recreation is for all and, in an effort to ensure that people with disabilities have full access to sport and active recreation, several organisations have been set up to facilitate this. One such organisation is Disability Sport NI.

"**Our Mission:** To ensure that people with disabilities have an equal opportunity to live a full, active and healthy lifestyle through sport and active recreation.

"**Our Vision:** An inclusive society where people with disabilities fully participate in all aspects of life, including sport and active recreation."

It has **five strategic priorities:**

1. Community sport – improving health and well-being

"To improve the health and well-being of people with disabilities and long-term health conditions through increased participation in community sport and active recreation opportunities."

2. Performance sport – developing sporting talent

"To lead the development of performance pathways, facilities and support programmes which enable people with disabilities to achieve higher levels of performance in their sport."

3. Training and sports facility access

"To develop and deliver training and access programmes which will contribute to a sports and active recreation sector in Northern Ireland which is more inclusive of people with disabilities."

4. Communications and engagement

"To inspire and encourage people with disabilities to become more active by providing information on the opportunities available, by highlighting positive role models and by challenging negative attitudes and misconceptions about people with disabilities."

5. Governance and income generation

"To manage an effective well governed organisation with the capacity to lead the development of disability sport in Northern Ireland."

[*information taken from* dsni.co.uk/about-us/ *and* dsni.co.uk/about-us/what-we-do]

FURTHER THINKING

Northern Ireland's councils have a responsibility for provision in the active leisure industry. Use the Internet to find their present goals, and their strategies for achieving those goals.

- note the similarities and differences between their goals.
- note the similarities and differences between the strategies to be used to achieve those goals.

ANALYSIS, INTERPRETATION AND EVALUATION

ASSESSMENT FOR LEARNING

1. You, your classmates and your teacher should provide information and/or data on Sport NI, local councils or Disability Sport NI. Some information should be accurate and some not so accurate.

2. Study the information provided. Assess, analyse, interpret and evaluate the information and based on your knowledge and understanding, explain your reasons for believing the information refers to Sport NI, local councils or Disability Sport NI. Back-up your findings with references to what is factual, sound or recommended (the 'ideal').

   For guidance on how to do this, use Steps 1–3 on page 6.

FURTHER THINKING

1. Based on the mission statements and strategies of Sport NI, Belfast City Council and Disability Sport NI, can you explain possible opportunities where you believe all three could work together? Carry out some research to see if you can find examples of cases where this actually happens.

Factors that determine the successful operation of active leisure facilities

When setting up a facility for the active leisure industry, whether in the public, private or voluntary sectors, the following factors – which are important on their own, but also interlink with each other – need to be successfully addressed for it to be viable and to thrive:

Accessibility

This factor considers how easy it is to get to the facility. This depends on the:

- location of the site.
- road infrastructure serving the site.
- road signage.
- public transport service (bus and train).
- parking at the site.

Ideally the facility would be in the middle of a large populated area that has a good road network and is easy to find. It would have lots of car parking spaces at the site and a reliable and frequent public transport system serving it.

Quality of facility

This factor considers the suitability of the facility for the intended purpose and its condition. This depends on the:

- original design.
- quality of the original build.
- efficiency of operating the facility.
- programme of maintenance.

Ideally the facility would be designed for the purpose intended, whether for one activity or for multi-purpose use. It should be constructed of quality materials and have systems that make it efficient and easy to operate. It should have a detailed programme for maintaining the facility and be refurbished frequently.

Cost to join or to participate

This factor considers how the membership fees can affect the success of a facility. This depends on:
- the costs to operate and maintain the facility.
- which sector controls and manages the facility.

Ideally the facility should make sufficient profit to be able to maintain and refurbish the facility often; to have it well managed and staffed; and for members or customers to feel that they are getting good value for money.

Opening hours

This factor considers the optimum times to have the facility open. This depends on:
- the costs to operate and maintain the facility.
- the demand for use at different times during weekdays.
- the demand for use at different times at weekends.
- the demand for use at different times during the year and at holiday times.
- which sector controls and manages the facility.

Ideally the facility should be open when customers want to use it. For instance, it should be open early in the mornings and in the evenings to cater for customers who work during the day. During daytime working hours, it can attract retired workers, older adults, parents and toddlers, school children, and those not working during the day. The facility also needs to be open at the weekends, but for less time (e.g. 8 a.m. to 6 p.m.).

Incentives, such as reduced entrance or membership fees, can be offered to attract customers at off-peak times.

Range of activities offered

This factor considers what activities should be offered at the facility. This depends on:
- the design of the facility.
- the demands of the customers.
- the cost of providing specific activities.
- which sector controls and manages the facility.

Ideally the facility should offer activities that the customers want: activities that are best performed in purpose-built facilities and that provide good value for money.

Timetable of activities

This factor considers when particular activities should be offered at the facility. This depends on:
- the demands of the customers.
- opening hours.
- which sector controls and manages the facility.

Ideally the facility should provide activities that customers want and at the times they want them.

Quality of coaching

This factor considers the suitability of the coaches for the customers. This depends on:
- the demands of the customers.
- the cost of providing the coaches.
- which sector controls and manages the facility.

Ideally the facility should be able to offer quality coaching appropriate for the age and performance level of the various customers. This can range from recreational level to elite performers. If customers find they are not improving, or are not satisfied with the quality of the coaching, they will leave.

Opportunities to improve and compete with other facilities

This relates to the management's desire to improve and compete in the active leisure industry. This depends on:
- the facility management reviewing their operation.
- the facility management listening to the customers' demands.

- the facility management drawing up and implementing an action plan to improve.
- which sector controls and manages the facility.

Ideally the management of the facility should be the best that it can be. A team should frequently review its customer wishes and needs, and its provision and operation then, based on the reviews, draw up and implement action plans for improvements.

Provision for disability and special needs

This considers the suitability of the facility and of the programmes offered. This depends on:
- implementing the law.
- listening to those with disabilities or special needs.
- the facility management providing opportunities and programmes for those with disabilities or special needs.

Ideally the facility should be designed to allow easy access at the entrance and to all areas of the facility for all those with disabilities or special needs. The facility and staff should be able to cater for their needs. The management should listen to the needs of these customers and offer a suitable programme of activities.

ASSESSMENT FOR LEARNING

1. Explain how each of the following factors can determine the success of an active leisure facility.
   - Accessibility
   - Quality of facility
   - Opening hours

2. How would you apply the following factors to create an ideal active leisure facility?
   - Costs for customers
   - Improvement of the facility and services
   - Provision for disability and special needs

ANALYSIS, INTERPRETATION AND EVALUATION

ASSESSMENT FOR LEARNING

1. You, your classmates and your teacher should provide information and/or data relating to the factors that determine the operation of active leisure facilities. Some information should be accurate and some not so accurate.

2. Study the information provided. Assess, analyse, interpret and evaluate the information and based on your knowledge and understanding:
   (a) identify and explain what information is inaccurate and what information is missing, if any, and how this would affect your analysis and evaluation.
   (b) identify and explain what information is positive and the benefits; what information is negative and the consequences. Back up your findings with references to what is factual, sound or recommended (the 'ideal').

For guidance on how to do this, use Steps 1–3 on page 6.

Career opportunities in the active leisure industry

There is a wide variety of employment and career opportunities in the leisure industry, including:

Leisure centre assistant
This job involves various maintenance and repair tasks, assisting and supervising centre users and administering first aid.

Leisure centre manager
This job involves planning the centre's programme, marketing it to potential users, recruiting and managing staff, dealing with customer feedback, managing the financial affairs of the centre and ensuring that it meets its legal obligations to health and safety.

1.3 THE ACTIVE LEISURE INDUSTRY

Poolside lifeguard
This job involves ensuring that swimmers behave in a safe fashion and obey poolside rules; removing distressed swimmers from the pool; administering first aid; and regulating the temperature and hygiene of the pool water.

Health and fitness instructor
This job involves helping users to set and achieve their fitness targets; supervising the use of equipment and running classes. Instructors should also stay ahead of developments in health and exercise practice and keep fit.

Professional sportsperson
This job involves training and taking part in matches, races or competitions; appearing in public and on the media; and networking with club and/or personal sponsors. A high standard of behaviour is expected in both professional and personal life.

Keith McClure

Sports coach
This job involves developing a programme of relevance to the individuals being coached and attending their competitive events. Coaches should also keep up to date on developments in sports science; understand the importance of diet; and the causes and implications of injuries.

Sport and exercise scientist
This job involves the application of science to sport and exercise; working with sport coaches, therapists, doctors and equipment designers to improve the performance of individuals and teams. These scientists must keep abreast of advancing knowledge and applications in physiology, and may take part in research.

Sport psychologist
This job involves helping athletes, sports teams and coaches mentally prepare for competitions, for example to overcome problems, improve focus and reduce anxiety. These psychologists also assist with conflict issues; motivating sportspeople; and helping coaches with team building.

Sport physiotherapist
This job involves diagnosing injuries, identifying their causes and planning treatment programmes. Physiotherapists also advise on how to avoid sports injuries and are required to keep up to date with new techniques and technologies available for treating patients.

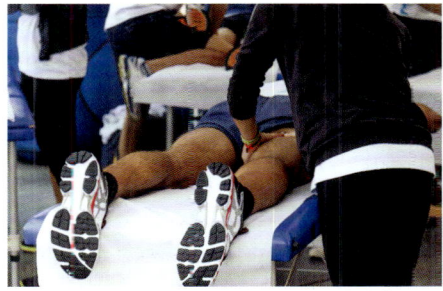

Activity leader
This job involves instructing people on a particular activity, for example hill-walking or mountain biking. Leaders design the programme and resources and deliver the training either outdoors or in a classroom. They are required to carry out risk assessments and comply with health and safety regulations.

Playworker
This job involves designing and supervising educational or developmental activities specifically for children. Playworkers are required to help children develop skills such as reading and the use of cutlery. They must be aware of all health and safety procedures and of child protection procedures, and be able to report a child's progress to parents.

Administration or management roles
This job involves the smooth and effective running of an office, which includes dealing with communication by post, email or phone; record-keeping; greeting visitors; and ensuring the office functions efficiently.

Sports development officer

This job involves raising public awareness of health and fitness issues, and promoting participation in sport, particularly amongst underrepresented groups. This often means proactively setting up new activities in targeted areas and recruiting staff. These officers need to work with stakeholders and national governing bodies (NGBs) to secure funding, support and strategic partnerships, and then work within the limits of these resources and relevant regulations. Some sports development officers may specialise in developing opportunities and activities for people with physical and mental disabilities.

ASSESSMENT FOR LEARNING

1. Choose any one of the possible careers in the active leisure industry that would interest you. Outline what this particular career involves.

2. Compare your career choice with the other careers to answer the following questions.
    - Which of the other careers would involve similar work to your career choice? Explain the similarities.
    - Which of the other careers would be most different from your career choice? Explain the differences.

FURTHER THINKING

Use the Internet to compare and contrast the career opportunities to discover:

1. Which career is most likely to have the highest salary, and which is most likely to have the lowest salary?
2. Which careers are most likely to involve working with elite sportspeople, and which careers are most likely to involve working with recreational sportspeople?
3. Which careers are most likely to require the highest educational training or qualifications to get started? Which careers are most likely to require minimal educational training or qualifications to get started?

Event management

If you are involved in the active leisure industry, it is not enough to build and maintain facilities. It is necessary to provide opportunities, experiences and events.

Ensuring an active leisure event is successfully organised

To organise and run a successful event, event managers need to do a lot of work, and the following principles and actions need to be applied:

The event

Event managers need to be clear on the objective and purpose of the event and what they are trying to achieve by holding the event.

Feasibility

This involves objectively and rationally researching and considering everything about the proposal in order to decide if it is worthwhile and viable to run the event. The feasibility study can range from a brainstorming session between event managers and organising committees, to commissioning a professionally written feasibility report. The brainstorming or feasibility study report should answer things like:

- is it a good idea?
- will it work?
- is there a market?
- is anyone else doing this or something like this?
- is there a suitable venue?
- is there the money to do it?
- will it make a profit?
- will we have the right staff to organise it?
- is there enough time to organise it?

If the event has been held before, the event manager should study the evaluation reports that were written. These can help to inform future events.

Cost

In order to determine whether an event is viable, event managers need to produce some basic financial information. A budget outline should be produced to include likely income (from, for example, ticket sales, catering or parking) and all possible expenditure (including, for example, hire of facilities, staff payments and advertising). It is best that the outline budget underestimates income and overestimates expenditure costs.

Event managers must have a means of covering the expenditure if the event is to be viable. A budget with likely income and expenditure should be agreed. All income and expenditure must be accounted for and a financial record kept for analysis and evaluation.

Timelines

In addition to the event being feasible and the costs being covered, there must be enough time to get everything agreed, planned, booked and organised. The timeline – setting out when everything should be done – should ensure that there will be enough time, thus preventing potential problems occurring later. This has to be managed and coordinated throughout.

The scheduling of matches for sports events has also to be planned. The type of competition (whether it will be knock-out, round robin, etc.), the number of entries and the playing areas available all dictate the scheduling and the overall time needed to run a tournament.

Facilities

Events can be held outdoors (e.g. a park), or indoors (e.g. a leisure centre), but in choosing the facilities, event managers need to assess the suitability of things like:
- the size of the facility.
- access to the facility.
- traffic control.
- parking at the facility.
- security at the facility.
- first aid at the facility.
- access for emergency vehicles.

Event managers also need to consider, for example:
- whether there are any potential hazards.
- any additional equipment that will be needed for the event – this will need to be set up, and then removed after the event.
- whether hospitality will be needed/provided.
- the effect the event will have on residents in the area.
- whether bad weather may affect the event.
- facilitating the media.
- whether any licences will be required: for example, to sell alcohol; play recorded music; or provide other forms of regulated entertainment.

Event managers need to visit and thoroughly assess the facility or amenity for their needs. If a facility is judged to be suitable for an event, then it has to be available to be booked on the chosen date(s). Event managers need to know and understand the conditions of use and be able to negotiate a price for its use.

Health and safety

This would require doing a risk assessment for organising the event at the facility and getting insurance cover. The risk assessment involves identifying hazards; evaluating the existing control measures; and, if they are considered inadequate, adding and implementing further control measures. Event managers also need to provide sufficient first aid cover; toilet facilities (if the facility is solely in an outdoor area); traffic management and an emergency plan in case of fire, accident, crowd disturbance, bomb scare, adverse weather, etc. The emergency plan should be discussed with the emergency services.

Staff

Event managers need to decide how many members of staff will be needed to run the event, and the responsibilities and duties of each. They will need to recruit the staff and train them for their roles. They will also need to consider: Will any staff be paid, or will the volunteers be given anything? Will the staff be insured? How will staff be identified at the event? Will they need to be fed?

Hospitality

In the case of an event, hospitality covers everything from welcoming those attending the event; organising guest speakers; meeting and greeting special guests (e.g. sponsors); providing transport and maybe accommodation; and providing appropriate catering for all those in attendance. Hospitality would also include having staffed information stands; good standard of toilets; facilities for people with a disability; and a good public announcement system. Everyone should leave the event feeling they were made welcome, the event was well organised and their needs were met.

Marketing

The scale of the event and the availability of funds for marketing will determine the range of promotions event managers can undertake.

When promoting an event, event managers need the public to know:
- what the event is.
- where the event is being held.
- when the event is being held.
- if the event is for a special occasion.
- who the event organisers are.
- how much tickets cost and how to get them.
- where they can get further details about the event.

Marketing can be done through local newspapers, community notice boards, banners, leaflets, local websites, local radio stations, local television, social media and so on. Newspapers, radio and television stations should be given the contact details of an organiser so that they can conduct interviews or obtain further information.

ASSESSMENT FOR LEARNING

1. What things do event managers have to consider in order to organise a successful event?

2. Within the school context, demonstrate that you can apply all of the necessary considerations in order to successfully organise a sporting event.

FURTHER THINKING

Select a number of well-known annual events. What evidence can you provide for each that would demonstrate that:
- the event had an objective or purpose?
- the event was feasible?
- the event was financially viable?
- the event was successfully organised on time?
- the facilities were suitable?
- health and safety issues were covered?
- the extent and quality of the marketing was good?
- there were sufficient staff, and they were effective and friendly in doing their jobs?
- hospitality was good?

Successful event management

It is the event manager who has overall responsibility for planning and implementing everything for an event, from beginning to end. If the event is small, the event manager may fulfil all of the roles and jobs. However, if the event is a massive undertaking, the event manager will have a team of managers who will have responsibility for organising particular parts. These managers will have teams of workers to do the jobs.

Skills needed

To be successful, event managers need to have, and be able to apply, the following skills:

Leadership skills

The success of events is the responsibility of the event managers. They are the leaders. To paraphrase American leadership guru, John C. Maxwell: an event manager would be the one who knows the way, goes the way, and shows the way.

1.3 THE ACTIVE LEISURE INDUSTRY

Examples of applying good leadership skills are:
- **Planning**, including researching, then drawing-up, a detailed plan with a budget. If the plan is agreed, the event manager is then responsible for leading the implementation of the plan and managing others to do the many tasks involved in making it a success.
- **Coordinating the work of many people**, knowing how to delegate tasks, and inspire and motivate other managers and their teams to do their jobs well and on time, so that the end goals and targets are met, and the event is a success. To do this successfully, event managers must have, for example, good communication, organisational and time management skills, as outlined in the points below.
- **Making decisions in the face of tough situations**. Also knowing that all managers and employees will respect and implement those decisions. Everyone should know that the event manager is in control, has a clear sense of direction, and empowers and inspires their teams to carry out given tasks to achieve the goals.
- **Staying calm when something goes wrong**. A good leader does not make rash decisions or crack under pressure. They resolve problems and issues quickly.
- **Maintaining the 'big picture'** at all times while still being mindful of all the details. A good leader is also a good multi-tasker.
- **Working with people**, including high-level executives, government officials, vendors, co-workers, sponsor representatives, customers, supervisors, suppliers, full-time staff, part-time staff, volunteers and more.

Communication skills

Communication is about clearly conveying information and ideas through a variety of media to individuals or groups in a manner that engages them and helps them understand and retain the message.

The ability to communicate is a key skill that underpins many of the other skills needed for successful event management. For example, good communication skills are important for customer service; interpersonal relationships; leadership; negotiation; conflict resolution; sales and marketing; and working as part of a team.

Examples of applying good communication skills are:
- **Picking the right medium**. A good leader should choose the most appropriate form of communication for the specific situation (e.g. face to face, phone, letter, email, text message). If they select the most appropriate medium, people will appreciate their thoughtful choice and will be more likely to respond positively to them. For example, serious conversations are almost always best done in person.
- **Conveying a message clearly** and in as few words as possible. A good leader should say what they want clearly and directly, whether they are speaking to someone in person, on the phone, using email or if they are undertaking a presentation. They should communicate on a level that is respectful to everyone and not talk down to anyone, regardless of their role.
- **Listening**. A good leader should pay close attention to what other people are saying; ask clarifying questions; and rephrase what the person says to ensure understanding ("So, what you're saying is …").
- **Understanding non-verbal communication**. A person's body language, eye contact, hand gestures, and tone all colour the message they

are trying to convey. A good leader should pay attention to other people's non-verbal signals.
- **Showing empathy, open-mindedness and respect**. A good leader should respect other people's points of view. They should be open, flexible, listen to, and empathise with, the other person's points of view, whether face to face, on the phone, or by email. They should be open to new ideas and accept criticism. It is team effort that leads to success.
- **Giving and accepting feedback**. This involves giving praise as well as correction. A good leader should be friendly and follow through on what they say they will do.
- **Using good IT skills**. This will ensure that a good leader can more easily communicate with others. They should have the ability to accept, learn and adapt to new technology as required by the job.
- **Using good coping skills**. A good leader should be able to handle a large volume of incoming communication: for example, a large number of emails, constant phone calls, and regular meetings.

- **Understanding and managing both their own emotions and the emotions of others** (emotional intelligence). Event managers must have the composure to stay calm under pressure.
- **Making decisions** or problem-solving in a positive, non-confrontational way when dealing with, individuals or teams.
- **Building and managing relationships**. Being tactful, assertive and, when necessary, reprimanding individuals or teams.
- **Working positively** as a member of a team.
- **Contacting and building relationships** either in person or through web-based tools, with sponsors; government agencies; and/or suppliers.
- **Reflecting and evaluating the work of individuals and teams**. Event managers must also be respected so their findings are accepted.
- **Effectively defusing, managing and resolving conflict situations**.

Interpersonal skills

Interpersonal skills are the skills that event managers use when they communicate and interact with other people, both individually and in groups/teams.

Examples of applying good interpersonal skills are:
- **Communicating appropriately and effectively with individuals and teams**. Without good communication skills, it is almost impossible for event managers to make themselves understood, to understand others, or to persuade and influence effectively.
- **Listening to, questioning, and empathising** with communications from individuals and teams.

Teamwork skills

Teamwork involves working collaboratively with others, to move the team toward the completion of goals. It is a shared responsibility. Individuals within a team often have specific tasks to complete. These tasks should be completed efficiently and effectively to meet deadlines. Event managers are in charge of all teams; they set the goals but must be able to work as a member of a team.

Examples of applying good teamwork skills are:
- **Inspiring** all individuals and teams to work together to achieve the goals within a tight schedule.
- **Applying** the interpersonal skills discussed.
- **Showing flexibility** to changing demands.

- **Working positively** as a member of a team. This could be leading one of the sub-teams for a time, or working as a team member to complete a task

Organisational skills

Organisation is the ability to be methodical and establish courses of action for yourself and others to ensure that work is completed efficiently and on time. Examples of applying good organisational skills are:
- **Planning** timelines and deadlines for all teams.
- **Coordinating** and managing many teams simultaneously.
- **Multitasking** effectively.
- **Seamlessly choreograph the planned course of action** so that each step of the event runs smoothly.
- **Using IT and management software** to help get things done faster. Event managers have access to a wide range of event management software (for instance, event ticketing software, venue management software and so on)
- **Keeping an eye on the detail**. Attention to detail allows event managers to ensure that everything is properly organised and in place for the event. A keen sense of detail will prevent small things from turning into big issues.
- **Effectively recording and evaluating** team performances.

Time management

Time management involves the ability to plan and prioritise workloads so that deadlines are met. Examples of applying good time-management skills are:
- **Setting realistic and achievable targets** with deadlines.
- **Prioritising**. This allows event managers to be more productive and achieve more within a limited time period.
- **Scheduling** one's own work and the work of all teams helping with the event. Everything must happen in the right order and at the right time.
- **Meeting deadlines** and also ensuring that all individuals and teams meet them too.
- **Developing strategies** and implementing them if deadlines are looming.
- **Coping with unexpected changes**. This can require replanning and rescheduling by event managers.

Financial skills

Involvement in event management means having a budget for each event. Event managers have financial responsibility for the overall budget and for the budget of each sub-team. Overall, total income should exceed total expenditure.

Examples of applying good financial skills are:
- **Understanding and following the principles of budgeting** when compiling and managing event budgets.
- **Understanding the difference between**: *income* and *cash flow*; *income* vs. *expenditure*; *gross* vs. *net* income; *estimated* vs. *actual* income/expenditure.
- **Understanding the necessity of contingency planning** where, for example, at least 20% of revenue is set aside to cover any unexpected costs.
- **Using a good accounting system**. Generating precise, accurate, reliable and prompt information.
- **Analysing budgets and making adjustments** when circumstances change.

Sales and marketing skills

Marketing involves doing everything that can be done to get people to participate in or attend an event, or to purchase services or merchandise. Sales of this merchandise, or of the tickets to the event, can be a source of income.

Applying good sales and marketing skills involves getting the '**4 P**'s right – product, price, promotion and place. Event managers must decide:

Product
- What is the right type of event (10K; marathon; indoor athletics meeting)? The event has to attract people to participate and/or attend.
- What services should be offered (catering; live music; master of ceremonies/announcer)? Attendees have to feel that it was a great event.
- What merchandise should be on sale (T-shirts; programmes)? What are attendees likely to buy?

Price
- What would people pay to participate or attend?
- What prices should the merchandise be?
- The smallest loss of profit through improperly priced entry fees, ticket prices or merchandise can scale up to be a huge loss at a big event. Overpriced entry fees or ticket prices can mean people do not attend; merchandise does not sell; and event managers are left with unwanted stock.

Promotion
- What means of promotion will work best, be best value and be within budget?
- How and when to use local newspapers, local radio and local television.
- How to best use social media.

Place
- Where is the best place to hold the event? This decision will involve evaluating and deciding where is best for competitors; spectators; access; parking; health and safety; and the hire of facilities.

Negotiation skills
Having good negotiation skills means being able to bring about agreement between parties through discussion in order to achieve mutually beneficial results. Examples of applying good negotiation skills are:
- **Agreeing event budgets** with the team of managers.
- **Attaining grants**, when available, from government.
- **Attaining sponsorship** deals with sponsors.
- **Getting the best price for hire** of venue or facilities.
- **Getting the best price for services** with chosen contractors and suppliers.
- **Rescheduling** targets and deadlines with teams when things do not go to plan.

Problem solving
Problem solving is the ability to think laterally; to research, analyse and evaluate information and develop informed solutions. Examples of applying good problem-solving skills are:
- **Analysing** the problem and effectively evaluating the information and/or data from the analysis.
- **Researching** the options, weighing up the pros and cons, and reaching a logical conclusion.
- **Taking advice** from others.
- **Being creative** in approach.
- **'Thinking on your feet'** and being ready to face any situation.

Customer service skills
Customer service skills revolve around an honest desire to help people. Examples of applying good customer service skills are:
- **Knowing everything about the event**. This is the foundation that allows event managers to help customers.
- **Dealing with and being aware of, requests, problems and complaints** – whether these are made in person, by phone, email, letter or through social media – as well as everything else. Event managers are good at multitasking.
- **Knowing the policy and guidelines** for dealing with customer requests, problems and complaints.
- **Using good organisational and time management skills** so that there is no delay in dealing with customers.

- **Effective listening** and interpreting written communication, to understand the request or problem.
- **Empathising with the customer** when relevant.
- **Being attentive, polite, respectful, and tactful** with the customer.
- **Using problem-solving skills** to find a satisfactory solution.
- **Communicating** clearly and concisely using positive language.
- **Agreeing and confirming solutions**, then promptly delivering them.
- **Using IT skills** to log requests, problems and complaints, answering them and recording outcomes.
- **Handling difficult situations** by being professional, keeping a level head, diffusing tension, and by being calm and patient.
- **Showing willingness to learn** and improve.

ASSESSMENT FOR LEARNING

1. Give examples of what you would witness in observing an event manager who demonstrates great interpersonal skills at work.
2. Explain how an event manager would demonstrate excellent time-management skills at work.
3. Explain what is involved in having excellent leadership skills as an events manager. Give examples to show how communication skills, problem-solving skills and financial skills are important in this role.

Qualities needed

To be consistently successful, event managers need to have the following qualities:

Motivation

Motivation is a desire, drive, willingness or enthusiasm to do something.

Successful event managers must have the motivation to organise events as they are responsible for everything and are on call all the time. Without motivation, things would not get done.

Event managers are mostly self-driven and show a positive, can-do attitude. They are the driving force in the set-up and someone everyone can look up to. They want all events to be successful.

They motivate others. Event managers acknowledge and praise the work of their teams. Getting this recognition and appreciation from the event manager boosts the team's morale, and motivates them to do their best and complete all goals and targets within the time frame. Mutual respect is created, and everyone is motivated.

Initiative

Initiative involves taking the lead by taking action.

Event managers are leaders. They are resourceful; they can assess situations when things are not right and provide different solutions as to what could be done. They are prepared to put themselves forward and take the appropriate action.

If an individual or a team is having difficulty with a task, event managers do not abandon them. They get involved and help.

When an event manager shows initiative (for instance, when changes have to be made), this in turn encourages individuals and teams to take the initiative themselves and suggest solutions.

Creativity

Creativity involves thinking outside the box and coming up with new ideas or new solutions.

Not all event managers are creative, but the great ones are. They can identify new opportunities and, creatively and enterprisingly, make them a success.

Successful event managers can put new ideas to, and seek new ideas from, their teams. This makes all individuals and teams feel respected and wanted, and this can help identify future event managers.

In today's ever-changing, fast paced world, nothing stands still. To stand out from the crowd, event managers must be creative and innovative at the same time, for them and their teams to succeed.

Problems and challenges are not an issue for good event managers, as they have an innate ability to resolve them creatively.

Inspiration

Inspiration involves being mentally stimulated to do or feel something.

Good event managers are creative, highly motivated and take the initiative. They think positively and this positive approach should be evident in their actions.

By leading by example they also inspire others. When the workload is massive, deadlines are looming and morale is low, event managers find ways to inspire and motivate their teams. They encourage others and let them know that their hard work is appreciated.

Enthusiasm

Enthusiasm involves having an intense interest in something and an eagerness to be involved in it. Enthusiasm and passion generate excitement and bring about creativity and a productive workforce. When individuals and teams encounter the enthusiasm and passion of event managers, it inspires them, in turn, to do their best. If teams feel that their event managers are not enthusiastic they too are less likely to be motivated.

Positive attitude

Event managers are purposeful and goal-directed. They maintain a positive attitude and are long-term thinkers. They see opportunities and possibilities in everything that happens, positive or negative – viewing 'failures' as 'learning experiences'. They are optimistic and inspire others with their positive attitude.

ASSESSMENT FOR LEARNING

1. Describe a work situation that would demonstrate an event manager showing great motivation.

2. Describe a work situation that would demonstrate an event manager showing exceptional creativity.

3. Describe a work situation that would demonstrate an event manager showing an outstanding positive attitude.

Knockout, league and ladder competitions

Planning successful tournaments

Event managers have overall responsibility for planning successful tournaments, and one aspect of this is in deciding which type of tournament format to use – knockout, league or ladder. The decision is based on factors such as the likely number of entries; the time available for the tournament; how many matches/games would be needed to complete the tournament; the importance of continued participation in the tournament; and the number of playing areas available.

Knockout tournaments

Single elimination tournaments

You will be expected to deal with between 4–32 entries. In single elimination tournaments, winners advance to the next round and losers are eliminated. This continues until there is only one competitor or team left. They are the tournament champions.

Advantages
- Simple – easy to understand.
- Can deal with large numbers of entries.
- Less time is needed compared to other tournaments – fewer matches involved.
- Good when there are few playing areas.
- Good for playoffs.

Disadvantages
- Half of the competitors are eliminated after one game. Only a quarter remain after the second game.
- If participation is important, this is not the best tournament.
- Accurate seeding is important (see overleaf).
- Does not make the best use of multiple playing areas.

Number of matches/entries

For single elimination tournaments the total number of **matches** for the tournament is always the number of entries minus one, so if there are 19 entries there will be 18 matches needed to decide the overall winner.

In this type of tournament, the number of **entries** will ideally be 128, 64, 32, 16, 8 or 4 to allow for a 50% reduction in numbers at each stage. So, if you have 17–31 entries, the first round of the tournament will reduce the number of entries down to 16 (or if you have 9–15 entries, the first round will reduce the number of entries down to 8). This is achieved by the top seeds being given 'byes' in the first round of matches. The lower seeds play first round matches and the winners progress into the second round of matches. The number of 'byes' given for the first round of matches and the number of matches played in the first round depends on the number of entries. The first round is arranged so that after these matches are completed there will be, for example, 32, 16, 8 or 4 competitors left to compete in 16, 8, 4 or 2 matches in the second round. This process is discussed in more detail below.

Seeding

Seeding – the process of ranking all the entries from the strongest down to the weakest prior to the tournament – is very important in single elimination tournaments. If there is no seeding, the two best players/teams could be drawn against each other in the first round and one would be eliminated straight away.

Seeds are placed on a draw sheet in such a way as to ensure that all of the top 16 seeds will make it through to the next round; the top 8 seeds will make it through to the quarter-finals; seeds 1–4 will be in the semi-finals; and seeds 1 and 2 will play in the final, with seed 1 winning.

How to place the seeds in position on a draw sheet:
1. Work backwards. Work from the final (seeds 1 and 2 in the final) backwards towards the first round. Remember that, ideally, seeds 1, 2, 3 and 4 will be in the semi-final, and seeds 1–8 will be in the quarter-final.

2. In all the rounds (e.g. semi-final, quarter-final), seed 1 will normally play the bottom seed; seed 2 will play the next lowest seed; seed 3 the next lowest, and this continues until all seeds are placed in each round of matches.
3. If there are to be byes in the first round, then seed 1 is the first to be given a bye; seed 2 is the next; seed 3 the next, and this continues for as many byes are needed.

The following draw sheet (figure 1) shows how seeding and byes work with 20 entries in a single elimination tournament.

The purpose of following this process is to establish who will get a bye and who will play whom in the first round. Once this is established, the winner of any given match progresses to the next round and the loser is eliminated from the tournament.

The draw table also shows the number and order of the matches. It assumes the ranking of the seeds was perfect, as the higher seeds in each round progress to the next round. It can also be used for 17 entries and up to 32 entries. The number in brackets – e.g. seed 1 bye (32) – indicates who that seed would play if there were the 32 entries.

Scheduling matches for the number of playing areas

If there are no problems with venues or playing areas (e.g. clubs visiting other clubs to play matches) and no restraints on time (e.g. matches can be played over a number of weeks or months), then matches may be arranged so that all of the first round matches are played during a set week; the second round matches played over another set week and so on. Full matches can be played for whatever time is normal or needed.

If the tournament is to take place at one venue, over a day or a limited number of hours, and the venue has only one (or up to three) playing areas, then an event manager would need to workout how best to use the playing areas and produce a time schedule for all the matches in order to complete the tournament within the given time frame.

The following are examples of time schedules for a single venue event with either two or three playing areas. The schedule shows:

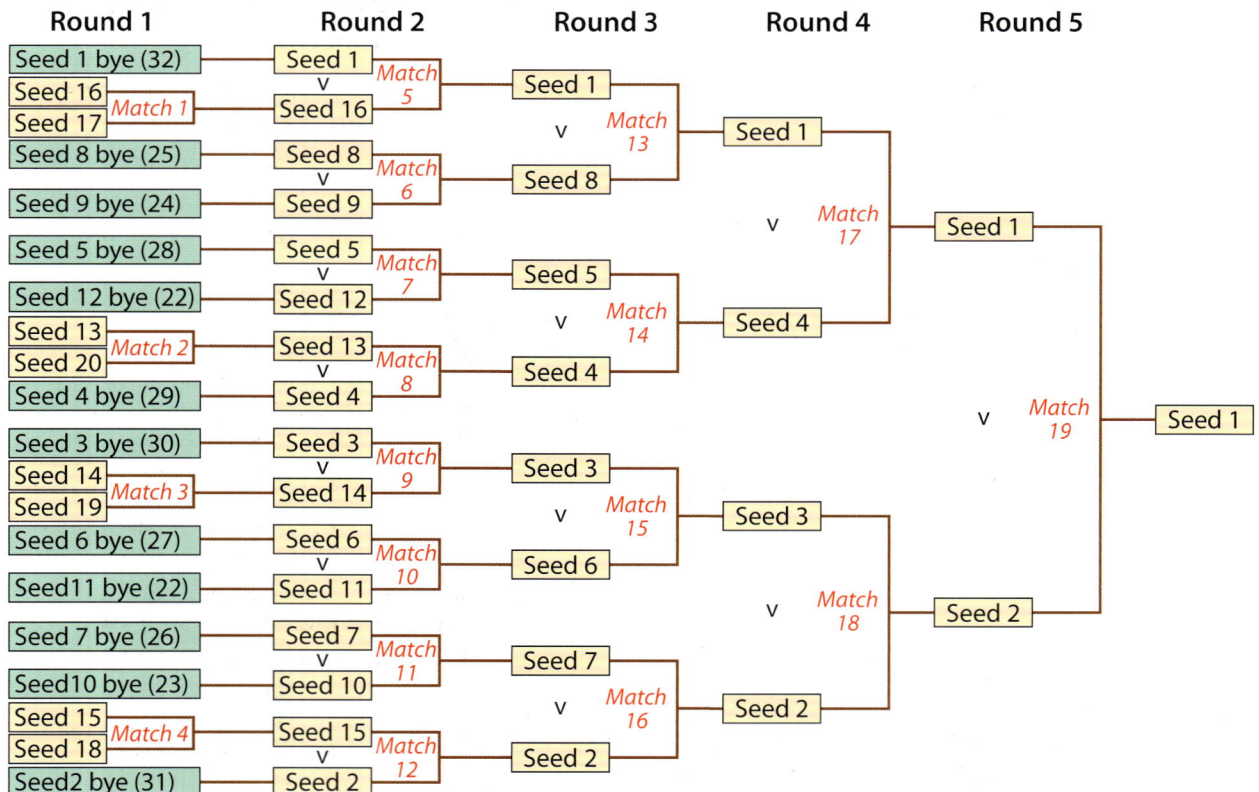

Figure 1: The draw sheet for 20 entries in a single elimination tournament

- the number of entries and the number of matches needed for the tournament.
- the allocation of the matches to the available number of playing areas.
- the duration and start times of the matches.
- the time allowed for changeovers between the sets of matches (in figures 2 and 3 below, up to 10 minutes has been allowed for changeovers).
- the number of sets of matches to complete the tournament for the number of entries and the number of playing areas.

		Play area 1	Play area 2
Order	Time	Match number	Match number
Set 1	10:00	1	2
Set 2	10:40	3	4
Set 3	11:20	5	6
Set 4	12:00	7	8
Set 5	12:40	9	10
Set 6	13:20	11	12
Set 7	14:00	13	14
Set 8	14:40	15	16
Set 9	15:20	17	18
Set 10	16:10	19	(20)

Figure 2: The time schedule for a draw sheet for a single elimination tournament with 20 entries (figure 1), two playing areas and matches that will last 30 minutes each.

		Play area 1	Play area 2	Play area 3
Order	Time	Match number	Match number	Match number
Set 1	10:00	1	2	3
Set 2	10:40	4	5	6
Set 3	11:20	7	8	9
Set 4	12:00	10	11	12
Set 5	12:40	13	14	
Set 6	13:20	15	16	
Set 7	14:00	17	18	
Set 8	14:40	19	(20)	

Figure 3: The time schedule for a draw sheet for a single elimination tournament with 20 entries (figure 1), three playing areas and matches that will last 30 minutes each.

So in figure 2 (in a venue with two playing areas), it will take 10 sets of matches to complete the tournament and under 7 hours to complete. In figure 3 (in a venue with three playing areas), it will take 8 sets of matches to complete the tournament, which can be completed in just over 5 hours.

If the overall tournament time is limited, the match and changeover times can be reduced (for example, from 30 to 15 minutes per match; and 10 minutes changeover reduced to 5). With these changes, in a venue with three playing areas, the tournament with 20 entries could be completed in 2 hours 35 minutes.

Whether there is one playing area or three, it is very important that everyone keeps to the schedule. Event managers draw up rules and conditions for the tournament to ensure that the schedule is followed. For example:

- all competitors and officials must be familiar with the order of play and the start times for all of the matches. The 5 minutes given between matches is to allow the next matches to start on time. Competitors must report to the officials in good time before their matches.
- if a match is a draw at the end of the 15 minutes, there will be a sudden death option to decide the winner.

It is normal to have a set amount of time for sports like football, rugby, netball and so on. It is not so for sports like badminton, table tennis or volleyball, but it is possible to successfully run tournaments for these sports using this format.

ASSESSMENT FOR LEARNING

1. Explain what method you would use to place the seeds in the first round of a single elimination knockout tournament.

2. Create a draw sheet for a single elimination knockout tournament for:
   (a) a group of 8 seeded players. Complete the sheet to show the sequence of matches for the number 1 seed to become the tournament winner.
   (b) a group of 11 seeded players. Complete the sheet to show who would progress in each of the rounds, if the seeding had been totally accurate.

Double elimination tournaments

You will be expected to deal with between 4–16 entries. The double elimination tournament allows a competitor to lose one match, but still to go on to win the tournament. Lose two matches and you are out.

Advantages
- Competitors play at least two matches. You can make it to the final if you lose only one match. It allows for one poor game.
- It allows for mistakes in seeding.
- It requires few playing areas.

Disadvantages
- Time needed to complete tournaments. Takes many sets to complete.
- Second and third seeds play many matches, others play few matches.
- Does not make good use of multiple playing areas.
- Takes many sets to complete.

Number of entries

Double elimination tournaments use the same principles to set up the first round of matches as would be used for a single elimination tournament. Again, seeding is very important.

The difference between the single and double elimination tournament happens when the first round has been completed. In a single elimination tournament, the losers of the first round can no longer take part. However, in a double elimination tournament, they have a further chance to continue in a separate (losers) single elimination tournament. The winner of this losers' tournament will play the winner of the first round winners' tournament and therefore could win the overall tournament.

The draw sheet shown in figure 5 (opposite) is for 16 entries in a double elimination tournament, and it shows:
- the principles applied for setting up the first round.
- the order of all the matches.
- how a player who loses one match continues in the tournament until they lose a second match.

Scheduling of matches for the number of playing areas

With two different, but interconnected, sections playing simultaneously (the winner and loser sections), an event manager will have to deal with an even more complex arrangement for matches. But with a bit of pre-planning and attention, a time schedule for all the matches can be produced in order to complete the tournament within the given time frame.

The example below (figure 4) is for the draw sheet of a double elimination tournament with 16 entries, three playing areas and matches that will last 30 minutes each (with an additional 10 minutes allowed for changeovers). It will take 12 (possibly 13) sets of matches to complete the tournament.

Order	Time	Play area 1 Match	Play area 2 Match	Play area 3 Match
Set 1	10:00	1	2	3
Set 2	10:40	4	5	6
Set 3	11:20	7	8	A
Set 4	12:00	B	C	D
Set 5	12:40	9	10	11
Set 6	13:20	12	E	F
Set 7	14:00	G	H	13
Set 8	14:40	I	J	14
Set 9	15:20	K	L	
Set 10	16:10	M		
Set 11	17:00	N	15	
Set 12	17:40	16		
Set 13	18:20	(17)		

Figure 4: The time schedule for a draw sheet for a double elimination tournament with 16 entries, three playing areas and matches that will last 30 minutes each.

1.3 THE ACTIVE LEISURE INDUSTRY

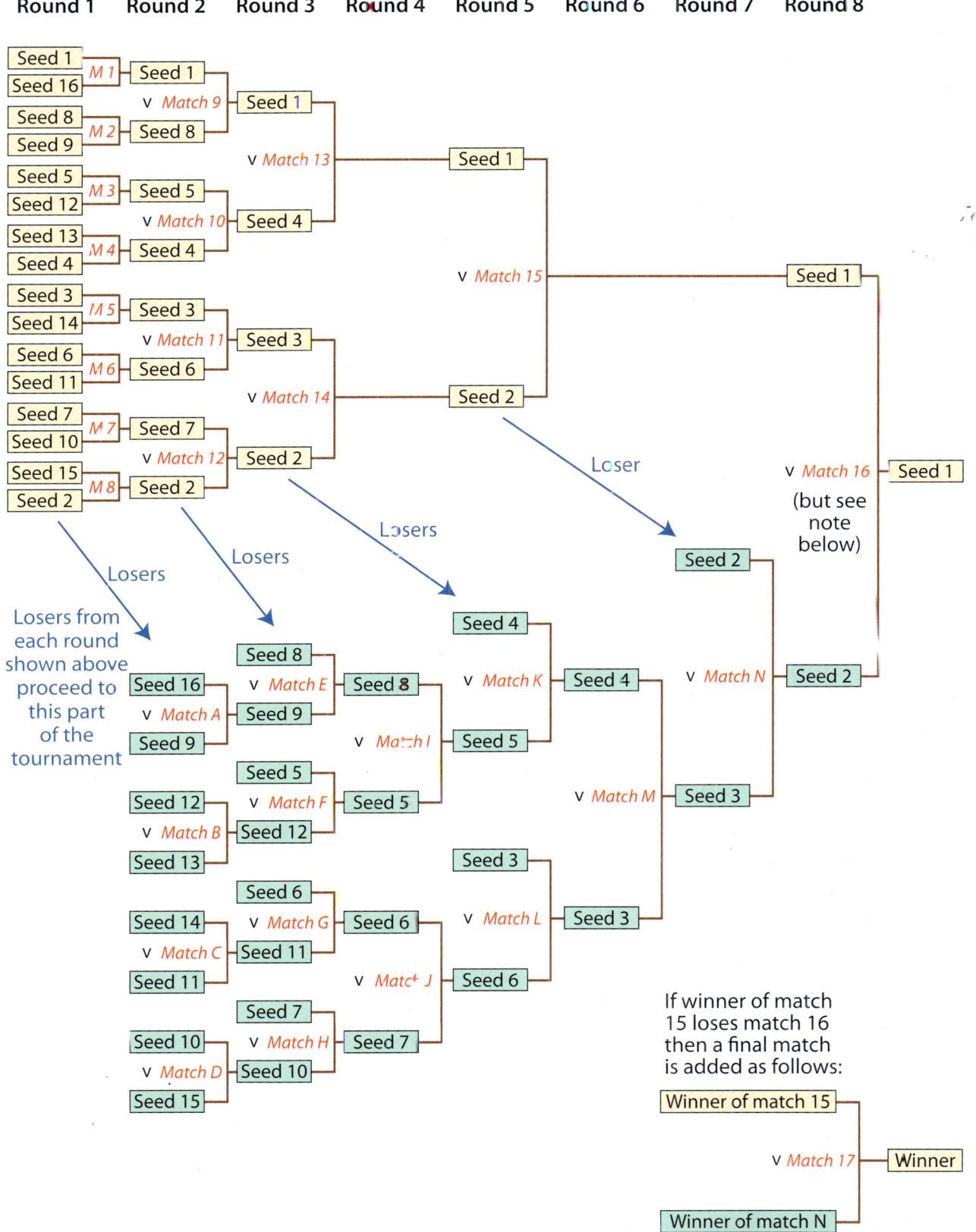

Figure 5: The draw sheet for 16 entries in a double elimination tournament

ASSESSMENT FOR LEARNING

1. What are the advantages and disadvantages of a double elimination tournament?

2. Below are four different schedules of matches for a double elimination tournament.

   (a) Which of the schedules, in theory, will work and which will not work? If you identify a schedule that is flawed, explain why it will not work and then explain how you would fix it for the tournament.

   (b) Identify and explain any observations that you feel could affect (positively or negatively) the effectiveness or success of the tournament.

Schedule 1		Play area 1	Play area 2	Play area 3
Order	Time	Match	Match	Match
Set 1	10:00	1	2	3
Set 2	10:40	4	5	6
Set 3	11:20	7	8	9
Set 4	12:00	10	11	12
Set 5	12:40	A	B	C
Set 6	13:20	D	E	F
Set 7	14:00	G	H	I
Set 8	14:40	J	13	14
Set 9	15:20	K	L	
Set 10	16:10	M		
Set 11	17:00	N	15	
Set 12	17:40	16		
Set 13	18:20	(17)		

Schedule 2		Play area 1	Play area 2	Play area 3
Order	Time	Match	Match	Match
Set 1	10:00	1	2	3
Set 2	10:40	4	5	6
Set 3	11:20	7	8	A
Set 4	12:00	B	C	D
Set 5	12:40	9	10	11
Set 6	13:20	12	E	F
Set 7	14:00	G	H	13
Set 8	14:40	I	J	14
Set 9	15:20	K	L	
Set 10	16:10	M		
Set 11	17:00	N	15	
Set 12	17:40	16		
Set 13	18:20	(17)		

Schedule 3		Play area 1	Play area 2	Play area 3
Order	Time	Match	Match	Match
Set 1	10:00	1	2	3
Set 2	10:40	4	5	6
Set 3	11:20	7	8	9
Set 4	12:00	10	11	12
Set 5	12:40	13	14	15
Set 6	13:20	A	B	C
Set 7	14:00	D	E	F
Set 8	14:40	G	H	I
Set 9	15:20	J	K	L
Set 10	16:10	M		
Set 11	17:00	N	16	
Set 12	17:40	(17)		

Schedule 4		Play area 1	Play area 2	Play area 3
Order	Time	Match	Match	Match
Set 1	10:00	1	2	3
Set 2	10:40	4	A	B
Set 3	11:20	5	6	7
Set 4	12:00	8	C	D
Set 5	12:40	9	10	11
Set 6	13:20	12	E	F
Set 7	14:00	G	H	I
Set 8	14:40	J	13	14
Set 9	15:20	K	L	
Set 10	16:10	M		
Set 11	17:00	N	15	
Set 12	17:40	16		
Set 13	18:20	(17)		

1.3 THE ACTIVE LEISURE INDUSTRY

Multilevel tournaments

You will be expected to deal with between 4–16 entries. In a multilevel tournament, the first round is the same as a single elimination tournament: if a competitor wins, and keeps on winning, it is possible for them to go on and win the whole tournament. The important difference is that, if a competitor loses (whether in the first or other rounds) they are not eliminated: they get another chance to play in a lower level. If they continue to win, they can become the champion of the lower level and get the chance to challenge the winning competitor in the top level.

Advantages
- Competitors are not eliminated after a loss. They continue to play in the consolation rounds. Good for recreational use when elimination is not desirable.
- All competitors play about the same number of matches. This is good if participation is a focus.
- Competitors end up playing others of similar standard.
- Can make good use of multiple playing areas. This saves time.
- Competitors have more games than in single or double elimination tournaments.

Disadvantages
- Accurate seeding is important.
- Not the best if final standings are important.

Number of entries

Multilevel tournaments use the same principles to set up the first round of matches as would be used for a single elimination tournament. Seeding is very important.

Once a round is completed, the losers in that round get another chance to compete against other losers.

The following draw sheet (figure 6) is for 16 entries in a multilevel tournament, and it shows:
- the principles applied for setting up the first round.
- the order of all the matches.
- how players continue to be involved in the tournament.

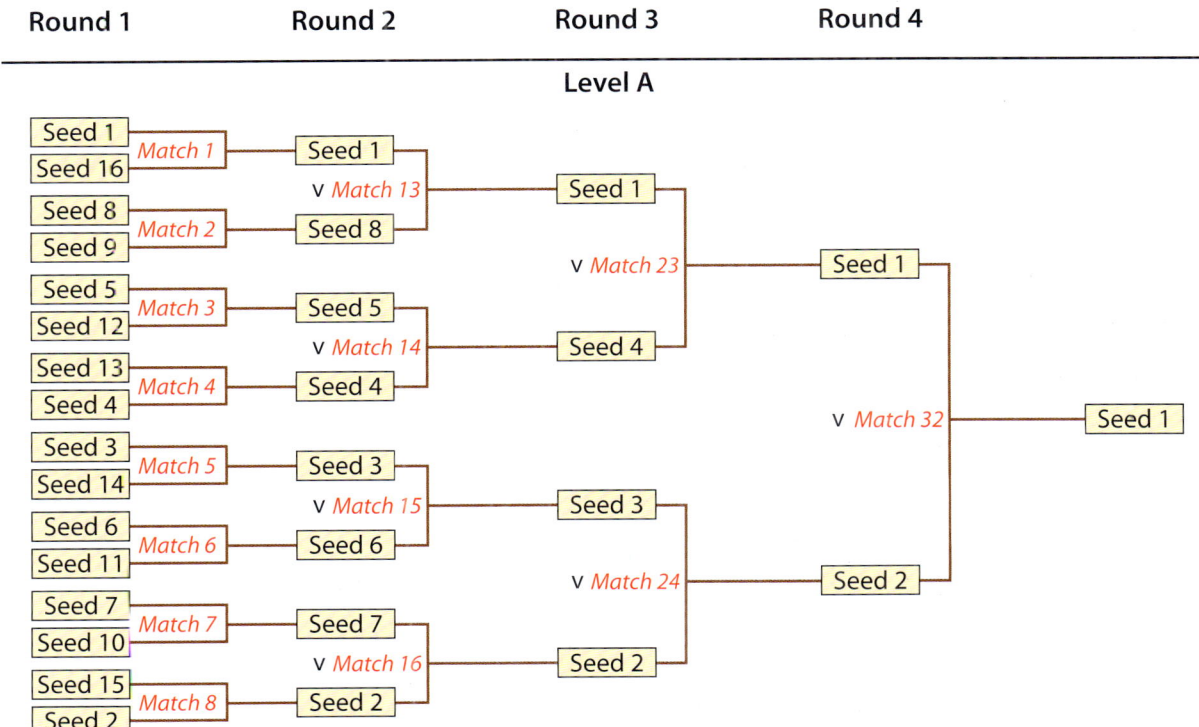

Losers from each round proceed down to lower levels of the tournament

Figure 6 (continued overleaf): The draw sheet for 16 entries in a multilevel tournament

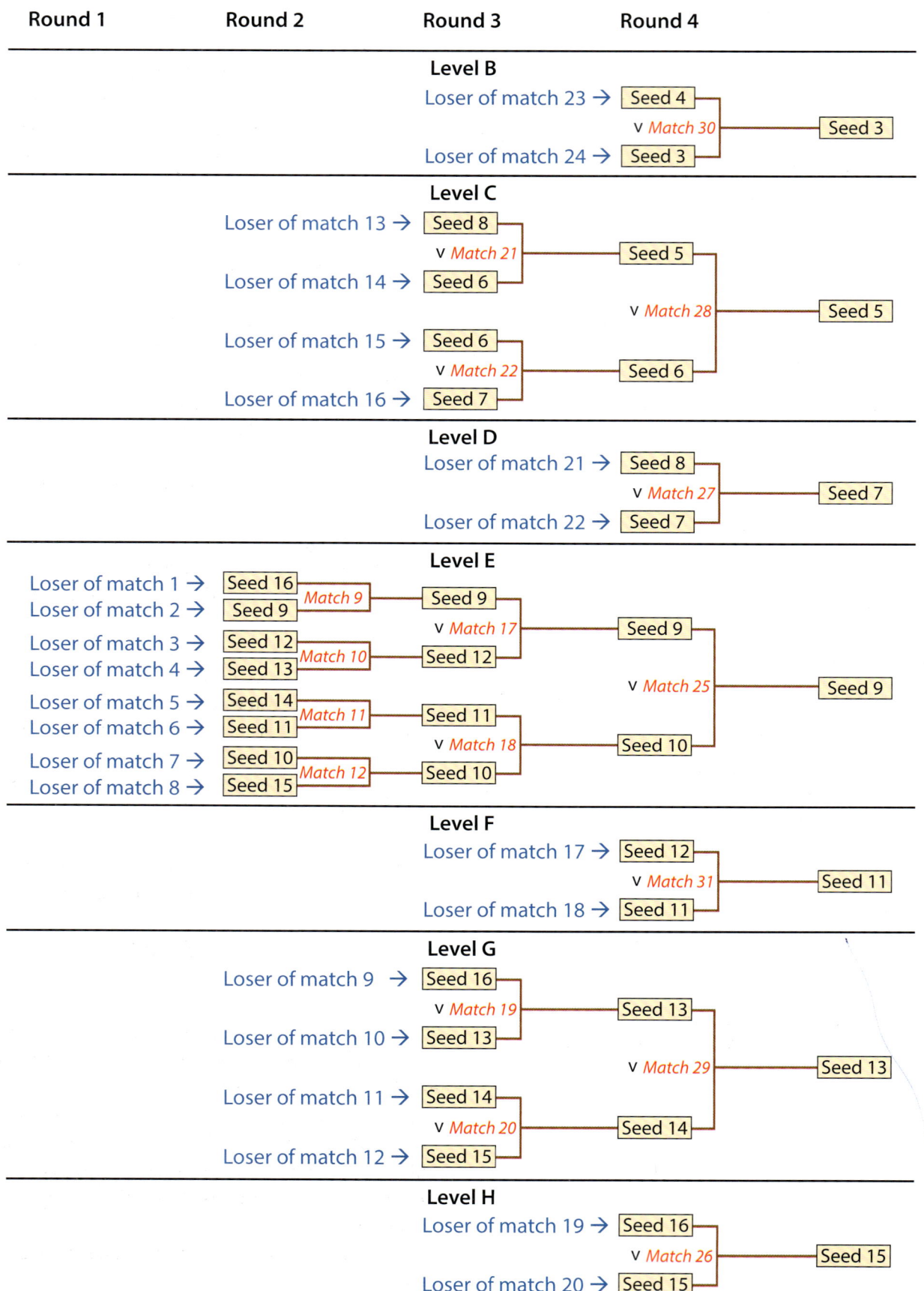

Figure 6 (continued): The draw sheet for 16 entries in a multilevel tournament

Scheduling of matches for the number of playing areas

The example below (figure 7) is for the draw sheet of a multilevel tournament with 16 entries, three playing areas and matches lasting 15 minutes each (with an additional 5 minutes allowed for changeovers). It will take 11 sets of matches to complete the tournament.

Order	Time	Play area 1 Match	Play area 2 Match	Play area 3 Match
Set 1	13:00	1	2	3
Set 2	13:20	4	5	6
Set 3	13:40	7	8	9
Set 4	14:00	10	11	12
Set 5	14:20	13	14	15
Set 6	14:40	16	17	18
Set 7	15:00	19	20	21
Set 8	15:20	22	23	24
Set 9	15:40	25	26	27
Set 10	16:00	28	29	30
Set 11	16:20	31	32	

Figure 7: The time schedule for a draw sheet for a multilevel elimination tournament with 16 entries, three playing areas and matches that will last 15 minutes each.

ASSESSMENT FOR LEARNING

1. What are the advantages of a multilevel tournament?
2. Create a draw sheet that will show how a multilevel tournament works for 8 entries.

League tournaments

League/round robin tournaments

A league tournament is often referred to as a 'round robin' tournament. In this type of tournament, all competitors/teams play each other an equal number of times.

Advantages
- Have fixed schedules if seasonal. Individuals or teams can prepare.
- Seeding is not important if it is a single league (though it is important if you have two or more groups/pools).
- Good when there are few entries.
- Good for a one-day tournament.
- Entries can be split into groups or pools. Winners of groups then compete in playoffs.

Disadvantages
- Not suitable for many entries as everyone has to play everyone else. This means many matches.

Number of matches/entries

You will be expected to deal with between 4–24 entries. The following formula calculates the number of matches needed for a specific number of entries:

$$\frac{[\text{entries} \times (\text{entries} - 1)]}{2} = \text{number of matches}$$

So, if there are 32 entries in a single group, it will require 496 matches to complete the tournament:

$$\frac{[32 \times (32 - 1)]}{2} = 496$$

A round robin tournament is ideal for a small number of entries because everyone plays everyone else. It is not, however, suitable for a large number of entries, especially if the tournament is to be completed within a day. In these cases, organisers will split the entries into separate groups/pools and the winners or qualifiers from the groups will compete in playoffs.

For example, by using the formula above you will see that:

- If there were 12 entries in one group, it would require 66 matches:

$$\frac{[12 \times (12 - 1)]}{2} = 66$$

- If you split the 12 entries into two groups (A and B), you would need 34 matches in total – both groups would have 15 matches and there would then be 4 playoff matches (the top two teams/people from group A and B go through to the playoff matches: Winner of group A will play second-place person/team from group B; winner of group B will play second-place person/team from group A. The winners or these two games will compete in the final; the losers will compete for 3rd and 4th place. That makes a total of four playoff matches.)
- If you split the 12 entries into three groups, you would need 21 matches in total – each of the three groups would have 6 matches and there would then be 3 playoff matches (it is likely that only one person/team from each group will go through to the playoffs and, as there are only three teams in the playoff matches, they would be able to play each other. That makes a total of three playoff matches.)
- If you split the 12 entries into 4 groups, you would need 16 matches in total – each of the 4 groups would have 3 matches and there would be 4 playoff matches (it is likely that only one person/team from each group will go through to the playoffs. As there are four players/teams in the playoff matches, there could be a draw to see who would play who in the first round of the playoff matches (so 2 matches) or it could have been stated in advance that Winner Group A plays Winner Group D, and so on. The winners would then play each other, and the losers would play each other (2 matches). These matches will decide 1st, 2nd, 3rd and 4th positions.)

The snake seeding system

If a round robin tournament has more than one group, seeding is even more important as it will prevent all the best competitors/teams from being drawn into the same group. The *snake seeding system* is usually used.

For example, if you had 12 seeded competitors/teams, divided across four groups, they would be placed as follows:

Group 1	Group 2	Group 3	Group 4
Seed 1	Seed 2	Seed 3	Seed 4
Seed 8	Seed 7	Seed 6	Seed 5
Seed 9	Seed 10	Seed 11	Seed 12

Working out the number of matches

In order to schedule the matches of a round robin tournament to the available playing areas, an event manager would need to work out the number of matches to be played. One method that can be used for this is as follows.

For an odd number of competitors/teams

Draw a shape that has the same number of vertices as there are teams (a vertex is a point where two lines meet; plural –vertices): so a triangle for 3 teams; pentagon for 5 teams; heptagon for 7 teams, and so on. Each vertex represents one team.

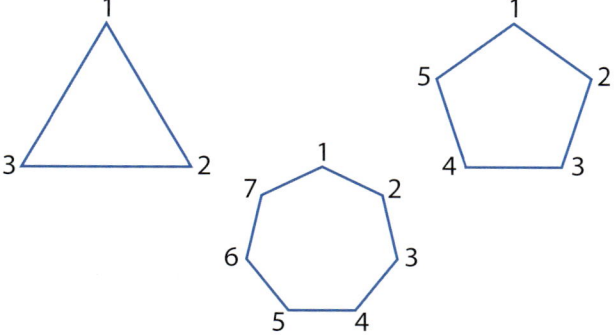

Matches in the first round will be between teams on the same (invisible) horizontal line. So with the group of 7 teams, for example, the first round of matches would be 5v4, 6v3 and 7v2, and team 1 would not play.

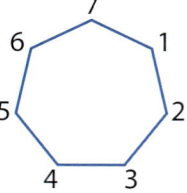

To work out the matches for the second round, the numbers rotate clockwise one position to the next vertex. Matches will once again be between teams on the same horizontal line: in this case, 4v3, 5v2 and 6v1, and team 7 would not play.

This rotation continues until team 1 would once again be at the top.

For an even number of competitors/teams

Draw a shape that has one vertex fewer than the number of teams ($n - 1$): so a triangle for 4 teams; pentagon for 6 teams; heptagon for 8 teams. Each vertex represents one team, except for the last, which is placed in the middle of the shape.

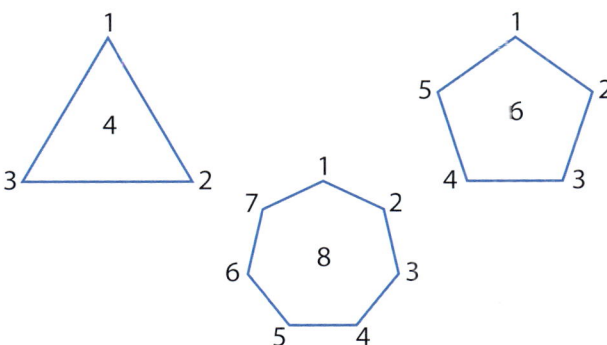

Matches in the first round will be between teams on the same (invisible) horizontal line, and between the two teams that remain (the one at the top of the shape and the one in the centre). So, with a group of 8 teams, for example, the first round of matches will be 5v4, 6v3, 7v2 and 1v8.

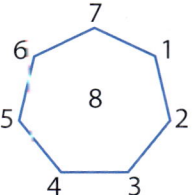

To work out the matches for the second round, the numbers rotate clockwise one position to the next vertex. Matches will again be between the teams on the same horizontal line, and the teams on top of and in the centre of the shape: in this case, 4v3, 5v2, 6v1 and 7v8.

This rotation continues until team 1 would once again be at the top.

Scheduling of matches for the number of playing areas

The examples below (figures 8, 9 and 10) outline instances where 12 entries have been split into multiple groups across either two or three playing areas. In each case, matches last 15 minutes each (with an additional 5 minutes allowed for changeovers).

			Play area 1 (G1)	Play area 2 (G2)
	Order	Time	Match	Match
Group Stage	Set 1	10:00	4v3	4v3
	Set 2	10:20	5v2	5v2
	Set 3	10:40	1v6	1v6
	Set 4	11:00	3v2	3v2
	Set 5	11:20	4v1	4v1
	Set 6	11:40	5v6	5v6
	Set 7	12:00	2v1	2v1
	Set 8	12:20	3v5	3v5
	Set 9	12:40	4v6	4v6
	Set 10	13:00	1v5	1v5
	Set 11	13:20	2v4	2v4
	Set 12	13:40	3v6	3v6
	Set 13	14:00	5v4	5v4
	Set 14	14:20	1v3	1v3
	Set 15	14:40	2v6	2v6
Playoffs	Semi-finals	15:00	WG1v2nd G2	WG2v2nd G1
	Final and 3rd/4th place	15:20	Winners of semi-finals	Losers of semi-finals

Figure 8: The time schedule for a draw sheet for a round robin tournament with 12 entries, two groups, two playing areas and matches that will last 15 minutes each. Group 1 will play its matches in area 1; group 2 in area 2 – this means that both playing areas should be of the same standard so that no one/team is disadvantaged.

	Order	Time	Group	Play area 1	Play area 2	Play area 3
				Match	Match	Match
Group stage	Set 1	10:00	G1	5v2	4v3	1v6
	Set 2	10:20	G2	5v2	4v3	1v6
	Set 3	10:40	G1	4v1	3v2	5v6
	Set 4	11:00	G2	4v1	3v2	5v6
	Set 5	11:20	G1	3v5	2v1	4v6
	Set 6	11:40	G2	3v5	2v1	4v6
	Set 7	12:00	G1	2v4	1v5	3v6
	Set 8	12:20	G2	2v4	1v5	3v6
	Set 9	12:40	G1	1v3	5v4	2v6
	Set 10	13:00	G2	1v3	5v4	2v6
Playoffs	Semi-finals	13:30		WG1v2nd G2	WG2v2nd G1	
	Final and 3rd/4th place	14:00		Winners of semi-finals	Losers of semi-finals	

Figure 9: The time schedule for a draw sheet for a round robin tournament with 12 entries, two groups, three playing areas and matches that will last 15 minutes each

	Order	Time	Group	Play area 1	Play area 2	Play area 3
				Match	Match	Match
Group Stage	Set 1	14:00	G1/2/3	3v2 G1	3v2 G2	3v2 G3
	Set 2	14:20	G4/1/2	3v2 G4	2v1 G1	2v1 G2
	Set 3	14:40	G3/4/1	2v1 G3	2v1 G4	1v3 G1
	Set 4	15:00	G2/3/4	1v3 G2	1v3 G3	1v3 G4
Plyoffs	Semi-finals	15:30		WG1vWG4	WG2vWG3	
	Final + 3rd/4th	16:00		Winners of semi-finals	Losers of semi-finals	

Figure 10: The time schedule for a draw sheet for a round robin tournament with 12 entries, four groups, three playing areas and matches that will last 15 minutes each

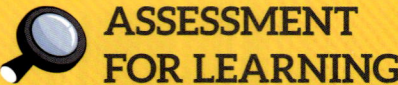

ASSESSMENT FOR LEARNING

1. In the time schedule in figure 9, team 6 play all their matches in play area 3. What are the potential issues with this?
2. Try to improve the time schedule in figure 9 so that all teams play the available areas in a more even and fair way.

Tables for recording results

For round robin tournaments the results are usually converted into points for a win, draw or loss. It can be as simple as 2 points for a win, 1 point for a draw and 0 points for a loss, or there may be opportunities for competitors/teams to earn bonus points. Event managers can decide this and, as long as all competitors know and understand the system before the tournament, it should be fair.

1.3 THE ACTIVE LEISURE INDUSTRY

Whatever system is used, points are usually entered on to a table that records the points awarded for all of the games/matches played by all of the teams in a group/pool (see figure 11). The table can be expanded to match whatever number of competitors/teams there are in the tournament or tournament group.

Name of tournament					
	A	B	C	D	Totals
A					
B					
C					
D					

Figure 11: A sample recording sheet for 4 competitors/teams

ASSESSMENT FOR LEARNING

1. Explain how you can use a pentagon to work out the matches to be played when you have 6 teams in a league competition.

2. Create a time schedule for a draw sheet for a round robin tournament with:
   (a) 12 entries, three groups, two playing areas and matches that will last 15 minutes each.
   (b) 12 entries, three groups, three playing areas and matches that will last 15 minutes each.
   (c) 12 entries, four groups, two playing areas and matches that will last 15 minutes each.

Ladder competitions/tournaments

In a ladder tournament, players are listed as if on the rungs of a ladder. The objective for a player is to reach the highest rung of the ladder.

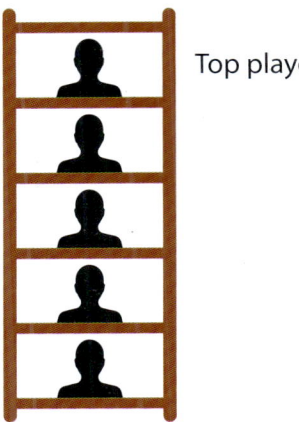
Top player

A pyramid tournament is similar to the ladder tournament in that the objective of a player is to get to the top. The difference in the pyramid tournament is that you can have a number of players on the same level.

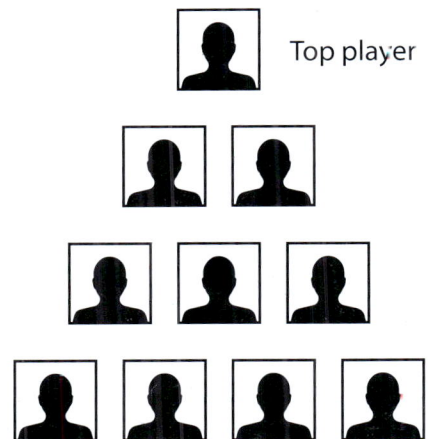
Top player

Advantages
- Easy to organise.
- Can be held over any length of time.
- No one is eliminated if they lose. Can play unlimited matches.
- Do not have to provide match schedules.
- Participants arrange matches.
- Limited supervision.
- Simple win/loss system.
- Good for ranking participants.

Disadvantages
- Participants have to arrange matches.
- Some participants are not challenged or do not challenge, so have few matches; others are continually challenged or are challenging.
- Not suitable for some sports (e.g. team sports, since it is more difficult to arrange a suitable

date and time when more people are involved).
- Interference with ladder, if it is in public place.
- Can be kept going for too long.

Number of entries

You will be expected to deal with between 4–21 entries. Theoretically, you could have any number of competitors in a ladder or pyramid tournament. However, for a single ladder or single pyramid tournament, it is best to have 21 or fewer competitors. If you do have more competitors than this, you can have ladders or pyramids at different levels, but linked. A competitor can move from one level to another, as shown in the diagram below. Challenges are vertical within a pyramid and horizontal between pyramids. To encourage participation and challenge from the beginning, the best players are often placed, by the event manager, at the bottom of the ladder.

Scheduling of matches

No matches are scheduled. Competitors arrange the matches between themselves, but there are some rules about challenging that usually apply. For example:
- You may only challenge someone who is one or two places above you on the ladder.
- Challenges must be accepted. Matches must be played within a set time limit.
- If the lower-placed player wins the match, then the two players swap places on the ladder.
- If the lower-placed player loses, then they may not challenge the same person again without challenging someone else first.

For ranking to be accurate at the end of the tournament, there must have been lots of appropriate challenges at all levels on the ladder.

ASSESSMENT FOR LEARNING

1. What are the advantages and disadvantages of extended tournaments like ladder or pyramid tournaments?
2. What ideas, conditions and rules would you have for a ladder competition to make it continually active and fair for the participants?

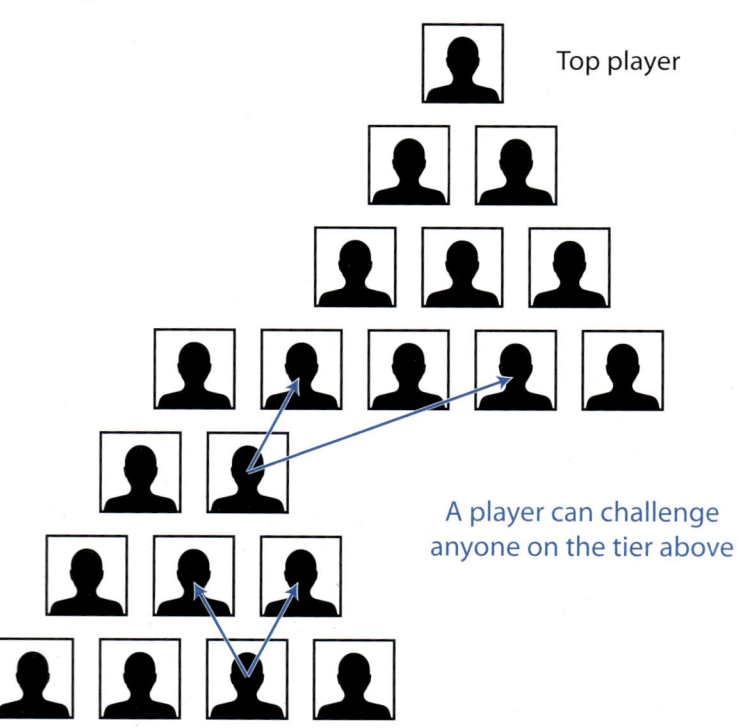

A player can challenge anyone on the tier above

Evaluating the success of active leisure events

Event managers have the skills and qualities needed to plan and run successful events. One skill that keeps them improving and being successful is the ability to analyse and evaluate everything that they, and their teams, do to plan and run the events.

This means analysing and evaluating the overall planning and staging of an event, and any of the following areas: **feasibility; costs and budget; timeline of work; facilities and resources; risk assessment for health and safety; hospitality; staffing; advertising and marketing** (see pages 114–116).

A good event manager will learn from the analysis and evaluations and make changes so that future events will be managed even better. They may use one or all of the following methods:
- SWOT analysis
- SMART principle
- Financial analysis
- Statistical analysis
- Questionnaires
- Verbal feedback

SWOT analysis, financial analysis, statistical analysis and the use of the SMART principle are usually internal evaluations carried out by the event managers and their teams. Questionnaires and verbal feedback are usually used with clients or people who experienced the event.

SWOT analysis

In using this method, there is an analysis and evaluation of:
- **S**trengths: Identifying strengths will be beneficial in helping to capitalise on opportunities to plan and stage future events. The more strengths a person/project/team has, the less threat there will be of being unsuccessful.
- **W**eaknesses: By identifying weaknesses, it becomes possible to devise a plan that will eliminate or minimise these and reduce the threat of failing or being unsuccessful.
- **O**pportunities: Did the team take advantage of all opportunities available – whether that meant opportunities for funding, publicity or in utilising available resources, or were some opportunities missed? An event manager should try, for example, to keep on top of interesting trends; changes in technology; local events, and so on. This helps keep the team in a good position to secure future contracts.
- **T**hreats: When in competition with others to plan and stage events, then those competitors are a threat when it comes to securing management of future events. This makes it even more important to build on strengths and eliminate or minimise weaknesses.

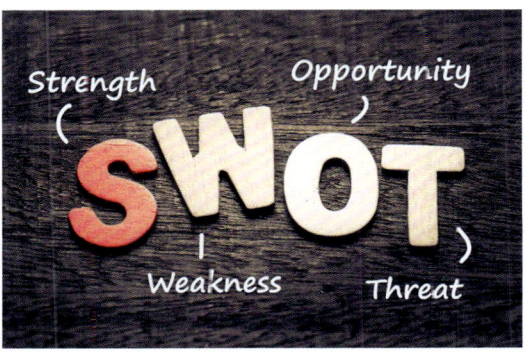

Strengths and weaknesses usually relate to internal issues (things you can control), while opportunities and threats usually relate to external issues (over which you may not have control).

Performing a SWOT analysis can help in developing a future strategic plan. However, it is important to remember that the analysis can be influenced (and often quite strongly) by those performing it. Not everyone may be open and honest.

SMART principle

In theory, the SMART principle should have been used from the start of the project to agree objectives and decide planning actions. It can also, however, be used after the event, allowing analysis and evaluation of the various points – an event manager can evaluate to what extent the SMART principles have been successfully applied, enabling them to discover weaknesses that may have lessened the event's success (see page 11 for further information on applying the SMART principle).

To what extent did the objectives and actions remain:

- **S**pecific – did you know exactly what had to be done with regard to the objectives and actions?
- **M**easurable – did you know when the objectives and actions were completed?
- **A**ttainable – did the objectives or actions become difficult or impossible to attain?
- **R**elevant – were the objectives or actions relevant/irrelevant?
- **T**ime-bound – to what extent were the objectives or actions completed (or not completed) on time?

Financial analysis

This method involves an analysis of the overall expenditure compared to the overall income. It includes an examination of all areas where income was generated – including a look for further opportunities to increase this income – and a look at all areas of expenditure to see if this could be reduced.

A financial analysis and evaluation would be carried out both before the event – in order to decide upon the budget that will estimate income and expenditure – and after. By evaluating finances after the event, an event manager can develop strategic plans to increase income and reduce expenditure for future events.

Statistical analysis

In this method, information and data is collected so that it can be analysed and evaluated. Based on the analysis and evaluation, lessons can be learnt and adjustments or improvements made.

A statistical analysis can be general (e.g. the number of people who attended) or very specific (e.g. how many bottles of water sold compared to bottles of a soft drink sold).

A statistical analysis can stand alone or be part of a SWOT analysis.

Questionnaire

When compiling and issuing questionnaires, organisers must be clear on what areas require feedback. This will depend on who is being asked. All questions must be worded carefully, so that those completing the questionnaire understand clearly what they are being asked. In answering the questions, are they required to: use written communication? tick a box? answer yes or no? give a rating from 1–10? or complete any combination of these? How long will it take to complete the questionnaire? How will the answers be collated, analysed and evaluated?

Verbal feedback

This involves listening to what people have to say about the event. Verbal feedback can be informal, or structured with an interview and formal questions. It can be with those who were involved in planning and staging the event; those who were staff; or those who experienced the event. More and more feedback from those who attend the event is now obtained through social media platforms.

1.3 THE ACTIVE LEISURE INDUSTRY

 **ASSESSMENT FOR LEARNING**

Take a look at:
- feasibility
- budget
- timeline of work
- facilities
- safety
- hospitality
- staffing and marketing

For each of these:

1. Give examples of what would be regarded as **strengths** in a SWOT analysis.
2. Give examples of what would be regarded as **weaknesses** in a SWOT analysis.
3. Provide a **SMART objective** for each of the areas.
4. Give examples to show how **income** could be maximised and **expenditure** minimised.
5. Give examples to show what **information/data** you would want from a statistical analysis.
6. In compiling a questionnaire to evaluate the degree of success of an event, what questions would you ask?

ANALYSIS, INTERPRETATION AND EVALUATION

 ASSESSMENT FOR LEARNING

1. You, your classmates and your teacher should provide information and/or data relating to the factors that can determine the degree of success of active leisure events. Some information should be accurate and some not so accurate.

2. Study the information provided. Assess, analyse, interpret and evaluate the information and based on your knowledge and understanding:
   (a) identify and explain what information is inaccurate and what information is, if any, missing so will not allow a comprehensive evaluation.
   (b) identify and explain what information is positive and the benefits, and what information is negative and the consequences. Back up your findings with references to what is factual, sound or recommended (the 'ideal').

For guidance on how to do this, use Steps 1–3 on page 6.

COMPONENT 2
Developing Performance

2.1 DEVELOPING PHYSICAL FITNESS FOR PERFORMANCE

Learning outcomes

In this section, you will learn:

- the concept of physical fitness
- the components of physical fitness
- the principles of training
- the methods of training
- assessment of physical fitness
- planning and evaluating training programmes
- planning and evaluating training sessions

Physical fitness

The concept of physical fitness

Physical fitness is the ability to perform physical tasks efficiently and effectively.

Therefore, whether you are physically fit or not depends on the physical task you are set. Physical fitness is a **relative concept**. You can be fit for one task yet not be fit for another. It will depend on the type and level of fitness required for the task. For example, a top athlete could be physically fit to win a gold medal at putting the shot in athletics because the task requires strength and power, but be unfit to run a 10,000 m track race because the task requires aerobic and muscular endurance. Someone could be fit to play a full game as a goalkeeper but unfit to play a full game as a midfield player.

The difference between physical fitness for health and physical fitness for performance

To maintain physical health, you need to do appropriate and sufficient exercise/activity to keep your body in reasonable working order. This would be your baseline or benchmark. If you do less exercise than this, it could lead to poor health.

To be physically fit for performance, you want to go above this baseline or benchmark. You want your body to be in better shape than normal, so you do more exercise/training. Ultimately you want to exercise/train so that your body is in the best shape possible to perform your physical task or challenge as efficiently and effectively as possible. This is **peak physical fitness**.

Keith McClure

In Section 1.2 on page 50, a continuum was used to illustrate the difference between physical fitness for health and physical fitness for performance. The following diagram illustrates the difference between the two with regard to the quantity and quality of training needed.

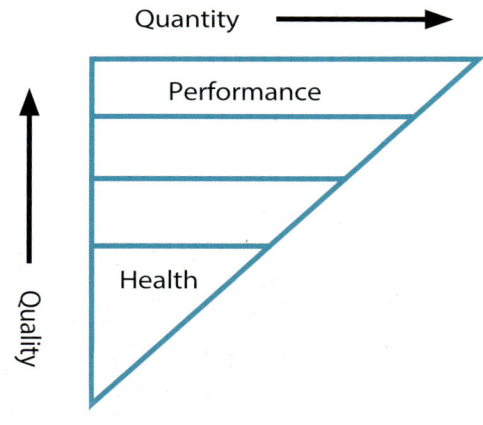

2.1 DEVELOPING PHYSICAL FITNESS FOR PERFORMANCE

> **ASSESSMENT FOR LEARNING**
>
> 1. What is the definition of physical fitness? Explain why physical fitness is a relative concept.
>
> 2. Using the diagram on the previous page, explain the differences between physical fitness for health and physical fitness for performance.

Components of physical fitness

There are seven components of physical fitness. You will need to know and understand them and what determines physical fitness in each. They are:

- aerobic energy production
- anaerobic energy production
- muscular strength
- muscular power
- muscular speed
- muscular endurance
- flexibility

To perform any physical task, you require energy. Energy can be produced **aerobically** or **anaerobically**.

Aerobic energy production

Aerobic energy is produced **with the use of oxygen.**

Aerobic energy production is determined by the ability of the respiratory and circulatory systems to deliver nutrients and oxygen to the working muscles and the ability of the working muscles to use the supply.

This can be developed by using exercises and training methods that work the major muscles of the body hard and for long periods of time, but the respiratory and circulatory systems can meet the energy demands of the exercise.

Anaerobic energy production

Anaerobic energy is produced **without oxygen.**

Anaerobic energy production is determined by the ability of the muscles and liver to store fuel and the ability of the muscles to utilise this fuel.

This can be developed by using exercises and training methods that work the major muscles of the body at very high intensities or maximum efforts, where the respiratory and circulatory systems cannot deliver sufficient nutrients and oxygen to the working muscles. The working muscles have to use the fuel stored in the muscles and liver.

The use or predominance of the aerobic or anaerobic energy systems depends on the intensity of the effort required and the length of time for which the person has to maintain that intensity/effort. Generally, the higher the intensity of the physical activity, the less time it can be maintained, and anaerobic energy production becomes more and more important. The lower the intensity of the physical activity, the longer it can be maintained and aerobic energy production becomes more and more important.

Muscular strength

Muscular strength is about a muscle or group of muscles being able to apply maximum or near maximum force to overcome a resistance.

Muscular strength is determined by the size of the muscle and the ratio between the different types of muscle fibres (see page 19)

Muscular strength can be developed by using exercises and training methods that require the muscles to produce maximum or near maximum force.

Muscular power

Muscular power is about a muscle or group of muscles being able to apply force in an explosive effort to overcome a resistance. It involves strength with speed and can involve lifting, pushing, pulling or moving 'heavy' things.

Muscular power is determined by the size of the muscle and the ratio of the different types of muscle fibres (see page 19).

Shot put and hammer throwing are activities that require muscular power. In these activities force is applied in an explosive effort. So, if you had two shot putters with equal strength, the one who can apply that strength with greater speed, or more explosively, will have the advantage. Similarly, with two boxers of equal strength, the one who can apply that strength with greater speed, or more explosively, will have the advantage.

Keith McClure

Muscular speed

Muscular speed is about a muscle, or group of muscles, being able to move a moderate-to-light resistance explosively with speed.

Muscular speed is determined by the ability of a muscle or group of muscles to contract and relax quickly. This is, in turn, determined by the ratio between the different types of muscle fibres (see page 19).

Playing shots in badminton, tennis or golf, involve muscular speed, as the shots involve applying a force explosively at high speed to overcome a moderate-to-light resistance.

This can be developed by exercises and training methods that improve strength and explosive movements.

Muscular endurance

Muscular endurance is about a muscle, or group of muscles, being able to hold or to keep repeating a movement that requires less than maximum effort for a long period of time. The length of time will depend on the amount of force that the muscle, or group of muscles, is required to produce.

Holding two light dumbbells for as long as possible with your arms straight and your hands at shoulder height involves muscular endurance. Continually playing shots in badminton or tennis requires muscular endurance in the arms, wrists and fingers, and continually repeating cycling or running movements requires muscular endurance in the leg muscles.

Muscular endurance is determined by the ratio of the different types of muscle fibres (see page 19). This can be developed by using exercises and training methods that work the major muscles of the body at moderate-to-high intensities for long periods of time

2.1 DEVELOPING PHYSICAL FITNESS FOR PERFORMANCE

or for many repetitions, depending on the resistance, and depending on the ability of the respiratory and circulatory systems to deliver sufficient nutrients and oxygen to the working muscles.

Flexibility

Flexibility is about being able to bend, stretch, twist and turn easily. It is determined by the ability of the muscles and ligaments surrounding joints to stretch to allow the full range of movement at the joints.

This can be developed by using exercises and training methods that stretch the muscles and ligaments surrounding joints: for example, dynamic and static flexibility exercises.

>
> ### ASSESSMENT FOR LEARNING
>
> 1. Explain the differences between aerobic energy production and anaerobic energy production.
> 2. Explain the differences between muscular strength and muscular endurance.
> 3. For each of the components of physical fitness, explain what determines a person's ability in that component.
> 4. For each of the components of physical fitness, name activities associated with developing fitness in that component.

The relative importance of the components of physical fitness for physical activities and sports

To decide the relevant importance of the components of physical fitness when planning a training programme for a physical activity, sport or position within a sport, you need to:

1. know and understand each of the components of physical fitness.
2. be able to analyse and evaluate the physical demands of a physical activity or sport on the cardio-respiratory systems in terms of the intensities required and the duration of these intensities. Based on your evaluation, you determine the relative importance of developing the aerobic and anaerobic energy systems in the training programme.
3. be able to analyse and evaluate the physical demands on the musculatory system in terms of strength, power, speed, endurance and flexibility. Based on your evaluation, you determine the relative importance of developing each of the components in the training programme.

Athletics events

This would normally cover the track and field events – for example, shot put, long jump, javelin, high jump – and the marathon, sprint, middle distance and long distance running events.

Example of application

A 200 m sprint demands that a person runs at maximum intensity, or flat out, for 20–25 seconds. At maximum intensity, the aerobic energy system is not able to deliver sufficient oxygen and nutrients to the muscles, so the energy will be produced by the anaerobic energy system.

This means, for the 200 m sprint, the development of the anaerobic energy system will be a very important aspect of the training programme, and the development of the aerobic energy system will be of little importance.

To perform at your best in a 200 m sprint, you also need strong muscles that can work at speed. This means the development of muscular strength and muscular power would be very important in the training programme. Flexibility is also important, to allow the full range of movements for sprinting.

> ### ASSESSMENT FOR LEARNING
>
> 1. Choose a few contrasting track events and field events. Evaluate and explain the different physical fitness demands for these events.
> 2. Then evaluate and explain the relative importance of developing the aerobic and anaerobic energy systems in the training programme.
> 3. Finally, based on the physical fitness demands of the events, evaluate and explain the relative importance of developing muscular strength, power, speed and flexibility in the training programme.

Individual sports

This concerns any physical sport that you do as an individual – for example, swimming, cycling, rowing, dancing, gymnastics, orienteering – or singles participation in sports like badminton, tennis or squash. There are many possibilities.

Example of application

A 2000 m indoor rowing race demands that the person maintains a high pace working close to their aerobic/anaerobic threshold for most of the race. The aerobic energy system will therefore produce most of the energy, but the anaerobic system will also be involved at the start and finish of the race. This would mean the development of the aerobic energy system would be a very important aspect of the training programme, and the development of the anaerobic energy system would also be important.

This race will require the muscles to work without tiring, so the development of muscular endurance in the training programme would be very important. The race also demands muscular power at the beginning and end of the race, therefore, it is important to also develop muscular strength and then power in the training programme.

For many team sports, both aerobic work and bursts of anaerobic work are needed. Playing also requires muscular strength, power, speed and flexibility.

Example of application

In basketball or netball, players need to perform for more than 30 minutes, so the development of the aerobic energy system in the training programme will be important. However, within that time, the players will be required to move at speed; to start and stop quickly; to jump in the air and land; and be able to turn or change direction quickly. This means the development of the anaerobic energy system is also important. These movements are repeated continuously, which means muscular endurance is important; and to perform them well requires muscular strength, power and flexibility, so work on all these components should be included in the training programme.

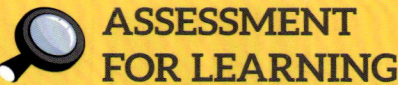

ASSESSMENT FOR LEARNING

1. Choose a few contrasting individual sports. Evaluate and explain the different physical fitness demands for these sports.
2. Then evaluate and explain the relative importance of developing the aerobic and anaerobic energy systems in the training programme.
3. Finally, based on the physical fitness demands of the sports, evaluate and explain the relative importance of developing muscular strength, power, speed and flexibility in the training programme.

Team sports

Team sports could range from playing doubles in badminton or tennis, to playing a team game like rugby. In doubles badminton, both players have similar physical fitness demands, however, in rugby the physical fitness demands can be different depending on the position being played.

ASSESSMENT FOR LEARNING

1. Choose a few contrasting team sports. Evaluate and explain the different physical fitness demands for these sports (or positions within these sports).
2. Then evaluate and explain the relative importance of developing the aerobic and anaerobic energy systems in the training programme.
3. Finally, based on the physical fitness demands of the sports, evaluate and explain the relative importance of developing muscular strength, power, speed and flexibility in the training programme.

2.1 DEVELOPING PHYSICAL FITNESS FOR PERFORMANCE

ANALYSIS, INTERPRETATION AND EVALUATION

ASSESSMENT FOR LEARNING

1. You, your classmates and your teacher should provide examples, with some accurate and some inaccurate information and sometimes missing information. The examples should cover the physical fitness demands for events and sports and the relative importance that is being given to the components of physical fitness in the training programme. Make sure to cover athletic events, individual sports and team sports.

2. Study the information provided in the examples. Assess, analyse, interpret and evaluate the information, and based on your knowledge and understanding:
   (a) identify and explain what information, if any, is missing and how this would affect your analysis and evaluation.
   (b) identify and explain what information is sound, positive and accurate; and what information is negative or inaccurate and needs to be changed. What changes would you recommend? Back up your findings with references to what is factual, sound or recommended (the 'ideal').

   For guidance on how to do this, use Steps 1–3 on page 6.

and these, along with **periodisation** and **peaking**, should be applied to plan effective training programmes for performance.

Specificity

Since the effects of training are very **specific**, the training and training methods must match, as much as possible, the physical fitness demands of the chosen event, sport or position within a sport. You need to be able to analyse the physical demands of an event, sport or position and, based on this, decide the relative importance of the components of physical fitness for inclusion in a performance-related training programme.

For example, in order to devise a training programme for running a marathon, you would need to look at the physical demands of the event. The marathon requires a person to run (aerobically) for hours and, during that time, the legs are continually working. This means the emphasis in the training programme would be on developing aerobic fitness and muscular endurance through running.

Keith McClure

If you had to devise a training programme to run 100 m you would once again have to look at the demands of the event. The 100 m requires maximum effort for anything from 10–15 seconds. It also requires strength and power in running. This means the emphasis in the training programme would be on developing strength, power and anaerobic fitness.

Imagine having to devise the training programme for a decathlete in track and field athletics. You would have to consider the physical fitness demands

Principles of training

SPORRT, FITT, periodisation and peaking

The basic principles of FITT – **F**requency, **I**ntensity, **T**ime and **T**ype – and SPORRT – **S**pecificity, **P**rogressive **O**verload, **R**est/Recovery, **R**eversibility (maintenance) and **T**edium (variety) – have already been covered in chapter 1.2 (see pages 56 and 57), for the following events and make sure the decathlete is prepared to perform well in all of them: 100 m, long jump, shot put, high jump, 400 m, 110 m hurdles, discus, pole vault, javelin and 1500 m.

Overload

If you want to develop your physical fitness in any of the components, then you must work the body systems harder than they are being worked at present. In other words, you must **overload**.

For example, if you were doing continuous steady-pace running for three nights per week at a rate of perceived exertion (RPE) of 5/10 and for 30 minutes each run, then you would have achieved a certain level of aerobic fitness. If you wanted to improve on this level of fitness, then you would have to apply the principle of overload. This can be done by using the **FITT principle**:

- **Frequency:** you could run one extra night per week.
- **Intensity:** you could run at RPE 7/10 instead of 5/10 on one or more of the runs.
- **Time:** you could run for 40 minutes instead of 30 minutes for one or more of the runs.
- **Type of exercise:** running.

If you did any one of these or any combination of these, you would have applied the principle of **overload**.

The overload puts added stress on the body, and the body gradually adapts to cope with it. This adaptation is due to the body systems changing and becoming more efficient. Because of this increased efficiency (improved physical fitness), what was originally a stress on the body becomes normal. The skill in applying the principle of overload is to add enough stress to make a difference and make the body adapt, but not to add so much stress that it leads to fatigue or injury.

Progressive overload

If any of the body's systems are subjected to an overload through training, then they adapt to cope more efficiently with the overload: the body becomes fitter. To become even fitter, overload again and the body systems will once again adapt to cope. This is the principle of **progressive overload**. It is important that the overload at the beginning of the training programme is at an appropriate level for the individual and their circumstances, and that the overload is increased gradually and sensibly over the training programme.

To apply the principle of progressive overload effectively, you need to understand the components of physical fitness and how the training methods are used to develop these components. For example, the way you progressively overload to improve muscular strength differs somewhat from the way you would progressively overload to improve muscular endurance. For muscular strength, you would first look at increasing the resistance or the weight to be lifted – the number of repetitions would stay much the same. For muscular endurance, you would first look at increasing the time you spend on each exercise or increasing the number of repetitions – the resistance or weight would stay much the same.

Rest/Recovery

You will benefit from a hard workout only if you allow your muscles time to recover and your body time to replace the fuel that has been used up. It is during rest/recovery periods that improved biological adaptations take place in the body.

2.1 DEVELOPING PHYSICAL FITNESS FOR PERFORMANCE

In performance-related training programmes, a recovery period does not necessarily mean that you do nothing. You may still train but at a lower intensity (e.g. RPE 4/10 instead of RPE 8/10). Training at a relaxed and easier pace may even help recovery. Alternatively, you could work on a different component of physical fitness, or work a different part of your body. For instance do a hard run one day, and the next, work on developing muscular strength in the trunk and upper body.

The best guide for achieving balance between training effort/intensity and rest/recovery is: the harder the training effort/intensity, the more time should be allowed for rest and recovery.

Tedium (avoided through variety)

You are less likely to experience *tedium* – where you become psychologically and physically bored – and less likely to stay on a plateau without improving, if you use a *variety* of training methods and venues.

If you are training for a particular event or sport (for example, a 10 km road run), then variety should be provided by changing the training methods and/or the venues. For example, you could do a continuous steady-pace run in the park for one session, a fartlek run in the forest for another, and an interval training session on the 400 m track for another.

You have variety through the range of training methods and venues, yet the principle of specificity has still been applied.

Reversibility (avoided through maintenance)

If you stop training, then the biological adaptations produced by the body will be *reversed* and you will lose your level of physical fitness. This is to be avoided. So, if you want to *maintain* your level of physical fitness, then you need to continue to train.

Everyone is different and we all respond differently to training. Effective training programmes take this into account. The principles of training may need to be applied differently to get the best results for individuals. For example, some individuals may respond better to higher volumes of training and others to higher intensities. Some will respond better to complete rest/recovery where nothing is done, and others respond better to doing light training for rest/recovery. It is important to find out what works best for each individual.

Periodisation, including peaking

Periodisation is a principle that is applied to performance-related training programmes. It splits the training programme into different phases (or periods) and each phase has a different training focus. This is to effectively prepare the body and bring it to its peak level of physical fitness. It will enable an athlete to perform at their very best on the day of an important competition, or for a period of time. The phases are:

1. **foundation phase:** This comes at the start of a training programme and helps to develop all-round, general physical fitness.
2. **development phase:** This maintains general fitness but concentrates on building up the components of physical fitness specific to the event, sport or position. This is when the volume of work is at its highest.
3. **sharpening phase:** For this, specific fitness is maintained but the amount or volume of training is reduced. The emphasis is on high intensity, sharpness and speed.
4. **peaking phase:** This is the stage prior to competition. The athlete will perform much less work, but that work is at a high intensity and specific. Then, some days before the competition training will ease right off (or taper off) to allow the muscles time for complete recovery and for the fuel stores to be full.
5. **competition phase**
6. **rest/recovery phase**: After a competition there would be a short rest/recovery period, and after a season of competitions, a longer rest/recovery period.

The variety of sports, the range of competition structures and the differences among individual athletes, mean that there can be no set time frame for each of these periods/phases. Instead, the aim is to find the best way to prepare individual athletes so that they are at their peak level of physical fitness, which will enable them to perform at their very best when it is most needed.

ANALYSIS, INTERPRETATION AND EVALUATION

ASSESSMENT FOR LEARNING

1. You, your classmates and your teacher should produce examples where any one, or any combination of, the principles of training have not been applied safely, appropriately or effectively. Make sure to cover athletic events, individual sports and team sports.

2. Study the examples. Assess, analyse, interpret and evaluate the information, and based on your knowledge and understanding:
   (a) identify and explain what information, if any, is missing and how this would affect your analysis and evaluation.
   (b) identify and explain what information is sound, positive and accurate; and what information is negative or inaccurate and needs to be changed. What changes would you recommend? Back up your findings with references to what is factual, sound or recommended (the 'ideal').

   For guidance on how to do this, use Steps 1–3 on page 6.

ASSESSMENT FOR LEARNING

Explain how each of the principles of training should be applied in the following examples:

1. Specificity applied to a chosen athletic event; an individual sport; and a team game.

2. Overload applied to two workouts where the person is currently swimming 100 m in 120 seconds × 10 repetitions with 60 seconds rest between repetitions.

3. Progressive overload applied to each of muscular strength; muscular endurance; and aerobic fitness.

4. Rest/recovery applied to an athlete training six days per week.

5. Variety applied to a competitive cyclist.

6. Periodisation applied to a training programme for a seasonal team game.

7. Peaking applied to running a half marathon on a Saturday.

8. Reversibility applied to any training programme.

Methods of training
Developing aerobic fitness and anaerobic fitness

Some key terms

Continuous steady-pace, **fartlek**, **interval** and **circuit training** are well-established training methods that can be used to develop either aerobic or anaerobic fitness.

The variables of **intensity** (how hard you work), **work time** (how long you work) and, with some training methods, the **recovery time** you take, are adjusted so as to develop either aerobic or anaerobic fitness. The variables are all **interrelated**.

A **repetition** is a short burst of work or a particular exercise being performed once. After each repetition in aerobic and anaerobic workouts, there will be a rest/recovery period. This may be complete rest where nothing is done, or it may involve doing low-intensity work/exercise. It is likely to be short for aerobic and longer for anaerobic.

A **set** is the number of repetitions completed *in a row* before a *significant* rest/recovery period is taken.

Continuous steady-pace training

This method of training is normally associated with developing aerobic fitness. It involves **continuous** work (for example, **running**, **cycling** or **swimming**) at a **steady** rate. Once the heart rate reaches a desired **intensity** (how hard the heart has to work) or a rate of perceived exertion (RPE), it is then maintained at that intensity for a period of time (for example, anything from 30 minutes or more).

2.1 DEVELOPING PHYSICAL FITNESS FOR PERFORMANCE

Examples of this kind of training would be: running nonstop for 60 minutes at a steady pace, maintaining an intensity of RPE 7/10; a steady paced 6-mile run in 36 minutes; or a steady 10-mile run at 7 minute per mile pace.

Fartlek training

Fartlek is the Swedish word for 'speed play'. It is a method of training that can be used to develop aerobic or anaerobic fitness, although it is mostly associated with the former. It involves continuous training but includes working the body at high intensities for varying periods of time. Periods of high-intensity work are followed by periods of recovery. The intensities and the times for which they are maintained are decided during the training, depending on how you feel.

An example of fartlek training would be a 40-minute run with bursts of fast running (e.g. RPE 8 or 9/10) for varying lengths of time – anything from ten seconds to two minutes. After a burst of fast running you may run slowly (RPE 3 or 4/10) to recover then, for a time, increase your pace again before doing your next burst of fast running.

Interval training

This method of training can be used to develop aerobic or anaerobic fitness.

Like Fartlek, it also involves alternating periods of high-intensity work with periods of recovery, but this time the intensity, recovery time and the number of repetitions to be done are decided in advance.

An example of interval training would be running 200 m in 25 seconds, followed by 2 minutes recovery time, repeated 5 times. This would constitute one set. Three sets would be performed with 5 minutes rest/recovery between each set. All times, distances, repetitions and sets would be fixed: 200 m × 25 sec × 5 reps × 3 sets. Alternatively, it could be 200 m × 35 sec × 20 reps × 2 sets.

To tailor this training to develop either aerobic or anaerobic fitness, you must consider the following:

- **Intensity:** For developing aerobic fitness, the intensity should be near the aerobic/anaerobic threshold (e.g. RPE 8/10); for developing anaerobic fitness, the intensity should be over the aerobic/anaerobic threshold (e.g. RPE 9 or 10/10).
- **Time:** For developing aerobic fitness, the work time will usually be longer (e.g. 90 seconds) than the work time for developing anaerobic fitness (e.g. 30 seconds).
- **Repetitions:** For developing aerobic fitness, the number of repetitions in a set will be more (e.g. 20 repetitions) than the number of repetitions for developing anaerobic fitness (e.g. 4 repetitions).
- **Rest time between repetitions:** For developing aerobic fitness, the rest time between repetitions will be less (ratio of 1:1 or less) than the rest time between repetitions for developing anaerobic fitness (e.g. ratio of 1:4 or more).
- **Sets:** In developing aerobic fitness, the number of sets will usually be fewer (e.g. 2 sets of 20 repetitions) than the number of sets for developing anaerobic fitness (e.g. 4 sets of 4 repetitions).
- **Rest time between sets:** In developing aerobic fitness, the rest time between sets will be relatively short compared to those when developing anaerobic fitness.

Circuit training

This method can be used to develop aerobic or anaerobic fitness. It involves working the body by doing a series of different exercises in a sequence.

An example of circuit training would be:

1. box jumps onto a bench for 50 seconds, followed by 10 seconds rest.
2. squat thrusts for 50 seconds, followed by 10 seconds rest.
3. side-stepping shuttles for 50 seconds, followed by 10 seconds rest.
4. shuttle runs for 50 seconds, followed by 10 seconds rest.
5. sit-ups for 50 seconds, followed by 10 seconds rest.
6. step-ups on to and off a bench for 50 seconds, followed by 10 seconds rest.
7. burpees for 50 seconds, followed by 10 seconds rest.

The exercises would be done in this sequence and this would be one **circuit**.

The circuit could be repeated a number of times with a short or long break given between each one. The intensity or work rate can vary according to the exercises being done. It is these variables that make it either an aerobic fitness circuit or an anaerobic fitness circuit. If the exercises are very high intensity (e.g. RPE 9/10), they will develop anaerobic fitness. If the exercises are moderate intensity (e.g. RPE 6/10) they will develop aerobic fitness.

Given that genetic make-up, levels of physical fitness and the effort made, can vary so widely from person to person, the same circuit could develop anaerobic fitness for some and aerobic fitness for others.

> ### ASSESSMENT FOR LEARNING
>
> 1. Produce examples that show how the following methods of training are applied to develop both aerobic fitness and anaerobic fitness. Explain the difference between each.
>   - interval training
>   - fartlek training
>   - circuit training

Developing muscular strength, power, speed and endurance

Some key terms

Circuit training, **isotonic weight training** and **isometric training** are well-established training methods that can be used to develop muscular strength, power, speed and/or endurance, depending on how that training method is used.

As with aerobic and anaerobic workouts, it is the **intensity**, the **work time**, the number of **repetitions** and **sets** done and the recovery time between sets, that decide whether the workout will develop muscular strength, power, speed or endurance.

Circuit training

You have already explored how circuit training can be used to develop aerobic or anaerobic fitness (see above). This training method can, in theory, be used to develop muscular strength, power, speed or endurance, though it is probably best known for developing muscular endurance. A circuit should normally include exercises that work all the major muscle groups of the body. The exercise order should generally rotate around the different areas of the body to allow an area to rest before it is exercised again. However, pressure can be put on an area by having exercises for that area following on from each other.

Exercises like press-ups, sit-ups and star jumps use the person's body weight as the resistance. As the person gets fitter it becomes easier for them to perform these exercises. The resistance (body weight) stays the same, so the number of repetitions performed is usually increased, which is why circuit training is most often used for improving muscular endurance.

152

The intensity of the exercises will dictate the work time or number of repetitions to be completed. Moderate intensity (RPE 3/10) means many repetitions; hard intensity (RPE 8/10) means fewer repetitions.

To develop muscular strength, you need to make the exercises more difficult. For example, a high-intensity exercise to develop strength should be RPE 8/10 and therefore require a considerable effort. Exercises can be made harder by adjusting them (e.g. doing a press-up with your feet on a table and your hands on the floor) or by using equipment (e.g. weights and medicine balls, which can make the exercises more suited to improving strength).

To develop muscular power, you need **plyometric exercises, which require explosiveness in performing them** (e.g. jumping or hopping on to and off high platforms, or doing press-ups where you push up and clap your hands). An example of circuit training that includes some plyometric exercises would be:

1. box jumps onto a high bench for 30 seconds, followed by 10 seconds rest.
2. squat thrusts for 30 seconds, followed by 10 seconds rest.
3. squat jumps for 30 seconds, followed by 10 seconds rest.
4. press-ups with clap, for 30 seconds followed by 10 seconds rest.
5. sit-ups for 30 seconds, followed by 10 seconds rest.
6. two footed jumps on to and off a 1 m platform for 30 seconds, followed by 10 seconds rest.
7. burpees for 30 seconds, followed by 10 seconds rest.

Isotonic weight training

Isotonic weight training involves a muscle, or group of muscles, working against a resistance (a weight) where the movement of body parts takes place. Weight training exercises usually involve the muscle working **concentrically** (where the muscle gets shorter and bulkier as it works), and then **eccentrically** (where the muscle gets longer and less bulky as it works).

Isotonic weight training can be done by using:

- **free weights:** weights attached to a barbell or dumbbell; or pre-manufactured dumbbell weights. These can be moved freely about an area.
- **fixed weights:** weights that are part of a machine, moved by lever or pulley systems.
- **machines:** some machines provide various resistances without the need for actual weights.

Isotonic weight training can be used to develop muscular power, strength, speed or endurance and is the most easily adapted to specifically develop any, or all, of these components of muscular fitness.

Muscular fitness

To develop muscular fitness your muscles need to work against a resistance. The resistance – which can be a weight expressed in kilograms (kg) – will be different according to what type of muscular fitness you wish to develop. So, for one exercise you could lift 20 kg, and for another you could lift 10 kg. If you wanted to develop another component of muscular fitness, the weights you lift would change.

The weight (or resistance) can also be expressed as a **Repetition Maximum (RM)**, which is the maximum weight you can lift a certain number of times. For example, 1 RM is the maximum weight that can be lifted only once or for one repetition, and 10 RM is the maximum weight that can be lifted for 10 repetitions (and no more).

The advantage of using the RM method for expressing weight is that it means the principles for developing the components of muscular fitness can be explained and applied to a group of people without referring to specific weights. Everyone can be told that the weight they are to lift is 15 RM – the maximum weight they can lift for 15 repetitions (and no more), but they must discover what that weight is for them. In practice that could be 5 kg for one person, 10 kg for another person, and 20 kg for another. They all lift different weights but, for each of them, that is the weight that is appropriate for them (15 RM).

Muscular strength

To develop muscular strength, you need to use a weight between 1–12 RM: the lower the RM the better. However, the closer the weight is to 1 RM, the more the risk of injury increases, which is why inexperienced and young people using weightlifting to develop strength should use 6–12 RM.

The number of repetitions in a set should be as close as possible to the RM, and there should be about 3–5 sets. The lower the RM (i.e. the heavier the weight), the longer the rest between sets should be. For example, when using 3 RM, the rest time should be 5 minutes or more, compared to 1–2 minutes when using 12 RM.

can effectively develop this strength; see page 153). If you increase the explosiveness or speed of movement you will also develop more power (plyometric exercises can do this). For most sports, it is important to develop both.

First, you would develop muscular strength by using weight training, then you would apply this strength by doing plyometric exercises (see page 153). The plyometric exercises help develop the explosiveness. Doing both will maximise your development of power. This will be most beneficial in events like high jump and long jump where power is needed.

Also, in power events, like shot or javelin, the strength is developed through weight training, and the explosiveness through explosively putting or throwing shot or javelin which are either slightly lighter or slightly heavier than regulation weight.

Muscular endurance

To develop muscular endurance, you need to use a weight between 13–25 RM: muscular strength/endurance is developed the closer the RM is to 13 RM.

The number of repetitions in a set should be as close as possible to the RM, and there should be about 2–3 sets. The higher the RM (i.e. the lighter the weight), the shorter the rest between sets should be. For example, when using 15 RM, the rest time should be about 60 seconds, compared to 30 seconds when using 20 RM.

Muscular power

Muscular power is about applying force/strength with explosive speed.

If you increase the strength/force of muscles, you will develop more power (isotonic weight training

Isometric training

Isometric training involves a muscle, or group of muscles, working against a resistance, but no movement of body parts takes place. An example of this kind of exercise would be to put your back against a wall and move into a seated position that you would then hold: your muscles are working to hold you in this position, but no movement of body parts takes place.

Since isometric training develops only muscular strength or endurance in the position held, this training method is limited in its use – most sports are dynamic and involve movement – but it can be used in some sports, such as gymnastics, where static positions need to be held.

The same general principles that apply to the other methods also apply to isometric training: greater resistances will develop muscular strength; less intense resistances, held for longer, will develop muscular endurance.

2.1 DEVELOPING PHYSICAL FITNESS FOR PERFORMANCE

ASSESSMENT FOR LEARNING

1. Produce examples to show the differences between how the following methods of training are applied to develop muscular strength and muscular endurance:
   (a) isotonic weight training
   (b) circuit training
2. Explain how muscular power can be developed for athletic events like long jump.
3. Explain the limitation of isometric training.

Developing flexibility
Some key terms
Any physical activity or exercise that stretches our skeletal muscles can be used to develop flexibility, but the key training methods are **static flexibility training** (performed actively or passively), and **dynamic flexibility training** (also known as **active/ballistic training**).

Static flexibility training
This method involves slowly stretching the muscle to its limit and then holding it in this stretched position for anything from 10–60 seconds. An example would be sitting on the floor with your legs straight, and slowly reaching forward, toward your toes, until you feel mild tension in your muscles. You would then hold this position for at least ten seconds.

If you hold on to your lower legs and pull your body down to keep the muscles stretched and under mild tension, then you are performing the static flexibility exercise *actively*. If you get another person to push down on your shoulders to keep the muscles stretched and under mild tension, then you are performing the exercise *passively*. Performed actively, you provide the force to stretch the muscle and hold it in that position. Performed passively, another person provides this force.

To develop flexibility effectively, static flexibility exercises should be held under mild tension for 20–30 seconds. Two or three repetitions of the exercise may be done. The muscles should be relaxed during the rest/recovery period between the repetitions. This method is most often used in cool-downs after hard exercise.

Static performed actively

Static performed passively

Dynamic flexibility training (active/ballistic)
This method involves bouncing or swinging a part, or parts, of the body to put the muscle in a stretched position and produce greater muscle length. The exercise can be done for 20–60 seconds or for 20–60 repetitions. An example would be to bend forward to touch your toes, then, while still bent over, gently bounce up and down to stretch the hamstrings.

In dynamic flexibility exercises, the force to stretch the muscle is provided by the bouncing or swinging movement. This method is relevant to sportspeople whose movements involve this type of flexibility: for example, high jumpers and games players. Dynamic stretching is used in warm-ups before games.

ASSESSMENT FOR LEARNING

1. Produce a file of dynamic flexibility exercises that could be used in a general warm-up. Draw and label stick diagrams to explain how they should be performed.

2. Produce a file of static flexibility exercises that could be used to develop flexibility. Draw and label stick diagrams to explain how they should be performed.

ANALYSIS, INTERPRETATION AND EVALUATION

ASSESSMENT FOR LEARNING

1. You, your classmates and your teacher should produce examples of where training methods have not been applied safely, appropriately or effectively. Make sure to cover athletic events, individual sports and team sports.

2. Study the examples. Assess, analyse, interpret and evaluate the information, and based on your knowledge and understanding:
   (a) identify and explain what information, if any, is missing and how this would affect your analysis and evaluation.
   (b) If sufficient guidance is provided, then identify and explain what information is sound, positive and accurate, and what is negative, wrong or inaccurate and needs to be changed. Back up your findings with references to what is factual, sound or recommended (the 'ideal').

   For guidance on how to do this, use Steps 1–3 on page 6.

Assessment of physical fitness

Reasons for assessing levels of physical fitness

By assessing athletes' levels of physical fitness, you can:
- judge their baseline level of fitness before they begin training programmes.
- identify talent.
- discover strengths and weaknesses.
- set realistic short-term and intermediate goals and targets.

By having the results from fitness tests, and by setting goals and targets, this:
- provides incentives.
- helps keep athletes motivated.
- allows progress to be monitored during training programmes.
- allows adjustments to be made to training programmes (using information gained from the results of fitness tests).

2.1 DEVELOPING PHYSICAL FITNESS FOR PERFORMANCE

Factors that underpin fair assessments

If your testing is to be **valid** and **reliable**, and allow you to compare results, then there are certain principles that must be followed. You should know and understand the following:

- **Specificity:** The tests selected (or designed) by you should be suitable for the purpose. If you want to assess aerobic fitness, then the test must be able to do that. If you want to assess flexibility, then the test must be able to do that. This makes the tests valid.
- **Protocol** and **accuracy of measurement:** The protocol (procedures and rules) for the tests must be followed strictly. It would not be fair to compare results if the test was done differently on separate occasions. The same applies to the accuracy of measurement. This means the test results will be reliable.
- **Monitoring:** The same tests should be used before, during and after the training programme. If you want to measure your progress or to judge the effectiveness of your training programme, then the same tests must be used on all occasions to allow for a fair comparison of results. This makes the results valid.
- **Conditions and environment:** The tests should be carried out under the same, or similar, conditions each time. It would not be fair to compare the results of a 10 × 5 m sprint test if one time the test was performed inside on a non-slip floor, and the next time performed outside on wet, slippery grass. This makes the results valid.
- **Athlete's health:** The tests should be carried out when the athlete is healthy and hydrated. It would not be fair to compare results if the athlete was suffering from the flu, an injury, or is dehydrated.
- **Athlete's state of mind:** The tests should be carried out when the athlete is feeling positive, motivated and wants to perform. It would not be fair to compare results if the athlete was depressed or experiencing emotional problems.

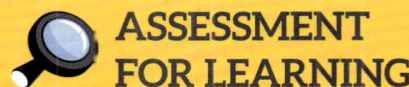

ASSESSMENT FOR LEARNING

1. For each of the four reasons for assessing levels of physical fitness, provide an example that would illustrate why that reason is important.
2. Explain the factors that underpin fair assessments.

Devising, selecting or using fitness tests

As you move up the continuum from being physically healthy towards achieving peak physical fitness, it becomes increasingly important to have specific tests that are valid, reliable and allow progress to be accurately measured and comparisons to be made between you and other people. This is where standardised tests are useful.

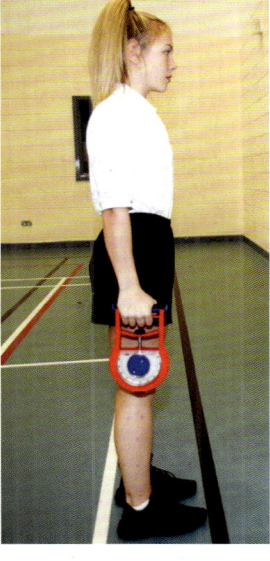

Keith McClure

You should be able to explain how the factors that underpin fair assessments are applied in administering the standardised fitness tests used by CCEA and outlined in the table overleaf.

Keith McClure

157

Component	Test(s)	
Aerobic energy production	Multi-stage fitness test* Cooper test (12 minute run)*	
Muscular endurance	60 second sit-up test* 60 second press-up test*	
Flexibility	Sit and reach test*	
Muscular strength	Grip strength test with dynamometer*	
Power	Standing broad jump*	
Agility	Speed and agility test*	

* CCEA fitness: Your teacher will explain the administration and protocol for these tests.

Images, Keith McClure

2.1 DEVELOPING PHYSICAL FITNESS FOR PERFORMANCE

ASSESSMENT FOR LEARNING

1. Choose two physical fitness tests and explain how the factors that interpin fair assessments are applied in administering them.

ANALYSIS, INTERPRETATION AND EVALUATION

ASSESSMENT FOR LEARNING

1. You, your classmates and your teacher should devise guidance for the administration of some physical fitness tests. However, some things in the guidance should make the tests and/or the results invalid or unreliable.

2. Study the examples. Assess, analyse, interpret and evaluate the information, and based on your knowledge and understanding:
   (a) identify and explain what guidance, if any, is missing and how this would affect your analysis and evaluation.
   (b) If sufficient guidance is provided, then identify and explain what information is sound, positive and accurate, and what is negative, wrong or inaccurate and needs to be changed. Back up your findings with references to the factors that underpin fair assessments.

   For guidance on how to do this, use Steps 1–3 on page 6.

3. Collate a wide range of fitness test results from the CCEA GCSE PE battery of tests so that you, and your class, can become skilled at analysing, interpreting and evaluating the results. (Your teacher will be able to give you, or tell you where to find, CCEA's GCSE PE battery of tests.)

4. Study the data. Assess, analyse, interpret and evaluate the data, and based on your knowledge and understanding:
   (a) identify and explain what data, if any, is missing, invalid or unreliable and how this would affect your analysis and evaluation.
   (b) If the data is all there and correct, then identify and explain what the data shows with regard to, for example, levels of physical fitness, identifying talent, discovering strengths and weakness and meeting goals and targets. Back up your findings with references to what is factual, sound or recommended (the 'ideal').

   For guidance on how to do this, use Steps 1–3 on page 6.

Planning and evaluating training programmes

What is a training programme?

A **training programme** is a planned series of training sessions that will enable someone to achieve a goal over a period of time.

Planning a training programme is a bit like baking a cake: there are certain principles that must be followed, but it is possible to change some of the ingredients, or mix them in different ways, in an attempt to bake a better cake. Sometimes it works and sometimes it doesn't, but people continually try to discover new or better recipes.

It is the same with planning training programmes: there are principles that must be followed, but people are continually trying out new methods and different ways of mixing the 'ingredients' of training programmes, in the hope of discovering something that makes training more effective.

In this section the focus will be on your ability to plan training programmes that demonstrate, in a clear and straightforward manner, your ability to apply the principles of training effectively, using safe and appropriate methods of training and exercise. In planning a training programme, you will need to consider the workouts – in planning a workout, you can assume that a warm-up and cool-down will be done before and after the workout.

The five-step process to bring about improvements (see page 6) applies to planning performance-related training programmes and performance. The focus in this section is not so much on the process to be followed but on how the principles of training and methods of training should be applied to the components of physical fitness during the process.

Planning performance-related training programmes

The following principles of training – specificity, variety, progressive overload, rest/recovery, periodisation, maintenance/reversibility and peaking (see also pages 147–149) – must be applied to performance-related training programmes for an event, sport, or position within a sport, for them to be safe, appropriate and effective.

Applying the principle of specificity

1. To plan an appropriate performance-related training programme, you must understand clearly both the physical demands required and the components of physical fitness (aerobic and anaerobic fitness; muscular strength, power, speed, endurance and flexibility).

    Based on your evaluation of the physical demands required of the performer, you will determine the relative importance of the various components of fitness. The performance-related training programme must reflect this. In other words, if aerobic energy production and muscular endurance are judged to be very important for the event or sport, then the majority of time in the training programme must be spent on developing them. The results of training are very specific, so it is important that you carry out this first step correctly.

2. To help identify the person's present level of fitness, you should select and undertake valid physical fitness tests for the relevant components of fitness for the event, sport or position within the sport. By testing the level of fitness in the relevant components, you will establish a baseline and identify strengths and areas needing improvement.

3. Once you have determined the relative importance of the components of fitness and have the baseline level from the fitness tests, decide what emphasis should be given to the components of fitness at various times over the time frame for the performance-related training programme. This is the **periodisation** of the training programme.

4. For each period or phase of periodisation, choose the types of exercise and training methods that will most appropriately match the emphasis to be placed on a particular component of fitness. In other words, if the sport required running and sprinting, and for a period the emphasis was on developing anaerobic fitness, then the type of exercise chosen for the training programme should be running, and the appropriate training method would be interval training.

5. To help decide realistic and achievable objectives and targets, you need to consider the individual's baseline level in the fitness tests. In addition, things like time available to train, access to facilities and disposable income can affect the implementation of a training programme. A person's age, gender, height, weight, body type, ratio of fast twitch to slow twitch muscle fibres, vital capacity and stroke volume will also affect what is possible.

6. Based on all this, set SMART/ER objectives and targets (see page 11) and check that the decisions you make are:
    - **Specific:** It's not enough to decide that aerobic training will be done – you must specify the type of exercise and method of training (e.g. a continuous steady-pace run).
    - **Measurable:** For example, the training will be a continuous steady-pace run for 60 minutes with a RPE of 7/10.

- **Attainable/agreed:** The person who is to follow the training programme must be aware of the decisions and agree with them.
- **Relevant:** The type of exercise chosen, the training methods used and how they are used must be appropriate and relevant to the person's specific objectives.
- **Time-bound:** The person will achieve their target within a set period of time.
- **Exciting:** The person is more likely to carry out the training if it is exciting for them.
- **Recorded:** You want to record what is actually being done so that you can check on progress being made and on the effectiveness of the training programme as it is followed.

Applying the principle of variety (avoiding tedium)

In performance-related training programmes, you must be specific with your training. For example, if the event or sport involves running and aerobic energy production, then your training must involve running and the development of aerobic energy production. You cannot provide variety in the programme by offering swimming, dancing and cycling as well as running, as these will make the training programme less effective (even though they all develop aerobic energy production). Instead, variety can be provided by using different training methods, using different venues for the training, training at different times, or training with different people.

Applying the principle of progressive overload

Improvement can only happen if you apply the principle of overload, which can be achieved by increasing the frequency, intensity or time spent training (FITT), or by increasing any combination of these variables (see page 148).

With performance-related training programmes, overloading often means working at your upper limits. This means it is very important to know *when* to add a further overload, and *what* form that overload should take.

The initial overload and subsequent overloading will depend on the individual and their circumstances. The results of the tests, together with the amount and intensity of the exercise and knowing how the person is progressing, will help you decide on appropriate overloading throughout the training programme.

Applying the principle of rest/recovery

In developing peak physical fitness, you work close to your upper limits when training. This means many workouts have high intensities. The harder you work the more important it is that you get rest/recovery time. Sometimes it can be total rest, but in training programmes that develop peak physical fitness, an easy training session is often used as the recovery. Ice baths, massage and the use of a roller are also used to aid and speed up recovery.

Applying the principle of peaking

In the peaking phase you perform much less work, but the work you do is at a high intensity. Then, some days before competition, you ease right off (or taper off) with your training. This is to allow your muscles time to recover completely and your fuel stores to be full.

Applying the principle of maintenance (avoiding reversibility)

You need to continue to train or you will lose your level of physical fitness (reversibility). During a series of competitions, you will maintain your physical fitness due to the physical demands the competitions place upon you. Recovery will come immediately after each competition, and then the peaking phase should be used again before the next competition.

Monitoring and reviewing progress

Performance is important in developing peak physical fitness. It is therefore essential to monitor the progress being made during the training programme to judge its effectiveness. This can be done by using the tests that established the baseline before the beginning of the programme. Results can be compared, progress monitored and analysed, and adjustments to the training programme can then be made.

Monitoring should also involve investigating and recording how the person feels before, during and after training sessions. This feedback can be used to adjust the training programme if necessary, and ensure progress rather than regression.

PHYSICAL EDUCATION for CCEA GCSE LEVEL

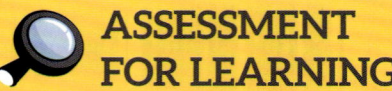

ASSESSMENT FOR LEARNING

1. Provide examples that show clearly that you understand how each of the principles of training are applied safely, appropriately and effectively to a performance-related training programme.

ANALYSIS, INTERPRETATION AND EVALUATION

ASSESSMENT FOR LEARNING

1. You, your classmates and your teacher should produce examples of performance-related training programmes where one or more of the principles have not been applied safely, appropriately or effectively. Make sure to cover athletic events, individual sports and team sports.

2. Study the examples. Assess, analyse, interpret and evaluate the information, and based on your knowledge and understanding:
   (a) identify and explain what information, if any, is missing and how this would affect your analysis and evaluation.
   (b) If sufficient information is provided, then identify and explain what is safe, appropriate, sound, recommended and effective, and what is not safe, appropriate, sound, or effective and needs to be changed. Back up your findings with references to what is factual, sound or recommended (the 'ideal').

For guidance on how to do this, use Steps 1–3 on page 6.

Planning and evaluating training sessions

A training session is the time spent exercising for one period of time. It normally includes a warm-up, a workout and a cool-down.

Warm-ups

A warm-up will prepare your mind and body for the workout, helping to minimise the risk of muscle and joint injury. Generally, the harder your workout is going to be, the longer you should spend warming up.

A safe, appropriate and effective warm-up should include:
- **pulse-raising activity**
- **dynamic flexibility exercises**

If performing in a sport, the warm-up before a match will also include skill-related practices.

Planning the pulse-raising activities

Pulse-raising activity involves working the major muscles of the body in rhythmic movements (e.g. jogging, though you could use a variety of other activities, like cycling or rowing). It is included in the warm-up in order to:
- gradually and moderately work the heart and lungs in preparation for the workout.
- redirect blood from some internal organs to the muscles.
- increase the blood flow to the muscles.
- raise body temperature: warm muscles are less likely to tear.

The following process should be used to plan the pulse-raising activity:

1. **Choose safe and appropriate pulse-raising activities:** The activity should match the type of exercise that you are going to use in the workout or in the sport.
2. **Decide the intensity:** To start, use low-intensity work (e.g. jogging) and gradually raise the intensity towards the level to be used in the workout (e.g. short sprints at the end).
3. **Decide the time:** The time spent will depend on the individual and the outside temperature. Generally, when your body starts to sweat it means that you have warmed up.

2.1 DEVELOPING PHYSICAL FITNESS FOR PERFORMANCE

Planning the active or dynamic flexibility exercises

Dynamic flexibility exercises are used in the warm-up in order to loosen up the joints so that they move more freely, and to stretch the muscles, tendons and ligaments at the joints, so that there is less chance of muscle or joint injury. This involves gently and rhythmically moving the bones at the joints so that the synovial fluid is warmed and becomes less viscous (less thick and slippery) and the muscles, tendons and ligaments at the joints are stretched.

The following process should be used to plan the dynamic flexibility exercises:

1. **Choose safe and appropriate dynamic flexibility exercises:** The exercises should cover the muscles, tendons and ligaments surrounding the major joints – neck, shoulders, arms, spine, hips, knees and ankles – or, as a minimum, the joints to be used in the workout.
2. **Decide the intensity:** To start, the bones at the joints should be moved gently and rhythmically within their normal range of movement, then the movements will gradually be extended.
3. **Decide the time:** The time will depend on the individual and the outside temperature. The dynamic flexibility exercises should be done until the joints move freely.

Planning the skill-related practices

Skill-related practices are usually performed as part of the warm-up before a game or match, after the physical warm-up. They are designed to get players into the 'groove', so they are less likely to make mistakes when the match starts.

The following process should be used to plan skill-related practices:

1. **Choose appropriate skills:** Start with the general skills expected from all players. If there are specific skills for particular groups of players, do them next. If in team games there are specialist individual skills required from individuals, these can be practiced separately from the others or before the team warm-up. Skills practices can be incorporated into the physical warm-up.
2. **Decide the intensity:** At the start, skills may be performed without opposition, but the practices should be intensified so that they are performed in match-like situations.
3. **Decide the time:** This should be sufficient to allow practice of the main skills and sufficient to allow players to get into the 'groove'.

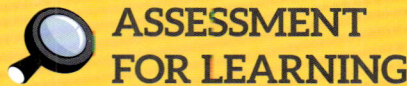

ASSESSMENT FOR LEARNING

1. Plan examples of warm-ups that will be safe, appropriate and effective for a range of events and sports.

ANALYSIS, INTERPRETATION AND EVALUATION

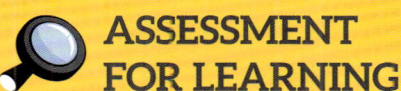

ASSESSMENT FOR LEARNING

1. You, your classmates and your teacher should produce examples of warm-ups where one or more of the principles have not been applied safely, appropriately or effectively. Make sure to cover athletic events, individual sports and team sports.
2. Study the examples. Assess, analyse, interpret and evaluate the information, and based on your knowledge and understanding:
   (a) identify and explain what information, if any, is missing and how this would affect your analysis and evaluation.
   (b) If sufficient information is provided, then identify and explain what information is safe, appropriate, sound, recommended and effective, and what is not safe, appropriate, sound, or effective and needs to be changed. Back up your findings with references to what is factual, sound or recommended (the 'ideal').

For guidance on how to do this, use Steps 1–3 on page 6.

Cool-downs

A cool-down will bring the body back to normal conditions gradually and safely.

A safe, appropriate and effective cool-down should include:
- **pulse-lowering activities**
- **flexibility exercises**

Planning the pulse-lowering activities

Pulse-lowering activities gradually ease the body out of the strenuous exercise in the workout. By continuing to exercise gently during the cool-down, you allow:
- lactic acid (which builds up during exercise) to be broken down and cleared from the muscles.
- the blood to be gradually redirected back to other internal organs.
- your body temperature to decrease gradually and return to normal.

The following process should be used to plan the pulse-lowering activities:

1. **Choose safe and appropriate pulse-lowering activities:** The activity would normally be the type of aerobic exercise that you were doing in the workout, but at a low intensity. For example, jogging and/or walking instead of running/sprinting.
2. **Decide the intensity:** You should gradually lower the intensity from the level at the end of the workout towards resting heart rate level.
3. **Decide the time:** This will depend on the individual and how hard or intense the workout was. The harder the workout, the longer the cool-down.

Planning the flexibility exercises

The first reason for including flexibility exercises in the cool-down is to ease the tension in tight muscles caused by the workout (elite athletes can often have their muscles massaged for them). The second reason is because the cool-down is the best time to develop flexibility, as the muscles are warm and pliable and can be more easily stretched.

The following process should be used to plan the flexibility exercises:

1. **Choose safe and appropriate flexibility exercises:** You can do *dynamic/ballistic* flexibility exercises, or *static* flexibility exercises. The latter can be passive or active (see page 155), though active is preferable, since you are in control of the tension. If static exercises are passive (i.e. another person provides the force to stretch the muscles under tension) there is a greater risk of injury.

   Normally flexibility exercises cover the neck, shoulders, arms, chest, trunk, hips and legs, and it is best to be systematic about the order. For example, start with the neck and work your way down the body. This helps ensure that you remember to cover all the areas of the body.
2. **Decide intensity:** With static flexibility exercises you slowly stretch the muscle to its normal limit, then stretch it a little bit further until it is under mild tension. This is an appropriate intensity.
3. **Decide the time/number of repetitions and sets:** With static flexibility exercises, you should hold the muscle in the stretched position under mild tension for 20–60 seconds. Repetitions of the exercises can be performed to develop flexibility further.

   With dynamic flexibility exercises you should do a fixed number of repetitions (e.g. 20 repetitions), for each exercise.

2.1 DEVELOPING PHYSICAL FITNESS FOR PERFORMANCE

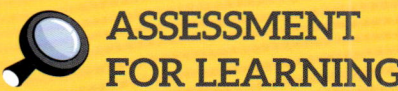

ASSESSMENT FOR LEARNING

1. Plan examples of cool-downs that will be safe, appropriate and effective for a range of events and sports.

ANALYSIS, INTERPRETATION AND EVALUATION

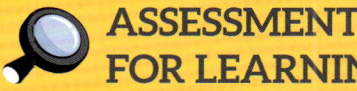

ASSESSMENT FOR LEARNING

1. You, your classmates and your teacher should produce examples of cool-downs where one or more of the principles have not been applied safely, appropriately or effectively. Make sure to cover athletic events, individual sports and team sports.

2. Study the examples. Assess, analyse, interpret and evaluate the information, and based on your knowledge and understanding:
   (a) identify and explain what information, if any, is missing and how this would affect your analysis and evaluation.
   (b) If sufficient information is provided, then identify and explain what information is safe, appropriate, sound, recommended and effective, and what is not safe, appropriate, sound, or effective and needs to be changed. Back up your findings with references to what is factual, sound or recommended (the 'ideal').

For guidance on how to do this, use Steps 1–3 on page 6.

Planning a safe, appropriate and effective workout

The workout is when the work is done to develop one or more of the seven components of physical fitness – aerobic and/or anaerobic energy production, muscular strength, power, speed, endurance and flexibility. Each workout is an important part of an overall training programme, just as one piece of a jigsaw puzzle is an important part of the overall picture. Each workout should have an objective and a target to be met.

To meet the objective and target, you need to consider the type of exercise(s) and training method(s) that should be used; the intensity of the workout and how the workout time will be used. These will vary depending on which components of fitness are to be developed.

In planning the workout, you also need to consider the individual and their circumstances: for example, their gender, age, weight, body type and present level of fitness.

Workouts to develop the aerobic or anaerobic energy systems

The objectives and targets of the workout should be kept in mind when using the following process.

Choose a safe and appropriate type of exercise and training method

Type of exercise: You should choose the type of exercise that is specific to the event or sport. If you are training to run a 10 km road race, then the type of exercise must be running.

Training method: For the development of **aerobic** fitness, you could choose from continuous steady-pace (CSP), fartlek, interval or circuit training. For **anaerobic** fitness, interval training is the most appropriate and most frequently used training method. Fartlek and circuit training can also be used.

Decide an appropriate intensity

Review the scale of intensities, from 1–10, on the Rate of Perceived Exertion (RPE) table (see page 54). The intensity of a workout will determine whether you develop aerobic or anaerobic fitness, as shown below:

Aerobic fitness	
CSP	The person should be working at an intensity near the aerobic/anaerobic threshold: a vigorous to hard intensity. For a CSP run, the intensity would be between RPE 7–8/10, depending on the length of the run.
Fartlek	For a fartlek run, the intensity for short bursts would be RPE 9/10; for longer bursts it would be RPE 8/10; and for periods of recovery in between bursts, RPE 4/10.
Interval	If the interval work times are long (e.g. 2 minutes), the intensity should be RPE 8/10. If the interval work times are short (e.g. 30 seconds), the intensity should be between RPE 8–9/10.
Circuits	The exercises in the circuit should be aerobic based and require RPE 8/10.

Anaerobic fitness	
Interval	The person should be working at an intensity above the aerobic/anaerobic threshold. With longer interval work times, the intensity should be RPE 9/10; and for shorter interval work times the intensity should be RPE 10/10.
Circuits	The principle used for anaerobic interval training should also apply to the exercises in circuit training. Exercises must be very demanding so that the aerobic energy system cannot cope.

Decide an appropriate time/number of repetitions and sets

The following work times are for running. Work times will differ for other types of activity (e.g. swimming and cycling) and depending on the individual's level of physical fitness.

Aerobic fitness	
CSP	CSP runs for workouts with an intensity of RPE 8/10 will be shorter: for example 30–40 minutes. CSP runs with an intensity of RPE 5/10 will be longer: for example 60–90 minutes.
Fartlek	A Fartlek run will be anything between 30–60 minutes, with various bursts of speed throughout ranging around RPE 8–9/10. Recovery running between bursts of speed will be around RPE 4/10.
Interval	Consider the work time for an interval/repetition; the rest time between each interval/repetition; the number of repetitions in a set; the number of sets to be completed; and the rest time between each set. For example, a person could run 600 m × 2 min × 10 reps × 2 sets with maximum 2 minutes rest between each repetition and 5 minutes rest between sets.
Circuits	Consider the time to be spent performing each exercise (e.g. 30–60 seconds); the rest time before starting the next exercise (0 seconds – move immediately to next exercise); the number of exercises in a circuit (e.g. 6–12); the number of circuits to be completed (e.g. 4); and the rest time between circuits (e.g. 1 minute).

2.1 DEVELOPING PHYSICAL FITNESS FOR PERFORMANCE

Anaerobic fitness	
Interval	Work time will be less than 60 seconds due to the high intensity (RPE 9–10/10); the rest time between will be longer than the work time to allow recovery (ratio of 1:4); the number of repetitions in a set will be small as the intensity is very high; and the number of sets will also be small. For example, a person could run 200 m × 30 sec × 4 reps × 3 sets, with a minimum of 2 minutes rest between each repetition and 5 minutes rest between sets.
Circuits	The exercises in the circuit (e.g. 4–8 exercises) will be high intensity or very hard (RPE 9/10) and performed quickly so that the aerobic energy system cannot cope: work time will be reasonably short for each exercise (e.g. 30–40 seconds). There will be a rest/recovery period between exercises of up to 2 minutes (e.g. ratio of 1:4). The number of circuits completed will depend on the number of exercises in the circuit.

ASSESSMENT FOR LEARNING

1 Plan examples of performance-based workouts that will be safe, appropriate and effective for developing *aerobic* fitness by using the following methods of training:
   - continuous steady-pace (CSP) training
   - fartlek training
   - interval training
   - circuit training

2 Plan examples of performance-based workouts that will be safe, appropriate and effective for developing *anaerobic* fitness by using the following methods of training:
   - fartlek training
   - interval training
   - circuit training

ANALYSIS, INTERPRETATION AND EVALUATION

ASSESSMENT FOR LEARNING

1 You, your classmates and your teacher should produce examples of performance-based workouts for developing aerobic and anaerobic fitness where one or more of the principles have not been applied safely, appropriately or effectively. Make sure to cover athletic events, individual sports and team sports.

2 Study the examples. Assess, analyse, interpret and evaluate the information, and based on your knowledge and understanding:
   (a) identify and explain what information, if any, is missing and how this would affect your analysis and evaluation.
   (b) If sufficient information is provided, then identify and explain what information is safe, appropriate, sound, recommended and effective, and what is not safe, appropriate, sound, or effective and needs to be changed. Back up your findings with references to what is factual, sound or recommended (the 'ideal').

For guidance on how to do this, use Steps 1–3 on page 6.

Workouts to develop muscular fitness – strength, power, endurance, speed

Choose a safe and appropriate training method

Weight training is the easiest method to develop any of the muscular fitness components (strength, power, speed and endurance) because the intensity can easily be changed by changing the weight. Circuit training can also be used by making exercises easier or harder and by using medicine balls and/or weights.

Choose safe and appropriate exercises

There are a wide variety of weight-training exercises and circuit-training exercises that cover all areas of the body. The exercises that are selected for workouts should be exercises that will work the muscles used in the event, sport or position in the sport.

Decide an appropriate order for the exercises

Generally, the exercises for the different parts of the body are done in rotation. For example, an exercise for the arms or chest, then one for the trunk, then the legs, and so on. The principle is to allow the muscles of one area to recover before they are worked again. However, the exercises can also be arranged to put more pressure on a particular area: for example, three exercises in a row that all work the legs.

Decide an appropriate intensity for the exercises

The intensity of the exercise will determine whether the exercise will develop muscular strength, power, speed or endurance. See figure 12 (opposite) for some guidance on the intensities to be used when using weight training or circuit training to develop the range of muscular fitness components.

To improve *strength* using weight training, you must use what feels to be very heavy weights for each of the exercises in the workout, but you must be able to perform each exercise safely, which is why it is sometimes better to use 8 RM rather than 3 RM. In circuit training, each of the exercises must be very demanding, for example RPE 9 or 10/10.

To improve *speed*, the '+ and −' in figure 12 indicate that the weight used should sometimes be just above the competition weight (e.g. shot, javelin, basketball, cricket ball, golf drive) and sometimes just below the competition weight. In both cases, however, the exercises must be performed explosively, with as much speed as possible. In circuit training, plyometric exercises can be used to develop speed.

To improve *power*, you must improve both strength and speed. You can have strength without power and you can have speed without power, but you cannot have power without strength and speed. Both strength and speed need to be developed. The weight training and circuit training exercises must be performed explosively.

To improve *endurance*, use weights that range from 13–40 RM, and exercises that range from RPE 5–7/10. The heavier the weight, or the harder the intensity of an exercise, the closer you get to the strength/endurance threshold.

Decide an appropriate number of repetitions and sets (or time)

The number of repetitions is determined by the intensity. There will be few repetitions with a high intensity workout and many repetitions with a low intensity workout. The number of sets will depend on the rest taken between them and whether further sets will make any difference to development.

See figure 12 for some guidance on the intensities (RM and RPE), the number of repetitions and the number of sets needed to develop the range of muscular fitness components.

Rest/recovery times are also shown, and these can be relevant in one of two ways:
- If the table represents a person doing sets of the *same* exercise for the *same* specific muscle

2.1 DEVELOPING PHYSICAL FITNESS FOR PERFORMANCE

Muscular fitness components		RM for weights	RPE for circuits	Reps	Sets	Rest between sets (min)
Power Perform reps explosively	Strength 1	1–4	10	1–4	2–3	5–6
	Strength 2	5–9	9	5–9	2–3	4–5
	Strength 3 /Endurance A	10–15	8	10–15	3–4	3–4
	Speed	+ and –	+ and –	5–10	3–4	3–4
Endurance B		16–25	7	16–25	3–4	2–3
Endurance C		26–40	6 or 5	26–40	3–4	1–2

Figure 12: Using weight training and circuit training to develop the muscular fitness components

group, repeated one after the other, the rest/recovery time refers to the time between each set.
- If a person moves on to a *different* exercise to tackle a *different* muscle group, then the change of exercise counts as a rest/recovery period. The times given in the table refer to the rest/recovery period needed before repeating the same exercise again.

The RM/RPE, number of repetitions, number of sets and rest between sets are variables that can be changed to suit individuals and their circumstances. What is best for one individual may not be for another.

Workouts to develop flexibility

Flexibility is an important component of fitness, but you would rarely have a specific workout for it unless it had to be developed to enable athletes to perform specific gymnastic or dance movements. Flexibility exercises would normally be done as part of every exercise or training session in the warm-up and, in particular, the cool-down (after the pulse-lowering activity).

The cool-down is the best time to develop flexibility as the muscles are warm and pliable and can be stretched much more easily (see 'Planning the flexibility exercises' under cool-downs on page 164).

ASSESSMENT FOR LEARNING

1. Practice planning examples of performance-based workouts that will be safe, appropriate and effective for developing *muscular strength* by using the following methods of training:
   - isotonic weight training and
   - circuit training

2. Practice planning examples of performance-based workouts that will be safe, appropriate and effective for developing *muscular speed* by using the following methods of training:
   - isotonic weight training
   - circuit training

3. Practice planning examples of performance-based workouts that will be safe, appropriate and effective for developing *muscular power* by using the following methods of training:
   - isotonic weight training
   - circuit training

4. Practice planning examples of performance-based workouts that will be safe, appropriate and effective for developing *muscular endurance* by using the following methods of training:
   - isotonic weight training
   - circuit training

ANALYSIS, INTERPRETATION AND EVALUATION

ASSESSMENT FOR LEARNING

1. You, your classmates and your teacher should produce examples of performance-based workouts for developing muscular strength, power, speed or endurance where one or more of the principles have not been applied safely, appropriately or effectively. Make sure to cover athletic events, individual sports and team sports.

2. Study the examples. Assess, analyse, interpret and evaluate the information, and based on your knowledge and understanding:
   (a) identify and explain what information, if any, is missing and how this would affect your analysis and evaluation.
   (b) If sufficient information is provided, then identify and explain what information is safe, appropriate, sound, recommended and effective, and what is not safe, appropriate, sound, or effective and needs to be changed. Back up your findings with references to what is factual, sound or recommended (the 'ideal').

   For guidance on how to do this, use Steps 1–3 on page 6.

2.2 DEVELOPING SKILLED PERFORMANCE

Learning outcomes

In this section, you will learn:

- the concept and assessment of skill
- factors that underpin the learning of skills

Skilled performance

The features of skilled performance

Skilled performance (skill) is the **learned** ability to bring about a predetermined goal or result with maximum certainty and efficiency.

In observing skilled performance, you will be aware that:

- the person has an **outcome** or **goal** that they wish to achieve: whether that is making a pass in netball, scoring a goal in football, or sinking a putt in golf.
- the skill or action is carried out **efficiently** – made to look easy, as if minimum effort is being used – and **effectively** – the pass in netball will go to the intended player at the right height and at the correct pace; the football will go into the goal beyond the reach of the goalkeeper; and the golf ball will follow the lie of the green at the right pace to drop into the hole.
- time after time, the skill or action will be carried out **fluently** with few mistakes being made – that is, with **consistency**. The person will be consistently successful.
- a skilled person is **recognisable**. They have mastered the techniques of the skill and consistently perform it efficiently and effectively with success. It is **aesthetically pleasing** to watch them perform.

However, it is worth remembering that, while the person may make the performance look easy and natural, skills are **learnt**. The person will have gone through the stages of learning a skill like everyone else: getting **feedback** on performances and spending hours **practising** in order to get to a stage where they can perform the skill automatically, without having to think about it.

Skilled performance for an individual is also **relative**: it depends on the context. A person may be skilled in one sport but not in another; and even within a sport, a person can be at various stages when mastering the skills of that sport. For example, in badminton a person could be skilled in performing a forehand overhead clear, but not in performing a backhand overhead clear.

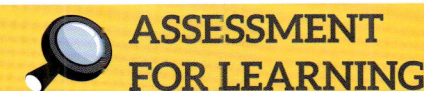

ASSESSMENT FOR LEARNING

1   Explain what makes a skill, a skill.

Classifying skills

There are endless skills that a person can learn and perform automatically: from an early age, we learn to hop, jump, read and write; we learn to ride a bike, to swim, to knit, to sew, and to cook; we learn skills from sports, from our families and from our peers.

One method of classification is to assign the skill a place on a continuum. One could indicate the difficulty (the basic to complex continuum) and another could reflect the number of factors outside your control (the closed to open continuum). You should be aware of the following:

The basic to complex continuum

Basic — Jumping

Complex — Back somersault with a full twist

The skills assigned to the **basic** end of this continuum are simple, more instinctive skills (e.g. hopping or jumping). The further along the continuum a skill is, the more it reflects the difficulty involved, until we come to skills classified as **complex**: these are more complicated, with more learning involved (e.g. a back somersault with a full twist on the trampoline).

The closed to open continuum

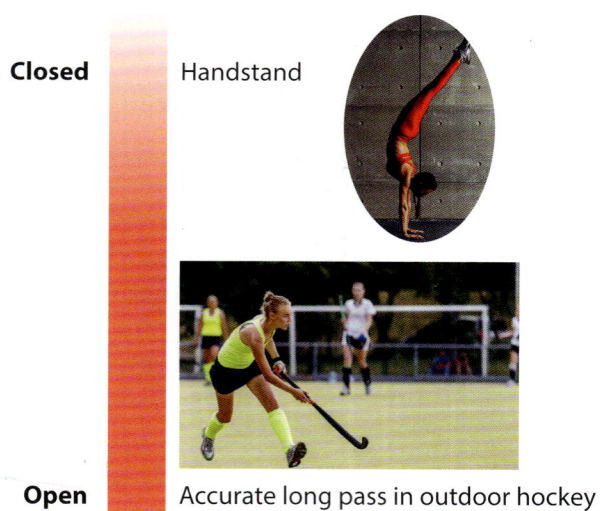

Closed — Handstand

Open — Accurate long pass in outdoor hockey

At one end of this continuum are **closed skills** – these have fewer factors that are outside the performer's control and/or these factors will have less impact on the performance of the skill (e.g. a handstand performed on a gym floor). At the other end are **open skills**, where there is a greater number of factors outside the performer's control, and/or the more likely it is that these factors will impact on the performance of the skill (e.g. a player in an outdoor game such as hockey has to take account of the movement and positioning of all other players, including the opposition, in order to deliver a quality long pass to the best-positioned teammate). A skill can be placed anywhere between these two extremes.

Discrete, continuous or serial skills

Finally, skills can be classified as discrete, continuous or serial.

- A **discrete skill** has a definite start and finish: it can stand alone. For example, doing a forward roll on a mat.
- A **continuous skill** is repeated over and over again. For example, rowing.
- A **serial skill** is a number of skills that have been linked together. For example performing a tumbling routine on the floor in gymnastics.

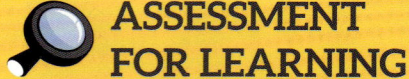

ASSESSMENT FOR LEARNING

1	What distinguishes a *basic* skill from a *complex* skill?
2	What distinguishes a *closed* skill from an *open* skill?
3	What distinguishes a *discrete* skill from a *serial* skill?
4	Provide examples of *basic* skills and *complex* skills.
5	Provide examples of *closed* skills and *open* skills.
6	Provide examples of *discrete* skills and *serial* skills.

The different types of skills

To perform skills efficiently and effectively, in many sports, you need to engage:

- **Cognitive skills:** These involve knowing and understanding the techniques used to perform skills. This can be achieved by listening to, reading or observing instructions. For example, reading instructions over and over again to learn how to serve in badminton.

2.2 DEVELOPING SKILLED PERFORMANCE

- **Perceptual skills:** These involve interpreting/evaluating a situation and then making decisions. For example, in badminton you look for your opponent's position in the service court and then decide which area of the court you will serve to.
- **Motor skills:** These involve the control of the muscles to perform the techniques of skills. For example, to hit the shuttlecock to the intended area of the service court, the brain tells the muscles the desired sequence of movements.
- **Perceptual motor skills:** These involve all of the above – the knowing and understanding; the interpretation/evaluation and the execution of techniques. In net games such as badminton and tennis, and in invasion games such as hockey and basketball, you need to know and understand how to do things (cognitive); you need to be able to read situations in the game and make the right decisions for those situations (perceptual); and you need to be able to execute the skills efficiently and effectively for your decisions to be carried out successfully (motor). In performing in sports such as gymnastics and trampolining, the main focus is on the successful execution of motor skills, perceptual skills are not so important.

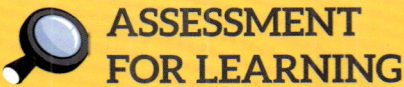

ASSESSMENT FOR LEARNING

1. What distinguishes a cognitive skill from a motor skill?
2. Explain why perceptual motor skills are very important if you want to be a good netball or basketball player.

Coordination, balance, reaction time and agility

Coordination is the ability of the brain and muscles to work together to perform smooth, accurate movements. It is about getting the timing of the sequence of movements right (the techniques). If you can consistently do this then you are more likely to be regarded as being skilled. If the timing is off and you are slightly late in playing a smash shot in badminton it can mean the shuttlecock is smashed on to your side of the court; similarly, if you are slightly early, it can mean that the shuttle hits the ceiling or goes high but lands mid-court on your opponent's side.

Balance is the ability to remain in a state of *equilibrium* (stable, not falling over), whether static or moving. Balance is about being in a position of control from which you can perform a skill's sequence of movements. If you can consistently

173

maintain that balance and control, then you are more likely to be regarded as skilled. If you are off balance when trying to play a smash shot in badminton, it may be impossible for you to go through the full sequence of movements and the shot will not be effective; or you may feel rushed when taking the shot, which will affect your timing.

Reaction time is your ability to react to a *stimulus*. It is the time that lapses from the presentation of the stimulus to the start of your response (for example, the time it takes for you to react to the starting pistol at the start of a 100 m sprint, or to react to your opponent's shot in a game of badminton). If you are consistently quick to react in an appropriate way, then you are more likely to be regarded as being skilled. The longer it takes for you to react to the opponent's shots in a game of badminton, the less time you have to move towards the shuttlecock, get balanced, and play an effective return shot.

Keith McClure

Agility is the ability to change direction efficiently and effectively when moving at speed. It is about being able to stop, start, or to change from going forwards to backwards to sideways quickly and with control. If you are consistently agile, then you are more likely to be regarded as being skilled. If you are slow to move, to stop or to change direction quickly in a game of badminton, you will often not be able to get into balanced positions to play your opponent's shots.

ASSESSMENT FOR LEARNING

1. Explain how each of the following factors may affect the performance of specific sports skills:
   (a) coordination
   (b) balance
   (c) reaction time
   (d) agility

Factors that underpin fair assessments

If your testing is to be **valid** and **reliable** and allow you to compare results, then there are certain principles that must be followed. These are outlined on page 157.

ASSESSMENT FOR LEARNING

1. What factors need to be met for assessment tests and results to be valid and reliable?

FURTHER THINKING

Put together a folder of standardised assessment tests that are considered to be valid and reliable when assessing coordination, balance, reaction time and agility.

ANALYSIS, INTERPRETATION AND EVALUATION

ASSESSMENT FOR LEARNING

1. You, your classmates and your teacher should produce examples of assessment tests for coordination, balance, reaction time and agility where one or more of the principles that underpin fair assessments have not been applied and should therefore make the tests invalid or unreliable.

2. Study the examples. Assess, analyse, interpret and evaluate the information, and based on your knowledge and understanding:
   (a) identify and explain what information, if any, is missing and how this would affect your analysis and evaluation.
   (b) If sufficient information is provided, then identify and explain what information is safe, appropriate, sound, recommended and effective, and what is not safe, appropriate, sound, or effective and needs to be changed. Back up your findings with references to what is factual, sound or recommended (the 'ideal').

   For guidance on how to do this, use Steps 1–3 on page 6.

3. Collate a range of results from standardised tests on coordination, balance, reaction time and agility so that you, and your class, can become skilled at analysing, interpreting and evaluating the results.

4. Study the data. Assess, analyse, interpret and evaluate the data, and based on your knowledge and understanding:
   (a) identify and explain what information, if any, is missing and how this would affect your analysis and evaluation.
   (b) If sufficient information is provided, then identify and explain what information is safe, appropriate, sound, recommended and effective, and what is not safe, appropriate, sound, or effective and needs to be changed. Back up your findings with references to what is factual, sound or recommended (the 'ideal').

   For guidance on how to do this, use Steps 1–3 on page 6.

Factors underpinning the learning of skills

Learning skills for physical activities and sports

The stages of learning

Learning can be said to take place in three stages:
- the **cognitive** stage
- the **associative** stage
- the **autonomous** stage

Cognitive stage

The cognitive stage is the first/beginner stage. It is the stage where you must really think about what you have to do in order to perform the skill. You must concentrate on, and give your full attention to, your attempts to perform the sequence of movements. At this stage, your movements are unlikely to be efficient, effective or coordinated, and you may make lots of mistakes. You may feel anxious, lack confidence, and worry that there is too much to take in. In a competitive situation you may feel lost.

However, if you persevere, you will pass from this stage to the next, and be able to perform the skill, even if not perfectly.

Associative stage

The associative stage is the intermediate, refining stage. Through repeated practice of the skill, and with feedback, you start to refine your technique (sequence of movements). Gradually, as you get 'into the groove', you may think less about the technique and more about timing and coordination. Your movements will become more efficient, effective and coordinated, and you make fewer mistakes. You will feel more in control and more confident. In a reasonably straightforward competitive situation (one without too much pressure), you can use the skill with success.

You pass from this stage to the next when you can perform the skill automatically, without having to think about your technique or timing.

Autonomous stage

The autonomous stage is the advanced stage. The skill has been learnt, and you are able to perform it automatically. Your movements are efficient, effective and coordinated, and you make few mistakes. You are in control and confident in yourself. In a competitive situation you can take account of relevant factors, such as opponents and environmental conditions, adjust yourself accordingly, and successfully perform the skill. You are also able to focus on other important factors of performance, such as strategies and tactics and successfully use the skills to implement them.

People learning new skills sometimes get no further than the cognitive stage, and some stay in the associative stage. There is no guarantee that performers reach the autonomous stage. Within the one sport you could have a performer at the cognitive stage for one skill, the associative stage for another skill, and the autonomous stage for another skill.

The three main types of guidance you can receive are **visual**, **verbal** (auditory) and **physical/manual**:

- **Visual guidance** is when your instructor *shows* you the technique or part of the technique being performed. This can be done through a demonstration, by watching a video, or by using photographs.
- **Verbal guidance** is when your instructor *tells* you what to do. This instruction should, however, be kept simple and short, especially during the cognitive stage. At all times the language should be clear, concise and consistent in the use of words.
- **Physical/manual guidance** is when your instructor physically *moves* you into position and takes you manually through the sequence of movements.

Keith McClure

The most appropriate method of guidance depends on the skill. For example, basic skills can usually be learnt quickly from a demonstration. Complex skills need to be broken down into parts, and a combination of visual and verbal guidance is usually most successful. Sometimes, even with clear visual and verbal guidance the learner still has difficulty and may need manual guidance.

The most appropriate method also depends on the learner. People usually have a predominant learning style or preferred way of processing information. For example, some people learn best with visual guidance, some with verbal guidance, and some with physical/manual guidance. Some learn best by doing or experiencing – these are **kinaesthetic learners**. Some are **analytic learners** – whether they see, hear or try the skill, they need to think about it, retry it, think about it again, and so on.

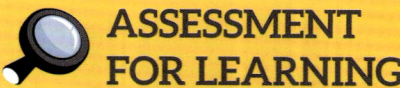

ASSESSMENT FOR LEARNING

1. Explain the differences among the three stages of learning.

Guidance and learning

To be able to move successfully through the stages of learning a skill, you need to know and understand the technique – the sequence of movements carried out to perform the skill efficiently and effectively. Techniques are the building blocks of skilled performance, so sound techniques have to be established in the cognitive stage.

2.2 DEVELOPING SKILLED PERFORMANCE

> **ASSESSMENT FOR LEARNING**
>
> 1 Choose a skill from a sport. Explain how you would use visual guidance and verbal guidance to teach the techniques of that skill.

Practice and learning

You can see the sequence of movements being performed, you can be told how to perform the sequence and you can be physically manipulated through the sequence, but if you don't actually do the sequence of movements yourself and practise them over and over, then you won't make progress through the stages of learning.

Practice is important. It is in practising a skill that we can develop sound technique and form a clear and precise memory of the skill. As the saying goes, 'practice makes perfect'.

However, it is important to realise that we must get the type and quality of practice right (this will depend on the complexity of the skill and the stage the learner is at in learning it), otherwise a different saying will be more applicable: 'practice makes permanent, but not necessarily perfect'.

There are different types of practice:

- **Whole practice** means practising the skill in its entirety. For example, when doing the long jump in athletics as you would in a competition – including the full sequence of movements for the run-up, take-off, flight and landing.
- **Part practice** means practising one part or section of a skill in isolation. For example, in the long jump, if you have been missing the takeoff board by quite a margin, you could sort out your run and markers and practise the run-up over and over to ensure you are hitting the take-off board correctly with your take-off foot. In some sports, like gymnastics and trampolining, certain skills can be too complex or dangerous to be attempted as a whole on your first attempts. Therefore, they are built up in parts, where you learn one part of the skill before moving on to the next part and so on.
- **Whole-part-whole practice** means practising the skill in its entirety in order to discover any weaknesses in the performance of the skill, then, if an area of weakness is identified, it is practised in isolation until corrected and the whole skill is then practised again. For example, if in practising the long jump as a whole skill you notice that your take-off is very flat or low to the ground, you practise the corrective actions in isolation until your take-off is corrected. You then practise the whole long jump again with the take-off now being correct within the performance of the whole skill.

Keith McClure

- **Mental practice** means visualising yourself doing the skill over and over again in your mind. For example, for the long jump you would visualise yourself setting a personal best jump. The image would include seeing yourself build up speed on the run-up, driving up powerfully from the take-off board, running or hanging in the air during flight, and finally, stretching out for the landing.

In using mental imagery, you should attempt to engage all your senses (seeing, hearing, feeling, touching and smelling) and perform the skill as successfully as you would want to in real life. Your mental image should include details for all aspects of the long jump (run-up, take-off, flight and landing) and for all parts of your body that are involved (leg actions, arm actions, position of the head, etc.). The image should also include environmental and other factors (wind, rain, surface, crowd, judges). Once you have the mental image you can focus on any part of it that you want.

Mental practice can be used at any time: when you wake up in the morning, before you go to training, during training, after training, or before you go to bed. It should take only a few minutes each time you practise it and can be effective in as little as 15 minutes per day.

- **Fixed/drill practice** means practising the skill repeatedly, and under the same conditions each time. This type of practice is most suited to skills from activities such as gymnastics and trampolining, where the environment and your opponents don't affect the performance of the skill in a major way. This method could also be used for long jump, or for a game in which one skill (or parts of the skill) could be repeated over and over with little variation in the playing conditions. For example, standing opposite a partner, about 5–10 m apart, to practise the chest pass, since no movement about the court is required in performing the practice.

- **Variable practice** means practising the skill in a variety of different contexts and conditions. This is most suited to net games such as badminton and volleyball, and invasion games such as netball and football, where the contexts and conditions are continually changing. Practice sessions that mirror these changes prepare you so that you can perform the skill in a wide range of situations.

- **Problem-solving practice** means being given situations in which you perform your skills while trying out different solutions. The sports most likely to use this type of practice are net games and invasion games. It involves thinking about strategies and tactics as well as practising your skills.

- **Conditioned games practice** means playing the game but with certain restrictions applied that are not normally part of the rules. For example, in hockey or football you could make a condition or restriction that you are only allowed two touches of the ball at any one time. The first touch could be to control the ball, and the second touch must then be a pass or a shot. This conditioned game practice could be used to encourage skill when passing the ball.

The type and difficulty of the practice you use depends on the complexity of the skill and the stage the learner is at in learning it.

Timing of practice

The timing of practice can have some effect on learning. Is it better to have one long continuous period of practice to learn new skills or to have the practice spaced out over time? The answer is that there are advantages and disadvantages to each.

Having one continuous block of time allows for continuity in the learning process. However, it can mean that people get tired and bored, and concentration is lost. A continuous block of practice is more effective with learners who have a high level of fitness and are highly motivated.

Having the time split up over a number of weeks allows for short sessions and therefore a shorter time for a focus to be maintained. There is also time for rest and time to practise before the next session. However, if practice is not undertaken between the sessions, then what was taught can be lost and little progress made from week to week. Spaced practice is more suited to learners who have lower levels of fitness and experience.

2.2 DEVELOPING SKILLED PERFORMANCE

ASSESSMENT FOR LEARNING

1. Provide an example that clearly illustrates the effective use of the different types of practice:
   (a) Whole practice
   (b) Part practice
   (c) Whole-part-whole practice
   (d) Mental practice
   (e) Fixed or drill practice
   (f) Variable practice
   (g) Problem-solving practice
   (h) Conditioned games practice

Feedback and learning

Along with good visual and verbal guidance, and consistent quality practice, you will also need regular and appropriate feedback – information on your performance – if you are to learn, and then execute, the proper techniques of a skill.

You need feedback throughout all stages of learning, but it is especially important in the associative stage. It is worth bearing in mind, though, that when detailed feedback is given during the cognitive stage (i.e., when the person is usually concentrating hard about performing the skill) it can often be confusing, and even a hindrance to learning.

Types of feedback
Intrinsic feedback

Intrinsic (internal) feedback provides information on the 'feel' of performing the sequence of movements. It includes information on balance and on the tension in the muscles. This information comes from the inner ear and from **proprioceptors** in the muscles, tendons and joints. It allows you to make fine adjustments to your movement. Some of the information is responded to without conscious control.

Intrinsic feedback also includes the information gathered from the **interoceptors** in the internal organs of the body (for example, the heart, lungs, stomach and intestines). This feedback allows the body systems to respond to the physical demands of the movements involved in the performances (see nervous system on page 33).

Extrinsic feedback

Extrinsic (external) feedback provides information on the performance from external sources, whether that is from a teacher, coach, video clip, a movement analysis programme, or even from your own experience and interpretation of the performance. When you gather information, you do it through **exteroceptors** (your eyes and ears). In the same way, when others give you feedback, it is usually presented visually or verbally.

There are two categories of extrinsic feedback:
- **knowledge of results** provides basic information on your performance – for example, you scored a goal; your service was in; your time was 12 seconds. This can be useful information, but it tells you very little about the quality of the performance.
- **knowledge of performance** provides information on the quality of your performance. You can get positive feedback on what you did correctly and negative feedback on what you did incorrectly. This feedback allows you to take corrective actions to improve your technique.

Feedback times
Concurrent feedback

Concurrent feedback is experienced or given during the performance of the skill. It can be both intrinsic (the performer's feelings) and extrinsic (the teacher's or coach's comments).

Terminal feedback

Terminal feedback is given after the skill has been performed, or after the training session. It is extrinsic and can be knowledge of results and/or knowledge of performance.

> **ASSESSMENT FOR LEARNING**
>
> 1 Explain the differences between intrinsic, extrinsic, concurrent and terminal feedback.

Arousal and learning

Arousal is your state of alertness. It is both a physical and mental condition. The physical is controlled by the autonomic nervous system; the mental is controlled by the brain.

Particular personality traits can have an influence on these levels of arousal. Some people tend naturally to get either overanxious or overexcited when they have to do certain things (for example, attend an interview; go to a concert; learn new skills; or perform in a competition) and these people often have very high arousal levels. On the other hand, some people tend naturally to be very relaxed and calm about the same things, and their arousal levels are often very low.

Often, it is the specific situation that has a greater influence on arousal levels. For example, you could get overanxious or overexcited, to the extent that you feel sick, when given the opportunity to go caving, whereas another person could be quite relaxed about it. Skydiving may not bother you, but it could make that same other person either overexcited or overanxious. Similarly, your level of arousal may be fine for playing in an ordinary league match in your sport but be very high for a cup-final match.

The point is that your personality traits, combined with the given situation, influence your level of arousal, and your level of arousal affects how you perform.

There are many theories that try to explain this. Generally, it is agreed that if your arousal level is either very low (if you are laid-back, uninterested, unfocused, bored or tired) or very high (if you are overexcited, overanxious, worried or tense), then you will perform poorly. This means there is an **optimum zone** in between. If your level of arousal is within this zone, then you will perform at your best.

Your challenge is to get your level of arousal into this optimum zone.

You can raise this level through, for example:
- mental imagery, in which you call up images of your goal (to win the league) and vividly remind yourself of what needs to be done to achieve it.
- a coach or manager motivating you with a pep talk.
- seeing the opposition and their determination.
- a coach or manager giving you a special role or job to do.

Keith McClure

You can lower your level of arousal through, for example:
- relaxation techniques, through which you can lower your heart rate, slow down your breathing and remove tension from your muscles.
- mental imagery, in which you imagine yourself performing well and being successful in the competition. This helps take away negative thoughts and worries.

It is a case of getting the balance right for each situation so that optimum arousal is achieved, and you can perform at your best.

The complexity of the sport can affect the optimum level of arousal required for peak performance. The greater the complexity of the sport the lower the level of arousal needed. For example, golf is more complex than weightlifting and requires finer motor skills, so it requires a lower level of arousal for peak performances; weightlifting is less complex a sport and requires gross motor skills, so it requires a higher level of arousal for peak performance.

> **ASSESSMENT FOR LEARNING**
>
> 1 What can a person do to try and get their level of arousal into the optimum zone?

Planning workouts

Planning workouts to develop skills at each stage of learning

Assessment of performance of an identified skill

For skills in physical activity and sports to be performed efficiently, effectively and accurately, athletes/players learn the 'ideal' **positioning**, **technique**, **timing** and **recovery** to perform skills. This 'ideal' is also known as the **full marks model**.

If you have a clear understanding of the full marks model for a skill you want to perfect, then you can compare any performance of that skill against it. This will enable you to judge how well the skill has been performed and help you identify areas of weakness. However, it is not always wise to judge a performance on one attempt, so your assessment should be based on patterns observed across many attempts.

Observation is key when judging how well a skill is being performed – whether that performance is live, recorded or even assessed through performance analysis software. If you are observing a live performance (where the skill is being carried out in front of you) you need to be able to remember accurately what you saw being performed and then compare it to the full marks model, in order to identify strengths and weaknesses. It is therefore more helpful if performances are recorded. Your judgement will still be based on observation, but you will be able to see one performance, or a number of different performances, many times before you reach a conclusion. The use of performance analysis software will allow you to take your observation one step further, enabling you to analyse recorded performances and compare one performance with another.

If working with recorded performances, you will also be able to observe, and make judgements on, your own performances; and while you cannot observe yourself performing live, you can *feel* how well a skill was performed. This is a kinaesthetic sense. With quality practice, you can get the feel of the full marks model, and with experience you can compare what you did to the ideal and be able to identify your strengths and weaknesses. This feeling of performing a skill, whether it has been performed well or not, is an important part in the mastery of learning a skill.

Your assessment of a learner will help them progress through the stages of learning (see page 175):

- **Cognitive stage**: Assessment should focus on the basic individual skills being performed in isolation. By judging performances against the full marks model, it will usually highlight obvious weaknesses in technique in performing the skills.
- **Associative stage**: Assessment should focus on the basic skills being performed when under some pressure or more challenging situations. These will find the weaknesses in specific parts of the technique of the skills and highlight how positioning, timing and recovery also affect the quality of performances.
- **Autonomous stage**: Assessment should focus on testing the consistency, efficiency and effectiveness of performing the full range of skills in challenging and competitive situations. This will highlight any minor weaknesses in positioning, technique, timing or recovery. Assessment should also focus on strategies, tactics and decisions in skill selection during challenging and competitive situations.

SMART objective for the workout

It is important that you have a clear objective for the workout and that this is based on the assessment and analysis of previous performances in the sport. This allows you to identify strengths and weaknesses in the range and mastery of skills. If you are serious about improving your overall performance, then your intention in the workouts will be to develop new skills or to work on eliminating areas of weakness in other skills. If you don't have clear intentions for your learner's workouts, then it can be very easy for them (and you) to remain in the comfort zone and only practise strengths.

One way to focus intentions and set new objectives is by taking your findings from the assessment and then following the SMART principle (see page 175 for each stage of learning):

- **Cognitive stage**: SMART objectives should focus on learning the techniques of the basic skills.
- **Associative stage**: SMART objectives should focus on correcting and improving the specific parts of the technique that did not match the full marks model and on improving positioning, timing and recovery. SMART objectives may also include learning new or more complex skills.
- **Autonomous stage**: SMART objectives should focus on improving decision-making in strategies, tactics and skill selection and in performing the range of skills efficiently, effectively and with accuracy.

Teaching/coaching a skill

To offer guidance on and teach a skill, you must have a thorough understanding of the full marks model and be able to communicate this to a learner. This can be done visually, verbally or manually (see page 176).

Your challenge is to encourage the learner to form a mental image of the correct technique (the full marks model), then provide opportunities for them to demonstrate the technique (in a way that does not put them under undue pressure). You then observe the learner's performances and provide feedback. They are then given further opportunities to demonstrate the correct technique for the skill. Once the learner has sufficiently grasped the technique, they can perform it in selected practices.

Your method of guidance may vary as the learner progresses through the stages of learning:

- **Cognitive stage**: At this stage, the individual is very reliant on the teacher/coach. Guidance provided should be both visual and verbal. Verbal guidance should apply the 'KISS' principle – **K**eep **I**t **S**hort and **S**imple. For some beginners, physical guidance may be needed.
- **Associative stage**: Both visual and verbal guidance should be used. The emphasis should be decided on what works best with an individual. Verbal guidance will be better understood as the individual, at this stage, should understand the sequence of movements to perform the skills.
- **Autonomous stage**: Guidance is more likely to involve discussions and practice with the teacher/coach about the use of strategies, tactics and decision-making in skill selection.

Giving feedback

You need to give regular and appropriate feedback on performances of the skill. This extrinsic feedback falls into two categories: knowledge of results and knowledge of performance (see page 179). The latter provides the most helpful feedback as it will focus on the technique and allow you to comment on the parts of the technique being performed well, and the parts that are not.

Your feedback can be visual, verbal or manual (see page 176), though visual and verbal feedback are usually combined to provide information on performances:

- **Visual feedback** is when you show the learner how they are performing the technique – perhaps by using recordings taken of their performance, or by reenacting it. You would then show them how the technique should be performed, either through a live demonstration (you, or someone else would perform the technique) or by showing the learner a video clip or photographs.
- **Verbal feedback** is when you tell the learner what they are doing well and what they are doing less well. This feedback should be straightforward and direct, using language that is clear, concise and consistent. You then tell the person how the technique should be performed.
- **Physical** or **manual feedback** is when you physically/manually take the learner through

2.2 DEVELOPING SKILLED PERFORMANCE

the sequence of movements to show how they were performing the skill. You then physically/manually take them through the sequence of movements as they should be performing it.

You can use the learner's own intrinsic (internal) feedback when assessing performances. This is getting information on the 'feel' of the performance and what was wrong in the sequence of movements. But whether the feedback is intrinsic, manual, verbal or visual, the whole point in providing it is to reinforce what is strong and to highlight what is perhaps weaker, so that corrective actions may be taken to improve technique at each stage of the learning process:

- **Cognitive stage**: Concurrent feedback is very helpful and should be used with beginners. The beginners will also rely on extrinsic feedback from the teacher/coach – both visual and verbal evidence should be provided. Terminal feedback can be helpful, but if the KISS principle is not applied, the feedback can be overwhelming and confuse the beginner.
- **Associative stage**: Concurrent feedback can still be helpful but is less important for the improver. Intrinsic feedback becomes more relevant and helpful. The individual should be able to work more with the teacher/coach and should be able to identify many of their own mistakes or weaknesses. Terminal feedback is better understood and becomes more useful.
- **Autonomous stage**: Concurrent feedback is unlikely to be used. The individual should be capable of effectively learning from intrinsic feedback. Extrinsic evidence from a teacher/coach, and video analysis or performance analysis programmes should be gathered and discussed as terminal feedback.

Selection of practices

The techniques for performing most skills are the same for beginners, improvers or advanced performers. All strive to perform the skill using the 'full marks' model. Once you have sound technique in place, practice is important. By practising a skill using sound technique, a person can develop and form a clear and precise memory of the skill.

The type and difficulty of the practice used depends on the complexity of the skill and on the stage that an individual is at when learning it. Practices must suit the stage of learning. It is through repeated quality practice of a skill that an individual is able to progress through the stages of learning.

- **Cognitive stage**: At this stage, practices should be simple with little pressure being put on the learner, allowing them to simply perform the skill repeatedly with good technique. It should allow for at least a 70% success rate. Types of practice most often used would be part, whole-part-whole and practice drills (see page 177).

- **Associative stage**: At this stage, practices can (and should) put some pressure on the learner, with greater emphasis on performing the technique efficiently and effectively. They should be more challenging and work on positioning, technique, timing and recovery. This will better reflect what will be required in a competitive situation and should allow for a success rate of around 70%. Any of the types of practice could be used (see page 177), but one particularly suitable example is whole-part-whole practice.
- **Autonomous stage**: At this stage, practices can be complex and put the learner under pressure. There is a greater emphasis on accuracy and it is expected that the technique will be performed efficiently and effectively, allowing for a success rate of around 80%. Any of the types of practice could be used (see page 177),

but one particularly suitable example is problem-solving practice.

Organisation

It is important that when you have a number of people of varying abilities and stages of development together, you manage them well. If you are playing in a competitive situation it is important to match people of similar abilities or stages of learning together. This will mean that the competition should be fair and close.

However, this is not the case when providing quality practice for an individual in the cognitive or early associative stages. If matched with someone at a similar stage of development, neither person will have the control necessary to provide the other with quality feed (the passing of the ball/shuttlecock/puck and so on, to another player).

If, however, you pair someone in the cognitive or associative stage with someone at the autonomous stage, then the latter will have sufficient control to provide the learner with whatever feed they require, thus allowing quality practice to take place. For example, to provide quality feed in badminton, a person should be able to consistently place the shuttlecock in the correct area of the court with the appropriate height, so that the learner can consistently practise the selected shot.

Time is not limitless for the development and practice of skills. It needs to be managed to get effective use from it. Within the part of a workout dedicated to developing skill, you may have to include, for example:
- an explanation of the intention of the workout – 2 minutes.
- an assessment of the performance of a selected skill – 5 minutes.
- analysis and feedback on the performances of the skill – 5 minutes.
- teaching or coaching the technique of the skill – 10 minutes.
- practising the technique using selected practices with feedback on the performances of the skill – 20 minutes.
- application of the skill in a competitive situation – 15 minutes.
- feedback on the performances of the skill – 3 minutes.

The times given above provide one example of how a 60-minute workout on a selected skill may be managed. How the time is divided up will depend on the stage of development that an individual is at, and on the type of practices to be used.

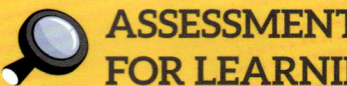

ASSESSMENT FOR LEARNING

1. Choose a skill and show that you can use the above process to plan an effective workout to develop that skill.
2. Practice doing this for other skills.

ANALYSIS, INTERPRETATION AND EVALUATION

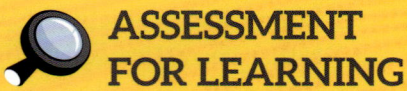

ASSESSMENT FOR LEARNING

1. You, your classmates and your teacher should produce examples of skill-related workouts to develop a specific skill where one or more of the principles, process or practices have not been applied safely, appropriately or effectively. Make sure to cover athletic events, individual sports and team sports.

2. Study the examples. Assess, analyse, interpret and evaluate the information, and based on your knowledge and understanding:
   (a) identify and explain what information, if any, is missing and how this would affect your analysis and evaluation.
   (b) If sufficient information is provided, then identify and explain what information is safe, appropriate, sound, recommended and effective, and what is not safe, appropriate, sound, or effective and needs to be changed. Back up your findings with references to what is factual, sound or recommended (the 'ideal').

For guidance on how to do this, use Steps 1–3 on page 6.

SAMPLE AUDITS

Mental and social health

Laura

Laura has confided to her friend that she has difficulty getting to sleep, as she is anxious that she will not be top of her class once again and that she will be letting her parents down.

She feels her friends look so much better than her without make-up and, although against the school rules, she wears some make-up to school each day.

She admits that she really appreciates her friend's dad giving them both a lift to school each morning and her mum bringing her home each day, but she has fond memories of the days when they both walked to school together and then home again – hail, rain or snow. School seemed so much more fun then.

Unlike her friend, Laura does not go to the netball club after school anymore, or play for the school team, because she feels she should be revising rather than playing sport.

Her mum and dad are very supportive and keen to find out how she is getting on at school each day, but she avoids this conversation as she feels she may be letting them down, so quite often she makes an excuse about needing to do homework and goes to her bedroom.

Her mum makes balanced, healthy meals at home and makes her a healthy packed lunch each day. She admits that she has started taking comfort snacks throughout the day. She thinks she is getting fatter.

She is friendly with the teenagers who live next door, and they recognise that she is doing too much school work and she needs to relax. They tell her a little alcohol would help her unwind and she is welcome to join them when they go out at the weekends. They also have friends who would let her try other methods that would take her troubles away.

Physical activity

John
Summary of physical activity done over three months

Day	Activity
Sun	Occasional easy walk: 30–60 min
Mon	Nothing
Tues	Nothing
Wed	Nothing
Thurs	Nothing
Fri	Nothing
Sat	Occasional easy walk: 30–60 min

Maria
Summary of physical activity done over one week

Day	Time	Physical activity	Work Load
Sun	14:00–15:00	Walk with dog: 4/10 RPE for 60 minutes	WL 240
Mon	08:30–08:50 15:30–15:55	Walk to school: 4/10 RPE for one mile in 20 minutes Walk home: 3/10 RPE for one mile in 25 minutes	WL 155

Tue	15:45–16:45	Hockey training :
		    Warm-up jog: (7 min)
		    Short intervals (10 × 50 m sprint): very hard intensity 9/10 RPE (10 minutes)
		    Skills practice: (15 min)
		    Match play: 7/10 RPE for 20 minutes
		    Cool-down with flexibility: (8 min)
			WL 230

Wed		No exercise	

Thu	15:45–16:30	PE school fitness suite:
		    Warm-up (5 min)
		    Exercise bike (120 watts): hard intensity 8/10 RPE for 20 minutes.
		    Bicep curl; shoulder press; front raise, sit-ups and squat jump exercises each done with 2 × 5 kg dumbbells: 10 reps, 20 sec rest × 3 sets for each exercise: intensity 8/10 RPE for 20 minutes
			WL 320

Fri		No exercise	

Sat	09:20–10:30	Hockey:
		    Warm-up (10 min)
		    Hockey match (mid field); hard intensity 8/10 RPE for 2 × 25 minutes
		    Cool-down jog (5 min)
			WL 400

		TOTAL Work Load (WL) for week:	WL 1345

RPE – Rate of Perceived Exertion. WL – Work Load: WL = RPE × Time.

SAMPLE AUDITS

Nutrition

Oliver
Typical food and drink consumed each week

Meal Day	Breakfast Home	Lunch School	Dinner Home
Mon	• No breakfast	• Chicken sandwich on white bread (2 slices) with butter and mayonnaise • 250 g bar of chocolate • 500 ml bottle of water	• Large bowl of pasta with cheese, chicken and cauliflower • 500 ml of tap water
Tue	• Large bowl of porridge made with semi-skimmed milk and 2 dessertspoons of sugar added	• Ham and cheese sandwich on white bread (2 slices) with butter • 250 g bar of chocolate • 500 ml bottle of water	• ¼ plate of battered fish; ½ plate of chunky chips; ¼ plate of mushy peas • 500 ml of tap water
Wed	• Large bowl of porridge made with semi-skimmed milk and 2 dessertspoons of sugar added	• Chicken and salad sandwich on white bread (2 slices) with butter and mayonnaise • 250 g bar of chocolate • 500 ml bottle of water	• 2 beef burgers with ½ plate of skinny chips; ¼ plate of baked beans • 3 scoops of ice cream for dessert • 330 ml can of cola
Thu	• Large bowl of porridge made with semi-skimmed milk and 2 dessertspoons of sugar added	• Ham and cheese sandwich on white bread (2 slices) with butter • 250 g bar of chocolate • 500 ml bottle of water	• Large bowl of pasta with chicken in tomato and basil sauce • 500 ml of tap water
Fri	• No breakfast	• School dinner of ½ plate of chips; ¼ plate of baked beans and 2 sausages • 250 g bar of chocolate • 330 ml can of cola	• Chinese takeaway meal: Egg fried rice with sweet and sour battered chicken or • Indian takeaway meal: Boiled rice with Madras vegetable curry • 500 ml of tap water
	Home	Home	Home
Sat	• 2 energy bars • 250 ml of energy drink	• Ulster fry cooked in sunflower oil in pan: 2 slices of bacon; 2 sausages; 2 pieces of soda bread; 2 pieces of potato bread; 2 eggs; cupful of mushrooms • 500 ml bottle of cola	• Thick homemade vegetable soup; 2 slices of toasted white bread with butter • 250 g bar of chocolate • 330 ml can of cola
Sun	• No breakfast	• 1 slice of roast beef; 3 medium-sized boiled potatoes; 3 tablespoons of cabbage and carrot; gravy • slice of chocolate cake with cream as dessert • 500 ml bottle of cola	• Large bowl of fresh fruit salad with natural yogurt • 250 g bar of chocolate • 500 ml bottle of cola

Snacks taken:
- Monday to Friday in school at break time: 25 g bag of potato crisps with 330 ml can of cola
- Monday to Friday immediately after school: 25 g bag of potato crisps with 330 ml can of cola
- Each night before bed: a hot chocolate drink made with milk

Sleep

Ciara
Sleep quality and pattern

Bedroom environment:
- The bed is comfortable, but the bedcovers are too warm when first in bed and so, to avoid sweating, are not used; later in the night, the bedcovers are used to avoid shivering.
- The bedroom is uncluttered, thanks to Ciara's mum.
- The bedroom is too hot when going to bed, but cool in the morning.
- The bedroom has curtains, but Ciara does not close them. Nothing overlooks the bedroom.
- The bedroom is quiet, if Ciara does not have music or the television on.
- The bedroom is Ciara's 'space': it has a television, games console, and tablet. She always has her smartphone.

Day	Time	Routine	Hours and quality of sleep
Sun	19:00 22:30 22:45 23:15 23:30	• Watch television and browse social media (study) • A hot chocolate drink made with milk (kitchen) • Play online game for 30 minutes (bedroom) • Get organised for school • Into bed	• Usually slow to get to sleep • Think about school • Alarm time 07:45 (Mon) – snooze then get out of bed at 08:00 (Mon) • Approximately 7 hours 15 minutes of sleep
Mon	19:00 20:30 22:30 22:45 23:00 23:30	• Do school work (study) • Social media (study) • A hot chocolate drink made with milk (kitchen) • Get organised for school (bedroom) • Internet browsing and social media (bedroom) • Into bed	• Usually slow to get to sleep • Alarm time 07:45 (Tue) – snooze then get out of bed at 08:00 (Tue) • Approximately 7 hours 15 minutes of sleep
Tue	19:00 21:30 22:30 22:45 23:00	• Training for sport (club) • School work (bedroom) • A hot chocolate drink made with milk (kitchen) • Get organised for school (bedroom) • Into bed	• Quick to sleep • Alarm time 07:45 (Wed) – snooze then get out of bed at 08:00 (Wed) • Approximately 8 hours 30 minutes of sleep
Wed	19:00 21:00 22:30 22:45 23:00 23:30	• Do school work (bedroom) • Social media chat (bedroom) • A hot chocolate drink made with milk (kitchen) • Get organised for school (bedroom) • Listen to music (bedroom) • Into bed	• Quick to sleep • Alarm time 07:45 (Thu) – snooze then get out of bed at 08:00 (Thu) • Approximately 8 hours sleep
Thu	19:00 21:00 22:30 22:45 23:15	• Do school work (bedroom) • Social media chat (bedroom) • A hot chocolate drink made with milk (kitchen) • Play online game (bedroom) • Into bed	• Usually slow to get to sleep • Alarm time 07:45 (Fri) – snooze then get out of bed at 08:00 (Fri) • Approximately 7 hours 45 minutes of sleep
Fri	19:00 19:30 22:30 23:30	• Internet browsing • Play badminton (youth club) • Social media chat and Internet browsing (bedroom) • Into bed	• Quick to sleep • Alarm time 07:45 (Sat) and out of bed 07:50 (Sat) • Approximately 8 hours of sleep
Sat	09:30 19:00 19:30 23:30 00:30	• Play for school team • Internet browsing (kitchen) • Hang out with friends (youth club) • Social media chat and Internet browsing (bedroom) • Into bed	• Quick to sleep • No alarm set, usually wake before 08:00 (Sun) – lie in bed and snooze then get up at 11:00 (Sun) • Approximately 7 hours of sleep and then snoozing

COPYRIGHT

Images in this book are copyright as detailed below. Numbers refer to page numbers in this book.

iStockPhoto: Front cover, 13 all, 14 top left, 14 middle right, 17 right, 18 bottom left, 22, 30 bottom left, 32 all, 38 left, 39, 40 left, 41 all, 42 all, 43 all, 44 all, 46 all, 47, 49, 50, 52 bottom left, 52 top right, 53, 57 top right, 58 all, 62 all, 63 all, 64 all, 68 right, 69 all, 70 all, 71 right, 76 all, 77 right, 78 left, 78 bottom right, 81 all, 82 all, 84 all, 85 right, 86, 87, 88 right, 89 all, 90 all, 91 all, 95, 96 all, 97, 98 all, 100 all, 102, 103 all, 104 top, 105 top, 105 bottom, 111 all, 113 right, 114, 117 all, 118 all, 119, 120, 123, 137, 138 all, 144 top right, 144 bottom right, 146, 151 left, 152, 154 left, 155 all, 156 top, 160, 164 all, 165, 172 all, 173 all, 176 right, 178 all, 179, 182, 183 all.

Shutterstock: 80, 85 left.

Derek Prentice: 14 middle left, 18 top left, 40 right, 48, 51, 52 bottom right, 56, 57 bottom right, 60 top, 68 left, 72, 77 left, 78 top right, 94, 104 bottom, 143 bottom right, 148 all, 151 right, 153, 154 right, 156 bottom, 168 all, 181.

Images that are copyright to other sources are acknowledged adjacent to the relevant image.

All images not covered by any of the above are copyright ©Colourpoint Creative Limited.

All text is copyright ©Derek Prentice and Colourpoint Creative Limited.

Copyright has been acknowledged to the best of our ability. If there are any inadvertent errors or omissions, we shall be happy to correct them in any future editions.